BREAKING THE

STUDIES IN LITERATURE AND RELIGION

General Editor: David Jasper, Principal of St Chad's College, The University of Durham

This series of volumes will provide an interdisciplinary introduction to the study of literature and religion, concerned with the fundamentally important issues of the imagination, literary perceptions and an understanding of poetics for theology and religious studies, and the underlying religious implications in so much literature and literary criticism.

Robert Detweiler
BREAKING THE FALL: Religious Readings of Contemporary Fiction

Max Harris
THEATRE AND INCARNATION

David Jasper
THE STUDY OF LITERATURE AND RELIGION: AN INTRODUCTION

David Jasper and R. C. D. Jasper (editors)
LANGUAGE AND THE WORSHIP OF THE CHURCH

Ulrich Simon
PITY AND TERROR: Christianity and Tragedy

Series Standing Order

If you would like to receive future titles in this series as they are published, you can make use of our standing order facility. To place a standing order please contact your bookseller or, in case of difficulty, write to us at the address below with your name and address and the name of the series. Please state with which title you wish to begin your standing order. (If you live outside the UK we may not have the rights for your area, in which case we will forward your order to the publisher concerned.)

Standing Order Service, Macmillan Distribution Ltd, Houndmills, Basingstoke, Hampshire, RG21 2XS, England.

Breaking the Fall

Religious Readings of Contemporary Fiction

ROBERT DETWEILER
Professor of Comparative Literature
Emory University, Georgia

MACMILLAN

First published 1989

Published by
THE MACMILLAN PRESS LTD
Houndmills, Basingstoke, Hampshire RG21 2XS
and London
Companies and representatives
throughout the world

Printed in Hong Kong

British Library Cataloguing in Publication Data
Detweiler, Robert
Breaking the fall: religious readings of
contemporary fiction.—(Studies in literature and
religion).
1. Fiction in European languages, 1945–. Religious
aspects
I. Title   II. Series
809.3′04
ISBN 0–333–45808–7

For Betty and Aaron, Richard and Mary Jane:
Religious Readers

Contents

Acknowledgements

The author and publishers gratefully acknowledge permission to use quotations from the following:

From *The Handmaid's Tale* by Margaret Atwood. Copyright © 1985 by O. W. Toad Ltd. Used by permission of the Canadian publishers, McClelland and Stewart, Toronto; of the British publishers, Jonathan Cape Ltd, London; and of the United States publishers, Houghton Mifflin Company, Boston.

From *Riddley Walker* by Russell Hoban. Copyright © 1980 by Russell Hoban. Used by permission of the British publishers, Jonathan Cape Ltd, London; and of the United States publishers, Simon & Schuster, New York.

From *The Woman Warrior: Memoirs of a Girlhood Among Ghosts* by Maxine Hong Kingston. Copyright © 1975 by Maxine Hong Kingston. Used by permission of Alfred A. Knopf, Inc., New York.

From *The Philosophy of Paul Ricoeur* edited by Charles E. Reagan and David Stewart. Copyright © 1978 by Charles E. Reagan and David Stewart. Reprinted by permission of Beacon Press, Boston.

The author is also grateful for permission to use, as the basis for the chapter on 'John Updike's Sermons', an earlier and shorter version entitled 'Updike's Sermons' which appeared in *Americana-Austriaca: Beiträge zur Amerikakunde*, vol. 5, 1980, edited by Klaus Lanzinger. Used by permission of Wilhelm Braumüller, Universitäts-Verlagsbuchhandlung, Vienna.

General Editor's Preface

Robert Detweiler's *Breaking the Fall* extends both our notion of reading and the concept of a religiously reading community. As our sense of textuality is expanded beyond the mere sense of words on a page and conventional linguistic idiom, so also our sense of the sacred is expanded. It may be that in our present time we are being called to live out the apocalypse and vitally, therefore, to seek the resituation of religious discourse. It may be that, in Martin Buber's words, distintegration of the Word has taken place, and that the familiar conventions of sermons and the liturgy are reappearing in fictive conditions and with a disturbing ambivalence. Such things are explored in this book.

Professor Detweiler is convinced of the importance of entertaining the energetic discussions of contemporary literary theory in the present debates in religious studies. The power of his writing reminds us of the relative neglect of modern and post-modern literature by most studies which are concerned with the relationship between literature and religion, and its sometimes disturbing qualities may draw us beyond our comfortable, conventional considerations to the point where we rediscover the inventiveness and creativity which flourish only at moments of ambiguity and recombination.

In our age we cannot afford to be timid in critical ventures. If we wish to continue in a belief in the possibility of religious interpretations of experience and literature, we must allow our horizons to be expanded and our pre-formed perceptions to be broken. Seeking new contexts and structures, our storytelling against despair may indeed be painful even as it represents a necessary and creative return to the semblance of faith and hope.

David Jasper

Preface

> . . . but as you go on, the writing – if you follow it – will take you places you never intended to go and show you things you would never otherwise have seen.[1]

Scholars of Bible and religion have been learning, in recent years and with increasing finesse, to adapt the methods of the literary critics to their interpretations of the sacred canons, while a number of literary critics have tried their hand at what we could call secular readings of the traditional sacred texts. Much of this crossing of old boundaries has been inspired by the flourishing of post-New Critical theory and practice that has also influenced theology and philosophy and even, to a degree, the social sciences. Yet in the midst of this stimulating inter-disciplinary activity, remarkably little writing has been produced in the area that was, for a time, the liveliest of the literature-and-religion nexus: the interpretation of narrative fiction, poetry and drama from a religious perspective. 'The triumph of theory in literary studies', as J. Hillis Miller has called it, seems to have caused a timidity among those of us interested in writing religious interpretations of literature, as if we feared that the theory had made, or would make, this interpretive endeavour – already under fire for some decades – invalid.[2]

This reticence is surprising for two reasons. First is that some of our prominent theorists, such as Jacques Derrida, Geoffrey Hartman and Frank Kermode, have suggested the value of recent theory for the religious interpretation of literary texts, causing one to wonder why their lead has not been followed more enthusiastically than it has. Second is that critics using other approaches – those that the New Critics labelled 'extrinsic' – such as the psychoanalytic, feminist and Marxist are busily appropriating the newer theory (often while challenging aspects of it) in their reading of literary texts, prompting one to inquire why the proponents of the religious approach are, in contrast, so unenterprising.

A probable explanation for this caution and quiescence is that the newer theory and criticism have complicated even more the issues of the religious interpretation of literature. We describe our hermeneutical scene not only as post-New Critical but also as the era of post-formalism, post-structuralism, deconstruction, post-representation, post-modern and even post-hermeneutic. These are all ill-defined and sometimes mischievous terms that obscure as much as they explain. Yet the obscuration in the terminology reflects an obscuration now at the centre (such as it is) of interpretation theory and practice. What has been understood as the substance of parable and a trait of metaphor has been expanded into a critical principle. *All* discourse, it is said, resists (like the parable) conclusive analysis, frustrates closure, opens up (like metaphor) to multiple readings, so that interpretation becomes less an effort to provide a text's 'proper' meaning and more an attempt to disclose its many possibilities of signification.

This is a hard hypothesis for critics who wish to interpret literature through a religious approach, for like their colleagues in biblical and religious studies they have tended to assume that the authority behind their project (a theology, a canon, an ecclesiastical tradition, a personal faith) would somehow, eventually, crystallize into definitive readings, aspects of a truthful vision of the nature of things. To put it in the concise terms of structuralism: the assumption of the reality of an Absolute Signified has led us to believe that we could both find and fashion absolute signifiers to determine our lives. This is not to say that such critics *necessarily* have more at stake than those who read from the perspectives of psychoanalysis, feminism, Marxism, etc.; only that they may think they do, since they have thought of themselves in closer, more self-aware proximity to personal and communal belief systems than other kinds of critics. Now, as virtually all discourse is viewed as overtly or covertly ideological, and as Christian and Jewish hermeneutics lose more and more of their privilege, the challenge to attempt literary interpretation in a religious-critical mode seems stronger than ever, yet we have been reluctant to take on something so formidable.

The critics who turn post-formalist theory into praxis do follow their New Critical forebears in one respect: they concentrate on literature from eras prior to their own, leaving the discussion of contemporary narrative fiction, poetry and drama largely to the reviewers. This is at least the case in Anglo-American criticism –

less so among the French, where the tradition of the critic who is also a literary artist is stronger and where a number of critics-cum-novelists (such as Philippe Sollers and Hélène Cixous) exert their dual influence. The reluctance among British and American critics to engage contemporary literature more generally is curious, for these are the texts that embody most attractively the tenets of current theory. In what is called post-modern narration or 'metafiction', for example, one finds an awareness of the artifice of the fictional texts emphasized – an exposure of the illusion of representation that is the artistic counterpart to the impasse or *aporia* that the deconstructionist critics insist inhabits *any* text and that triggers its disintegration as an inadequate model of presence. Almost needless to say, religious interpreters of literature have been as loath as the proponents of other approaches to take on the peculiar complexities of post-modern literature.

I have attempted in this study to read some examples of contemporary narrative fiction, along with a few older texts, from a religious perspective that interacts with post-formalist theory. My first chapter, however, is a foundational theory chapter that also proceeds via a reading of a short story by Milan Kundera. Placing this tale in dialogue with my knowledge of current critical discourse, I found that the ensuing 'conversation' between fiction and theory stressed three aspects of the post-modern literary temper: an emerging model of the self as an aggregate of selves; the complicated relationships among author, text and reader that often focus on plots and plotting; and the struggle simultaneously to accommodate notions of representation and to transcend them.

This dialogue, which would not respect the bounds of literary study but insisted on straying into philosophy, psychology, sociology and anthropology as well, prepared me for Chapter 2, 'What is Reading Religiously?' Here, rather than seeking yet another formula for the religious reading of literature, I tried first to imagine what a contemporary version of the old storytelling cultures might be like – those cultures in which the stories, formally recited and responded to, constituted much of the belief patterns. I discovered some characteristics of a writing and reading community with religious implications: the accent on community itself would offer a balance to our excessively privatizing tendencies; the communal interaction could counter our relentless drive to interpret (which this study cannot help but share) with attitudes of play and *Gelassenheit*; the writing and reading community,

especially as a liminal entity, could nurture a respect for the incomprehensibility of form and a reverence for mystery. Three kinds
of texts occurred to me as among those that could provoke or
inspire religious readings today in the community: texts of pain,
of love and of worship.

The remaining four chapters address such fictions of pain, love
and worship. I chose here to focus neither on traditional realistic
novels or stories nor on experimental ones, and I have not worried
a great deal about identifying these texts as modern or post-
modern. Most of them could be called, in literary-historical terms,
'transitional'. They are based in realism but slide, in varying
degrees, toward the surreal, the magical, the implausible, the
unthinkable. In this sense transitional, they are appropriate
vehicles for expressing the liminality that my projected writing
and reading religious community might feel. In almost every case
I have also selected texts that signal, one way or another, an
openness to a religious reading. Whether literary texts exist that
are outright hostile to such a reading I have not decided (probably
they do), but surely many exist that are indifferent, and I have
chosen instead of them some that seem congenial to my approach.

My approach is actually four approaches. Chapters 3 to 6 are
religious readings that are informed respectively by phenomenology, hermeneutics, deconstruction and anthropology of religion.
Although I did not want any of these four chapters to be dominated by any of these approaches, it seemed both potentially
helpful and in the spirit of play that marks this study (and that I
will expand on) to conduct the religious reading in each of these
chapters via a different interpretive strategy. The results will, I
hope, demonstrate the versatility and adaptability of religious
reading.

Chapter 3 on Walker Percy examines his fifth novel, *The Second
Coming*, as a text of love and pain (and to a lesser degree of
worship) that is formally realistic but flirts internally with the
implausible. One is encouraged to read this novel from the same
askew, off-centre perspective that the two main characters have,
whereby one is led to affirm the text's concluding, slightly mad
celebration of grace. The emphasis on falling in *The Second Coming*
reminded me of Heidegger's treatment of that concept and
inspired me to give this chapter an existential-phenomenological
slant. The stress on falling also provided me with a title for the
chapter, and for the study as a whole, that I intend as a *leitmotif*:

religious reading at least in the Western world finds itself still entangled, in the late twentieth century, in the mythology of the Fall and seeks in its fictions to brake/break the fall into meaninglessness and death.

The argument of Chapter 4 was provoked by my curiosity about John Updike's repeated use of sermons in his fiction. I discovered as I proceeded that these homilies are not only texts of worship but are employed in contexts of love and suffering to comment, against the grain of the plot, on matters such as carnality and theodicy. The relationship among sexuality, the problem of suffering and the nature of evil, and the effects of this relationship on an at least nominally Christian community, becomes prominent in Updike's 1984 novel, *The Witches of Eastwick*, and I have therefore devoted half of this chapter to that narrative. Because the sermons in Updike's stories and novels function as an interpretive discourse that *seems* to present judgements and convictions transcending the context of fiction, I borrowed Paul Ricoeur's 'hermeneutics of suspicion' and of 'affirmation'. Through it I could show that Updike's sermons are models of *in*authenticity that undermine the tradition of realism and prepare the reading community for a reconsideration of the possibility of mystery.

A contemplation on how sacred texts (some identified as such, some not) in recent fiction always appear to need a sacred space, and vice versa, led me in Chapter 5 to the widest-ranging discussion of my whole study. Narratives by Kafka, Borges, Réage, Patrick White and others that frustrate conventional resolution and call attention to their status as fiction invited a deconstructive strategy. Common to all of these narratives is the development of plots involving the inscription of texts on unusual places (such as bodies, walls, landscapes) in a process that valorizes, or sacralizes, the text or the space or both. These fictions call into question our definition of the oneiric by strange projections of where and how the sacred can be found or made. Such fictions thus appear to encourage not so much the resolution of mystery as its creation.

Chapter 6 began as an indulgence, as an occasion to explicate a favourite novel: Russell Hoban's *Riddley Walker*. Then, when in 1986 Margaret Atwood's *The Handmaid's Tale* was published, a comparative treatment of the two as novels of futurist dystopias presented itself as a promising venture – not least because in the months I had spent on the study thus far our global geopolitical and ecological crises seemed to have worsened, and these 'eco-apocalyptic' narratives offered me a chance to engage the prophetic potential of fiction. I took mainly an anthropology-of-religion perspective in this chapter, however, trying to describe the myth-lore, religious structures and worship patterns of the societies in the two novels (one a degenerate high-tech fascist state, the other a degenerate *post*-technological remnant) as if they were actual historical cultures. I have, as a result, allowed these two texts to speak themselves more expansively than the others I have studied, and I have tried to help them articulate, from imagined communities to real ones, concluding words of warning and hope.

In Chapters 3 to 6 I have not tried to develop a progressive argument, based on the first two chapters. Rather, I have taken up issues and concepts – role-playing and aggregate selfhood, plotting and community, fiction and representation, play, storytelling, mystery, liminality – from Chapters 1 and 2, maintained an alertness to texts of pain, love and worship described in Chapter 2, and (guided by my interpretive strategies of phenomenology, hermeneutics and so on) orchestrated these elements into four different patterns in the last four chapters. I do not offer this description of my procedure as an apology for not undertaking a more systematic and conclusive approach. The spirit of *Gelassenheit* and of deep play that marks my study is better served, I think, by a little less concern for control.

I have tried to honour the need for inclusive language by alternating at random throughout my study between the pronouns *she* and *he*, *her* and *him*. I hope that whatever irritations this practice initially causes the reader will be outweighed by its productive dissonance: religious readings no less than others, surely, should constantly promote awareness of the gender-based qualifications of any statement.

I am grateful to Joyce Alexander, Davis Perkins, Ann-Janine Morey, Vernon Robbins, William Doty, David Fisher and Daniel Noel for reading sections of my manuscript and offering helpful criticism, and no less to Gary Phillips and Lou Silverman for giving a thorough critique of Chapter 2 at a Society of Biblical Literature seminar in 1986. My thanks go to David Jobling for inviting me to give a version of 'Sacred Texts/Sacred Space' at St Andrews College in Saskatoon, to James B. Wiggins for asking me to present a version of the Walker Percy chapter at Syracuse University, and to Beatrice Batson for having me present early versions of both of

these at Wheaton College. To my editor David Jasper and to
Sharon E. Greene, who read the whole manuscript in many drafts
and gave many suggestions for revision, I can only express my
gratitude and my sympathy. All of these friends gave me faith in
the possibility of reading communities that can make a difference.
Once again, my thanks to June Mann, who prepared my manuscript with her usual efficiency and forbearance.

Notes

1. Margaret Atwood, *Second Words* (Boston: Beacon Press, 1984) p. 15.
2. J. Hillis Miller, 'Presidential Address 1986: The Triumph of Theory,
   the Resistance to Reading, and the Question of the Material Base',
   Publications of the Modern Language Association, vol. 102/3 (May, 1987)
   pp. 281–91.

Wir alle fallen. Diese Hand da fällt.
Und sieh dir andre an: es ist in allen.

Und doch ist Einer, welcher dieses Fallen
unendlich sanft in seinen Händen hält.

Rainer Maria Rilke, 'Herbst'

It was said that one of the worst tragedies of the spirit was to
be born with a religious sense into a world where belief was no
longer possible. Was it an equal tragedy to be born without a
religious sense into a world where belief *was* possible?

Julian Barnes, *Staring at the Sun*

Aber Freund! Wir kommen zu spät. Zwar leben die Götter,
    Aber über dem Haupt droben in anderer Welt.
Endlos wirken sie da und scheinens wenig zu achten,
    Ob wir leben, so sehr schonen die Himmlischen uns.
Denn nicht immer vermag ein schwaches Gefäss sie zu fassen,
    Nur zu Zeiten erträgt göttliche Fülle der Mensch.

Friedrich Hölderlin, 'Brot und Wein'

1

Playing for Real
Roles, Plots and (Non-)
Representations

Fiction is nothing less than the sublest instrument for self-examination and self-display that mankind has invented yet.

How simply the fictive hero becomes the real.

But this is the way life goes: A man imagines he is playing his role in a particular play, and does not suspect that in the meantime they have changed the scenery without his noticing, and he unknowingly finds himself in the middle of a rather different performance.[1]

'THE HITCHHIKING GAME': ROUT/E OF DESIRE

In a story entitled 'The Hitchhiking Game' the Czech writer Milan Kundera describes a young couple setting out for their two-week vacation in the Tatras Mountains.[2] During a stop at a service station the girl, who is very shy but impulsive, leaves the car, walks down the road and, pretending to be a stranger, thumbs a ride from her boyfriend. They develop the game as they drive, improvising roles opposite to their personalities. She becomes 'an artful seductress', 'a role out of trashy literature', and he plays 'the tough guy who treats women to the coarser aspects of his masculinity' (10). The fiction arouses and fascinates them to the point that it takes over their behaviour. Instead of continuing to drive on to the Tatras the young man turns off in another direction, and they end up for the night in the only hotel of an unfamiliar town. Over dinner they intensify the role-playing, which by now is aggressively erotic. The young man takes the girl to their room, pays her money and demands that she strip for him. But when she stands there naked, expecting that now they will drop the roles and make love as their real selves, the young man forces the game to its end, taking her as if she were a whore – while she discovers to her horror 'that she had never known . . . so much pleasure as at this moment' (25). The story ends with the couple's post-coital returning to themselves, with the girl sobbing and repeating, 'I am me, I am me', and the young man struggling to recall his compassionate nature.

This sad and profound tale embodies certain problems that attend the writing and reading of narrative fiction and that have become increasingly perplexing in contemporary novels and stories and the interpretation of them. All of these problems locate themselves at the intersection of 'fiction' and 'reality', terms that I place inside quotation marks to indicate how problematic they themselves have become. In the following pages of this chapter I will read Kundera's story in three different (but connected) ways in order to comment on three of these fiction-meets-reality problems. The first reading will explore the connection of narrative fiction to role-playing and concepts of selfhood; the second reading will deal with the complicated interactions between authors and readers of narrative fiction; and the third reading will examine the controversial concept of representation in relation to narrative fiction. I consider the articulation of these problems, along with some proposals toward their resolution, as a worthy undertaking in itself for students of narrative theory and praxis, but I also want to give them an airing in preparation for the second chapter, on the nature and possibilities of a religious reading of fiction. Indeed, my discussion of religious reading can proceed far more efficiently following this treatment of three fundamental narrational issues. Peter Brooks says in *Reading for the Plot* that 'Narratives both tell of desire – typically present some story of desire – and arouse and make use of desire as dynamic of signification.'[3] 'The Hitchhiking Game' is surely such a story of desire (a desire not limited to Brooks' fairly narrow Freudian definition of it), and I hope to show eventually how such articulation of desire leads to religious reading.

FICTION, ROLE-PLAYING AND THE MULTIFOLD SELF

The most obvious of these fiction-meets-reality problems manifest in 'The Hitchhiking Game' involves role-playing in relation to selfhood. The young Czech couple are not secure in their sense of who they are (she is, after all, only about twenty-two and he is twenty-eight), nor are they satisfied with who they appear to be to themselves and each other. She is highly-strung, inhibited, ill at ease with her body; he is naive, unhappy with his job, insecure and hypocritical. Both of them are jealous. The role-playing is for both a relief, a probe and a dare. It is a relief for them to engage in the fiction of being someone else, and it is not inappropriate for the pair, heading out on their annual holiday, to indulge a holiday from the self by adopting for a time the persona of another, even if that other is itself a borrowing, a cliché from 'trashy literature' and entertainment cinema. For them it is a relief because they do not particularly like who they are individually (although they seem to like each other well enough).

Such escape into the novelty of a fictive role need not be inspired by self-dislike; it can be undertaken for pleasure. Among my acquaintances are a lively young woman, a graduate student, who when travelling alone, for example on airplane trips, regularly lies to her seatmates and invents elaborate deceptions about who she is (this, at least, is what she tells me: she may be lying!); and a happily married couple who regularly play erotic 'chance-encounter' games with each other, benevolent variations of Kundera's story. Such brief excursions from the self via the constructive imagination can be refreshing, arousing and enriching.

In the Czech story, however, the relief engendered by the borrowing of another persona quickly becomes less important to the couple than the value of the role-playing as a probe, a testing to feel what it would be like to *be* someone else. They simultaneously invent and act out a 'script', a dialogue that they can create effectively because they know versions of it from the popular plots of literature and film and because they play, to each other, the opposites of who they normally are. Because they can immediately test the effect of their adopted role on the other person, they can develop it comprehensively – give it life and thus actually experience a simulacrum of otherness in a double sense: both of playing a different self that is validated by the other's complicity, and of responding to the other's assumed difference –

that makes him/her more different than usual and interprets the usual difference of the other. It is clear by the end of the story that the couple will never quite return to their earlier relationship: the probe has revealed too much to them about themselves and each other.

Few of us take our role-playing to this extreme; few of us collaborate with someone else in creating and acting out scripts of other selves – and why should we wish to? One reason would be to try out alternatives to the self we are that does not please us (and perhaps others), an intention more serious than a brief vacation from the self, because it indicates a desire for change, to become someone 'better', whatever that may mean, than we are. Things are not this simple, of course. Even if we could experiment, with someone else, in trying out other selves, the gap between acting and becoming is very hard to bridge. The neurotic protagonist of Max Frisch's novel *Mein Name sei Gantenbein* boasts that he tries on stories like clothes, but he does not therefore *become* any of the characters in these stories; he merely confuses his already precarious selfhood.[4] What we do undertake, far less dramatically than Kundera's lovers, is a performance of various roles, every day of our lives, that together help to constitute our self. These are roles of kinship (parent, child, spouse), vocation, power (chief, mediator, victim), faith (believer, doubter) and scores of others. Our lives consist in and progress by our ability to live these many roles, and sometimes we appropriate these roles as probes by performing them in unusual contexts, for example by acting as mediator in a marriage, or a believer in some business venture.

How do we know how to play these many roles? We have not been taught most of them. The Czech girl is astonished, as she strips seductively, to find herself doing it so well, for she has never done it before. Annis Pratt at the end of her *Archetypal Patterns in Women's Fiction* introduces the term *unventing* to describe 'a rediscovery out of oneself', and suggests that 'the writing and reading of women's fiction [is] a form of "unvention", the tapping of a repository of knowledge lost from Western culture but still available to the author and recognizable to the reader as deriving from a world with which she, at some level of her imagination, is already familiar'.[5] I believe that we are all, women and men both, more adept at such unventing and also at *living* fictions than we think we are. Although we assume that we live aligned to a solid selfhood, we actually improvise much of our lives, and the very assumption of a solid selfhood is disclosed as a fiction. The ambiguity of the term 'to act' – meaning simply 'to do' (as if there were any pure action) and 'to perform' – indicates the problematic interaction of fictionalizing and reflexive, habitual behaviour that characterizes us.

The Czech lovers' borrowing of other personae to play their game functions as something still more significant than a probe. It intensifies into a kind of risk or dare that gets out of hand, as dares tend to do. They lose control of the script they are improvising, so that they can no longer direct or even project its outcome. Thus they place themselves at risk and under the conditions of chance. This is, in good part, what arouses them: the unpredictability of their game creates a novelty in their otherwise staid lives that excites them to still more radical behaviour. They get caught up in the capriciousness of the fiction they have invented, let it take over their actions and discover that this surrender to chance is highly erotic. They are, indeed, seduced by it.

What is there in this yielding to chance, about the lure of the unknown and untried, that is so seductive? Freud argued at one stage in his career that *eros* is closely aligned to *thanatos*, that the death wish is always entangled in the forays of the libido; and enough nihilistic moments inhabit 'The Hitchhiking Game', especially the violently passionate climax when the couple endanger love for the sake of heightened sex, to support the theory of eros stimulated by death. But that seems only a partial answer to me. More substantial is that the couple glimpse, in their relentless playing out of the game they have initiated, the possibility that the self is a construct rather than merely a biological or historical given, that it is a complicated fiction with open-ended potential, and thus they are aroused by the realization that they can, to a degree, become what they imagine.

They are led to this half-conscious awareness by watching, and experiencing, their selves slip so easily into other roles. Performing a fiction, and finding how hard it is to stop it and return to their 'true selves', shocks them into sensing the flexibility, variability and untrustworthiness of what they had taken to be a firm and fundamental self-identity. They encounter what is becoming a common phenomenon of late twentieth-century humanity: the elusive and possibly illusionary self. The most powerful passage of the story occurs in the final paragraphs, after the climax, when the girl lies in bed sobbing and repeating 'I am me'. She needs to say that because her 'me-ness' has been so severely assaulted and must be repaired through language. As Kaja Silverman, summarizing the work of the French linguist Emile Benveniste, puts it, 'without language there would be no subjectivity. Benveniste insists that the individual finds his or her cultural identity only within discourse, by means of the pronouns "I" and "you".'[6] In Kundera's story the girl struggles to recover her *sexual* identity as well through repeating the personal pronouns.

Not only has the girl's lover, in his lust, betrayed her; her own body has caused her to trespass a boundary into forbidden territory. The risk and the dare have taken her into strange areas where she no longer knows herself. In our psychologized society we speak familiarly of the 'loss of self', of 'finding ourselves', of trying to learn who we are. This is transitional terminology that indicates a recognition of contemporary problems of selfhood and identity but still conceives of the self, at least under normal conditions, as something stable, foundational and singular for each of us. The implication is that we once possessed, or were, such selves that have lately faded or dissolved or been mislaid and can be reconstituted or relocated again. But nowadays such a self is looking ever more fugitive, and that concept is giving way to models of the self as an aggregate of many selves, as a linguistic creation and as a fiction. The model of an aggregate self can be enhanced by thinking of the self as a sort of corporation or holding company. This may sound like just another way of saying that each of us has many facets to our personality, but it means more than that, for it shifts the emphasis from the image of a substantial core of selfhood, around which one's personality develops, to the image of an empty centre that is occupied by a succession and interplay of selves, each of which, alone or in combination with others, is appropriate to a particular moment and condition of our existence. Howard Gardner, describing this model as prominent in social psychology and sociology rather than in depth psychology, says:

> According to this point of view, an individual is always and necessarily a set of selves, a group of persons, who perennially reflect the context they happen to inhabit at any particular moment. Rather than a centre 'core self' which organizes one's thoughts, behavior, and goals, the person is better thought of as a collection of relatively diverse masks, none of which takes

precedence over the others, and each of which is simply called into service as needed and retired when the situation no longer requires it and the 'scene' moves elsewhere. Here the accent in the 'sense of self' falls much more heavily on interpersonal knowledge and know-how.[7]

The suspicion that selfhood is like this – comprised of many selves – has led to the pejorative diagnosis of the modern personality as 'fragmented', 'split', 'disintegrating', but one could just as well view these modifiers as evidence of an outmoded sense of the self as a monolithic entity, a model now gradually being superseded by that of one's identity as an orchestration of many selves.

But if one wishes to understand the self as a unity of selves, one then needs to ask what it is that provides the unity, that makes them cohere and co-operate, and the answer is simply, as Benveniste has already shown us, language. The self however conceived is a linguistic structure. That we can name the 'I' as the experiential focus of the countless events we participate in daily, that we designate this 'I' as the protagonist of the many situations that comprise our time and space, provides a continuity and singularity to our existences derived from language. But we have mistakenly thought of this linguistically-constructed 'I', this grammatical 'I', as identical with a centrality of personal being called the self that exists 'before' and outside of language. We have thought of the 'I' as the personal pronoun that merely designates an absolute selfhood rather than as the term that allows us to conceive of a self at all. Now we are coming to recognize that 'I' and 'me' and 'you' are our constellating and orchestrating pronouns that enable us to think of our many selves as a unified self, and to use that fiction of a self as our model for identity and difference. As Benveniste argues, 'in some way language puts forth "empty" forms which each speaker, in the exercise of discourse, appropriates to himself and which he relates to his "person", at the same time defining himself as *I* and a partner as *you*.' Silverman, in turn, comments that 'subjectivity is entirely relational; it only comes into play through the principle of difference, by the opposition of the "other" or the "you" to the "I". In other words, subjectivity is not an essence but a set of relationships.'[8] This stress on relationships applies not only to our newer understanding of the formation of selfhood but also to our changing comprehension of the world itself. Gilles Deleuze above all has argued persuasively that external reality is most usefully envisioned as a multiplicity with no centre, a constellation of many discrete units interacting in a variety of complex ways, and his projection provides a fitting context for a theory of the relational or intrapersonal self.[9]

If the 'I' is indeed such an orchestrated fiction functioning in a world of decentred multiplicity, what happens to the 'believing self', the person wishing to live and articulate a religious faith? Is the believing self one of the many selves that constitute the 'I'? If the 'I' itself is a fiction, albeit a necessary and generative one, can such a fiction 'believe', have faith in anything that transcends fiction? I will return to these crucial questions in the next chapter.

FAMILY PLOTS: THE WRITING AND READING COMMUNITY

Such an approach to 'The Hitchhiking Game' that dramatizes our problems of selfhood, and that has led me to describe our transitional attempt to comprehend the 'I' as a fiction designating our orchestrated corporate and co-operative selves, is only one way of engaging the story. I find it just as instructive, building on this interpretation, to approach the tale as a model for the reading of contemporary fiction *per se*. The story is not only about two lovers playing a game with their identities that gets out of hand; it is also, on a non-literal level, about what transpires between author, text and reader. Realistic fiction, at least (and 'The Hitchhiking Game' is largely realistic), entices the reader into a game of role-playing not unlike the one that entangles the Czech lovers. Through involvement with the development of a plot, which occurs mainly through some degree of identification with characters who invigorate the plot and carry it through to its conclusion, the reader for a time forgets the self and participates in other selves.

To think of one's reading fiction as involvement in a plot takes advantage of the multiple meanings of 'plot'. A plot is a specific area, a territory that characters occupy and tend, and in which they act to make things happen – which events the reader shares by entering the plot. To put it like this is already to grasp a second sense of plot, in which it is the story's design, some sort of variation on the fundamental arrangement of conflict and resolution that constitutes narrative fiction. Peter Brooks, in fact, urges an epistemological function on plot, calling it nothing less than 'the organizing dynamic of a specific mode of human under-standing'(7). But because a plot is only gradually disclosed by an author and figured out by the reader, it assumes the meaning of connivance, a deception by the author at the reader's expense. The author delays the reader's enlightenment, plays with and manipulates the reader and in that manner 'plots' against him in order to keep him in his narrating power. As Brooks says, 'with the advent of Modernism came an era of suspicion toward plot. . . . If we cannot do without plots, we nonetheless feel uneasy about them, and feel obliged to show up their arbitrariness, to parody their mechanisms while admitting our dependence on them'(7). Such suspicion has intensified in our 'post-modern' era, in which authors of experimental and non-realistic fiction carry the plot against the reader still further by breaking the conventions of narration and thus making him unsure of what is 'happening' in the story.

In any case, the reader who becomes absorbed in the fiction and is thus made temporarily self-forgetful enjoys a respite from 'real life', just as the vacationing lovers in Kundera's story attempt a holiday from their ordinary identities. I do not see why this read-erly absorption in a fictive world should be denigrated as escapism, as it so often is. It is of course an escape to another world, but even the best-adjusted of us require such regular excur-sions of the imagination; it is a part of the play instinct that maintains us in balance, and even though the dominating work ethic of Western society has led us to undervalue play – and in recent decades has impelled us to work so hard at playing that it loses its ludic quality – we manage to find in the gratuitousness of fiction, and of reading it, a relief from our labour and achievement-oriented lives.

But even the least adeptly written narrative provides something more than escapism. One imagines that storytelling in pre- and non-literate (non-chirographic, in Walter Ong's terms) cultures had, along with its entertainment function, a recounting and a testing function.[10] Stories that were '*mythoi*', a blending of history (the wars, wanderings, tribulations of a people; the deeds of their leaders) and fiction (sacred tales about the gods, about cosmic beginnings and endings, deeds of superhuman heroes) served in their regular and ritualized retelling to confirm a people in their identity and challenged them to be worthy of their heritage through their own deeds of courage, faith, obedience, exploration. Since *mythos* also means plot, we see that these stories were meant to design the lives of the listening community. But in our secular age, in which the plots of our 'sacred texts' are taken from the sciences and technology, and in which urban living provides little space or time for ritual gathering, the communal storytelling activity has largely disappeared and has been replaced by substitutes from our entertainment and communications technology. We think immediately of television and cinema as such replacements, and they are. Television programming brings us occasionally a presentation of momentous events that form the plots, sometimes even the climaxes, of our national or even global 'narratives' (examples are the actions around the assassination of John F. Kennedy, the abandoning of Saigon at the end of the Vietnam war, Richard Nixon's public disintegration), but we do not share these communally; rather, we absorb them in our individual, private surroundings. One does watch cinema often in large groups, but fifty to two hundred people sitting together in a darkened room watching the flickering screen do not form a community.

An older technological replacement for ritual storytelling is the writing and reading of fiction. We tend not to think of these activities as shaped by technology, but they are. The mass printed and distributed book or magazine is just as much a technological production as a film or television show, even if a different kind of technology, and we should ask how the technologies of writing, printing, distribution and even reading influence the old dynamics of shared narrative. The novel in particular is a modern phenomenon. The condition of its artifice – that it usually has a single known author who claims the story as her own, that it is maintained and 'passed on', without alteration, in its tangible book form, that it is marketed rather than transmitted or 'handed down', that it is generally read by someone in solitude whenever she wishes, and not merely on a certain special occasion: all these distinguish it from the oral narrative, the story told in a group to nurture the group identity.

The conditions of the novel's interpretation, in contrast to the response to the oral narrative, are also instructive to recall. Whereas the formulaic recital of the tale and its recitation in the context of ritual constitute its form – it is part of a larger, more significant occasion – the novel's interpretation takes place via written explication in books and journals, or in classroom lectures and discussions. In both of these the novel's form is separated from the interpretive context and becomes the object of investigation, in other words, whereas the oral tale remains much more the nexus of the whole interpretive context, of which the hearing and responding community considers itself to be a part. What difference does this make? The novel, alienated from the communal roots of narrative, disseminated technologically and interpreted technically, becomes an ideal vehicle for the exploring self seeking to comprehend its separation, difference and individuality; but reading the novel also simultaneously undermines any secure sense of self-solidarity, because it is a kind of literature that by its nature promotes the notion of multiple selves. Jean-François Lyotard in *The Postmodern Condition* sees 'the dissolution of the self into a host of networks and relations, of contradictory codes and interfering messages', and contemporary narrative especially participates in this dissolution.[11]

In this sense, then, and by way of this comparison of oral and written narration, we see that reading fiction can serve as a probe by offering the self other versions of what it might be. Not only the novel provides this function; although the short story is older than the novel by many centuries, its form has become moulded by the same technology that has shaped the novel, and it is written according to a variety of chirographic formulas that are markedly different from the formulaic short stories of pre-print societies. Both of these literary forms, the novel and story, invite the reader to see herself in relation to the characters of the narrative, to put herself in some fashion in the place of those characters, to experience vicariously through them. Or, more reflectively, one can see oneself, traits of one's personality and behaviour, 'objectified' through such characters and in that way 'get a distance' on oneself, see oneself more clearly and thereby learn to confirm the patterns one approves and to modify those one does not. Reading fiction is thus a more comparative activity than we generally think it is. It somehow always involves an excursion from the self to examine other selves and at the same time an evaluation of the self in terms of similarities and alternate possibilities of behaviour exhibited by those other selves. Silverman, remarking on the 'discontinuous' or linguistically defined subject, says that it 'may depend for its emergence upon already defined discursive positions, but it has the capacity to occupy multiple and even contradictory sites' (199).

This seems also to describe the skill that the alert contemporary reader learns.

What makes this relationship between self and narrative both more provocative and frustrating nowadays is the recognition by scholars of narrative that literary texts, like our individual selves, are not necessarily coherent unities, totalities, wholes, but may consist also, like the self, of an aggregate of units that can be joined, shifted and rejoined in constantly changing patterns to produce (to borrow a phrase from Paul de Man) 'an infinity of valid readings'.[12] As Owen Miller says, 'There can be no doubt that a powerful link exists between theories of the self and theories of the text. In fact such a link seems a crucial aspect of the contemporary insistence on notions of textuality and the metamorphosis of the "literary work" into the "Text". The rejection of the text as an autonomous entity, as a self-regulating organic whole, seems logically consistent with the demise in belief in the Romantic notion of a discrete, independent, enduring self.'[13]

The Romantic writers themselves (such as the young Wordsworth and the young Goethe), celebrators of mutability that they were, did not in fact believe in a static, but rather in a developing self, one that could both grow and be transformed, so that we can understand their most radical, imaginative concept of self-identity as a sequence, or serial of selves. But they did not advance the concept of selfhood as an interacting aggregate of selves. This is a view that took shape – is still taking shape – in the twentieth century. Thus today's reader, learning to live with various incarnations of the self, 'tries on' characters from contemporary fiction to experience how they inform his own life, but then discovers that these fictive characters also often exhibit multiple selves. That is to say, characters in today's narratives not infrequently display orchestrations of selfhood such as I have been describing because many authors of the novels and stories recognize or at lease intuit that individual consciousness is structured in terms of multiple selves. Older literature, even that of the 'high modernism' of the early to mid-twentieth century, reveals very little of such an awareness – which means, of course, not that consciousness has not always consisted of a corporation of many selves, only that we have not discovered this model until recently.

It would be possible, I believe, to trace a history of the presentation of consciousness in creative literature from at least the Renaissance to the present in which one would find a movement from Christian dualism (in which a good and an evil self are locked in struggle) to an Enlightenment stable and unified self (established by the power and triumph of reason) to the progression of selves transforming one into the next in Romanticism, to the acutely self-diagnosing self of modernism (which conceives a fragmentation of the self that is neurotic if not outright psychotic), to the multiple selfhood recognized as common in postmodernism. Typical characters in this history would be Hamlet (Christian dualism), Samuel Johnson's Rasselas (Enlightenment rational wholeness), Goethe's Wilhelm Meister (a Romantic evolution of selves), Dostoevsky's Raskolnikov (the psychotic fragmentation of consciousness in modernism) and Toni Morrison's Sula (post-modern orchestration of selves).

Such a history would allow us to see more clearly how reading certain kinds of contemporary fiction functions as a probe. We find our sense of existing as intrapersonal selves articulated in the characters of this fiction, who themselves are presented as experimenting (in various degrees of awareness) with various selves and permutations of them. One could say that we readers of this literature play with the fictions of characters who are, in their plots, playing with fictions of characters.

We are now prepared to understand when and how reading as a probe turns into reading as a dare. It occurs when the reader, like the characters of his fiction, comes to suspect that the experimentations with the various selves are all there is, that no original or authenticating self exists for the experimenter to turn to when the experimenting stops; that the experimenting in fact never ceases. If – to play with Max Frisch's metaphor – trying on stories is like trying on clothes, reading as a dare is playing with the risk that one has no single, proper, identifying ensemble but that one constantly dresses oneself in different combinations. More philosophically stated, one reads daringly when one glimpses the necessarily nihilistic impulse of reading embedded in fiction (which I will discuss in more detail in Chapter 5) and continues to read and identify with the characters nevertheless.

A frightening aspect of Kundera's short story is that the players cannot quit the game. It gets out of hand, and they need to play it through to its end. Why are they unable to stop it? A 'literary' explanation is that they get caught up in a particularly powerful narrative, one fed by their erotic fantasies, and that they are therefore compelled to see how it 'comes out', to live it through to its

conclusion. Expressed psychologically (especially by the Gestal-
tists), it is that the need for closure comes to dominate: once we
humans begin something, we are restless and dissatisfied, at odds
with ourselves, until we have finished it. We apparently need to
complete an action, once started, because this is part of the
patterning and ordering process by which we make our lives
assume meaning.

One is helped at this point by Kenneth Burke's familiar thesis
that language is symbolic action.[14] Our designation of or reference
to anything takes the place of our immediate, visceral response to
that thing, and thus language always 'already' symbolizes and
gives us a 'secondary' relationship to things. Participating in narrative – telling or hearing, writing or reading it – with its beginning,
middle and end, then, is an elaboration of engaging in language
as symbolic action. The action symbolized in narrative is the life
cycle in miniature. It tells, in an infinity of variations, our birth,
maturation and death via its own structure of beginning, middle
and end. I believe that the innate and universal power of narrative
derives from this formal, structural articulation of our life-
progression and from the intuited awareness that, whenever we
tell or receive a story, we recall in intensely concentrated form the
relentless unfolding of our lives. As Brooks states it,

> plot is the internal logic of the discourse of mortality. . . . Walter
> Benjamin has made this point in the simplest and most extreme
> way, in claiming that what we seek in narrative fiction is that
> knowledge of death which is denied to us in our own lives: the
> death that writes *finis* to life and therefore confers on it its
> meaning. 'Death', writes Benjamin, 'is the sanction of every-
> thing that the storyteller can tell.' Benjamin thus advances the
> ultimate argument for the necessary retrospectivity of narrative:
> that only the end can finally determine meaning, close the
> sentence as a signifying totality. (22)

Reading is a dare for secularized individuals (who are not necessarily persons without religious faith but rather all those of us who
live in pluralistic societies no longer dominated by a traditional
belief system) in our age because its narratives cause us to dwell
more consciously and self-consciously on the patternlessness
within the birth-growth-death pattern, on the vagaries within the
structure, than the readers of older and more homogeneous

generations. One encounters a good deal of what Silverman calls 'writerly' fiction, a sort in which the author communicates her particular stresses and anxieties of composition (246–50). Prominent among these is the agony of choice – and I use the term *agony* because its Greek root *agōn* conveys the combined struggle, playfulness and anguish that accompany the author's labour. Anyone who has attempted to write fiction knows of the nearly paralysing force that the plenitude of possibilities – what John Updike called 'that beautiful blankness all around' – can induce.[15] The novelist has an infinity of settings, characters, perspectives, discourses, images, actions, to select from as she creates her fictions, and no assurance that her imagination's *agōn* will produce a cohesive, coherent, communicable something that a reader can accept as recognizable and eliciting response from his own imagination and experience. And indeed, this contemporary agonistic fiction is often a record of the author's difficulty in rendering compositional decisions, so that the narrative becomes an account and demonstration of how hard it is to compose *decisive* fiction.

This authorial dilemma – that her narrative can go anywhere, and that she must make significant choices at every stage along the way, with an overwhelming sense of too much to choose from and few guidelines for choice – is what makes fiction-writing a risk for the author, and it is part of what is conveyed as dare to the reader. For he comes to see this surfeit of possibilities, and the need always to choose specific ones, as indicative of his own condition: compelled to design his life on the basis of choices of action with far-reaching consequences, from too many options and with too little direction. Reading narrative, then, in which the author reveals her anxiety about the creative process – as so much contemporary writing shows – generates in the reader both a shared sense of the author's *agōn* and a reminder that one also always *lives* at risk – in doubt as how one's life will evolve and turn out. Reading narrative becomes a model for anxious open-endedness and self-doubt that inspires a desire for closure but simultaneously fears and avoids it. One seeks it because it is intolerable not to experience the completion of an action once launched. One avoids it out of fear that it may be an undesirable sort, and because one wishes to delay as long as possible the final closure of death. Especially in Chapter 6, my last chapter, I will pay attention to examples of contemporary fiction that seek to avoid closure and that struggle with (Frank Kermode's phrase) a 'sense of an ending'.

'The Hitchhiking Game', which plays out an action chosen impulsively and arbitrarily from many options, both in terms of the plot and of the author's formal composition, displays the ambiguity toward closure that the dare of fiction-writing and of designing one's life provokes. The couple in their roles of temptress and tough male – two of a great variety they could have adopted – lose themselves in their fictions until they act out the climax – sexual orgasm – that by its sheer visceralness (unconnected to any role) shocks them 'back to themselves'. But the girl says, again and again, 'I am me', trying to assure herself because her 'me-ness' has been attacked and made vulnerable, while the 'young man began to call compassion to his aid . . . There were still thirteen days' vacation before them' (91). After the closure that the sexual climax brings, another plot immediately develops, and the risk continues. The young woman sees that she needs to repair the structure of the self, and the young man sees that he needs to repair the relationship. Indeed, both of them need to do both of these.

What one risks, then, in reading fiction and in 'composing' one's life is the demand for ever new commitments. Reaching the end of the plot is only the prelude for beginning another one, or for discovering that this particular plot is just one sub-plot of a greater and more complicated action. Playing out a role is merely activating and invigorating one of the many selves available to us, or recognizing that this particular role/self is part of an orchestration of 'I's' that constitute our existence. We take risks in reading narrative and in shaping fictions of the self, but we have no other choice, short of living dumbly, unreflectively.

THE FULFILMENT OF REPRESENTATION

Kundera's tale can be read yet another way, as an allegory of the post-modern debate about representation. The young couple, in their game of role-playing, confuse the boundaries between common, everyday reality and fiction – that which is fabricated – to the extent that they set aside a certain part of their reality and live out a particular fiction. But in doing so, do they not transform the fiction into a reality? At the very least, once they have played these roles, the characters they have taken on, however temporarily, become part of their personalities – join their repertoire of selves – and hence become a part of their reality in that fashion. Thus the story leads one to return again to the old question of the difference between fiction and reality.

One difference, it seems at first, is that whereas fictions have to be imagined, reality is the given, the 'what is there'. But to say this is to suggest a simpler relationship between the two than is the case. To say that reality is 'what is there' is to state, more accurately, that it is what we *perceive* is there – and our perceptions are never purely sensory but also always involve the imagination, our image-making capacities. A blatant way of putting it is to say that we invent some of what we perceive. How much we make up has been the subject of philosophical argument for centuries and in our age has also become a focus of cognitive psychological and neurophysiological research. In the long philosophical debate the dominant position has been to distinguish between ordinary, everyday reality – the space-time-matter world in and around us – and a 'deeper' reality that inhabits transcendence (the so-called 'ultimate reality' of divinity), mind, nature, art, history, law, the virtues and so on, and that is hidden but can be disclosed by rational inquiry. That inquiry has evolved in scientific method in its various forms, mainly the reflective-analytical mode of philosophy and the experimental-inductive mode of the modern sciences. Language has been regarded mainly as an instrument, a means of recording and communicating our experience of ordinary reality and our discoveries of what the 'deeper' reality is.

Literature has accommodated this position by allowing itself to be described by the critics (and occasionally by describing itself) as the primary language of representation, with metaphor as its key operating agent. But in our century language *per se*, not just literary language, has come increasingly under suspicion regarding its reliability as a conveyer of our ordinary-reality experience as well as of our scientifically discovered reality, so that the philosophy of our era has consisted in good part in dealing with the realization that language will not behave itself, will not function passively or tractably as an information-carrying vehicle, but even at its most innocuous always has its own agenda, its own hidden discourses, even – perhaps – its own reality.

Language thus comes to participate in the discovery of reality, but its participation changes the nature of the search. Language reveals itself as not merely a vehicle of communication but a perceptual mode. In fact, it inserts itself between the philosopher/scientist and his study of reality, so that the perception of reality becomes thoroughly entangled in language, to the extent that we now sometimes refer to the 'universe of language' as the context and boundary of reality. Whether or not language is so totally dominating, we recognize its powerful influence in shaping our experience of both kinds, of ordinary and deeper reality. We can and do experience without verbalizing; our sensory apprehension and eidetic or image-making faculties can operate non-linguistically (but no more reliably than language for providing us a 'true' comprehension of reality), but language is necessary to organize, reflect on, interpret these experiences and to render them significant. This effort always fails, in a sense, because we never manage to say all that we mean or precisely what we mean – yet we do not know just what we mean until we say it. We all live with a sense of the inadequacy of our expression, and we tend to think that we fail at proper or complete expression because we are insufficiently literate, erudite or sensitive, but this inadequacy is actually a condition of our consciousness and our apprehension of reality. It is impossible for us ever to express our reality perfectly because that reality is partly our creation and takes shape only as we struggle to express it. What we call interpretation, giving signification, making meaning, are as much inventions as discoveries and organizations of reality, and they are bound to remain partial and insufficient because reality, thus understood, is always in process, unfinished, multifold and changing.

  If this is indeed how we think, perceive and articulate, then our traditional understanding of representation needs to be corrected. We must revise our view of language so as to see it not merely as a way of representing reality; of metaphorical language as not merely an imagistic, poetic way of illustrating facts and concepts; of fiction as not just a playful distortion of a more basic and more truthful language of scientific discovery, historical interpretation, diagnosis, philosophical analysis. What is referred to as the contemporary crisis of representation has to do with this realization that the relatively recently recognized new status of language as problematic (because it complicates the perception and interpretation process) no longer permits us to view language as simply conveying some objective reality. Above all, it no longer allows us to view the presentational, heavily metaphorical language of literature as merely reflecting the referents of the 'real' historical, natural, cultural world. Our struggle now is to learn what else a language complicit with shaping reality and making meaning does, if it does not only represent. Kundera's story will guide us in explaining three alternatives to thinking of the language of literature, of narrative fiction in particular, as representational.

First, we recall that the couple become involved in a *game*. It is not a formal game but an impromptu one initiated on impulse by the girl, and the two of them immediately establish rules, both by recognition and invention. They adopt and play roles, recognizing from their cultural experience which characters seem to fit, and they make up, via imaginative interaction, gestures and dialogue to animate the personae they assume. The nature of the game is erotic flirtation that intensifies into a seduction contest, and the goal is sexual consummation. But in 'representing' the characters they have chosen, their intention is not to achieve any serious authenticity of portrayal. They are merely *playing* at being the temptress and virile male, striving for a simulacrum of these two types (which are not well-defined culturally in any case) in order to excite each other and themselves. The key term here is 'playing'. Play is both an appropriation of what is there, of the given, and a refusal to put the components to 'serious' use. It appropriates persons in that it occupies them, causes them to devote themselves to an action and some mental, affective projection, yet it is also gratuitous, in that it produces no results.

The couple's playing instructs us in a role that language frequently takes on. It is, much of the time, playful, and a reason why we have underestimated the power of language to shape our reality is that we have undervalued the power of play itself. Children learning to talk demonstrate the force of language as play. The child is fascinated by naming and is intent on learning the terms that designate the objects, actions, relationships and so on of her experience. But she is not totally involved in this representational learning. In fact, children are not rational creatures and, unlike their elders, are not devoted to formal learning. The child is charmed by language itself, by the grand things it can do, by the power she achieves through it, and thus above all plays with language and transforms language into play. (Freud's famous interpretation of his baby grandson's 'fort' and 'da' game with language loses sight of just this, that it is, mainly and above all, play.) She can employ terms 'correctly', which is to say use them to match their mutually agreed-upon referents (for example, 'Teddy is sleeping'), but she will also, through repetition, incantation and random phrasing, construct word combinations gratuitously, for the pleasure of it (for example, 'Teddy Teddy Teddy', 'Teddy Beddy', 'Mommy is Teddy'). We assume that we outgrow this relationship to language as we mature, but we do not. It becomes less pronounced, but all of us retain a playful, non-rational liaison with language and enjoy it via puns, rhymes, chants, slips of tongue and pen, nonsense words and the like.

One of the ways, that goes largely ignored, in which Western culture combines representational language with linguistic play is in the naming of children. The selection of names for a daughter or son – surely a symbolic and literal act laden with social, cultural, sometimes religious and economic import – often happens in a remarkably haphazard manner. We may name our children 'for' someone; in that sense the names represent. But often – and increasingly so as we lose our religious heritage and close family ties – we select names merely on the basis of their sound, and of how they look when written; in this sense our most intimately identifying labels have been given to us playfully. Paradoxically, we are often named gratuitously in a society that values above all what is purposeful and meaningful.

The possibilities for playing in and with literary texts are virtually endless, and creative literature is in fact the kind of discourse in which linguistic play comes into its own, for literature is the most gratuitous kind of writing. Just as Kundera's couple resort to creative play as an escape from the duty and purposefulness of their lives, so too language finds its escape in the playfulness of literature. Does this literature construed as play not represent anything? Does it not point to some 'reality'? In so far as a literary text is an organization of words, a superimposition of structured language that interprets existence, it enacts the human compulsion to make order, just as every game played is, and reflects, a drive toward order – and this is a kind of representation. In so far as literary texts follow certain conventions – of genre, narrative format, tropes, etc. – they draw on the literary tradition and hence can be said to 'represent' the collective wealth of literature composed before them. But to argue that literature 'represents' in this fashion is not the same as stating that it exists by imitating the actions and characters of the historical world. It *plays* at imitating them, to greater and lesser degrees, and as a rule we mistake this playful imitation as standing, and standing in, for our lived world. Literature beguiles us into believing that its playful configurations of language are modelled on the components of our natural and cultural reality, when actually those configurations allow us to grasp the many possibilities – the inter*play* – of reality. The escape of language into the play of literature creates the conditions for new knowledge.

Literary language thus represents so much, no less than the conditions for a mode of knowing (as Brooks says of plot), that it represents nothing – no single thing – in the conventional sense of imitation or mimesis. Its method, enacted playfully, is to test limitations and push against boundaries, to see how far it can go and still 'make sense', which is to say still be coherent, communicable and in some fashion credible. We are of course describing metaphor and what metaphor does. *Metaphor* is derived from the Greek *meta* and *pherein*, 'to carry over' or 'to carry beyond', and denotes the process of transforming language beyond its wonted, literal meanings – as if these were the 'original' meanings. It occurs through the conjoining of dissimilar images that forces one's mind – first the imagination and then, sometimes, the analytical faculty – to conceive a new, often more complex, often strange and tentative image that acts as a probe for establishing a deeper and more encompassing view of our reality.

The young Czech pair engage in a metaphorical act when they assume different personae and bring them together, force them to interact as a probe toward some hitherto unexplored, unknown relationship. They leave, for a time, the tried, literal reflexes of their individual and common identities and 'become', which is to say represent, someone else, but they can do this only against the awareness of who they 'really' are, which is to say the awareness of their identities up to this point in their lives. The 'as-if' role merged with the familiar self (or familiar aggregate of selves) leads them into new insights about themselves alone, each other and the two of them together that indeed expand their reality. It is true that they are stunned by what they learn – by the intensity of their lusts and passions – to the extent that their lives are radically affected, but this is what powerful metaphoric experiences can do.

What is the role of representation in this metaphoric enactment, if we are illustrating here an alternative to mimesis? The roles of temptress and tough male that Kundera's characters take on are not so much imitations as they are creations. The young man and woman project and embody these roles in order to test what their actuality would be like – how it would be to live consistently as such persons. Such tentative actualizing of untried possibility is what happens, linguistically, in the appropriation of metaphor. When the new image joins the old in the dynamic of metaphor, something transformative occurs that we could describe, by analogy, as chemical. Both properties are changed by the contact, the intermingling (if they do not reject each other – as the poles of metaphor can also do if they are altogether too 'foreign' to each other).

Does this process represent or imitate anything? Only the manner in which language functions as a mode of knowing, for it shows language, in its play of familiarity and strangeness, similarity and difference, building on itself, evolving its own epistemology. And the stuff of narrative can be seen in good part as elaborated metaphor that builds on other narrative: all literature is part of a vast intertextual network.[16] In metaphor, then, we find a linguistic and literary probe toward new patterns of knowledge that offer us greater choices of what we might believe, how we might respond. Such imaginative playing with reality is risky, for it teaches us to suspect that everything we have accepted as foundational is open to question. We have seen this danger exemplified in the Czech couple, who once they have become absorbed by their game do not know how to stop it and feel themselves forcing it, driven against their wills, to a violent and destructive climax. Yet this willingness – sometimes this compulsion – to place everything at risk can be a third alternative way of comprehending how language engages reality without relying on the tradition of representation. Jacques Derrida in an essay on Plato locates this risk in the nature of the literary text itself and in the problem of its interpretation. After portraying texts as necessarily cryptic and deceptive, always resisting translation into perceptual statements, he writes of them: 'Always and essentially at the risk of being lost definitively.'[17] The 'being lost definitively' I take as a typical Derridean play on terms which refers both to the danger of the texts failing to inspire any adequate (whatever that may mean) reading whatsoever and of them remaining closed off to definition, which is to say closed off to interpretation from any approach seeking 'right' answers and solutions. Thus the risk comes to dominate the whole writing and reading scene.

What do author and reader stand to lose? They risk forfeiting their identities, their self-control and their control over their destinies. One observes in Kundera's story how the girl especially is victimized. Although she has initiated the game, she is the one who expects it to stop at the critical point; she assumes all along that she and her young man will quit their roles at the most intense stage of arousal and make love as their 'real' selves. But this the young man will not allow. He bullies her into continuing, now makes her play the role of whore and virtually violates her, although she then also discovers an unknown part of her responding lustfully to being taken. Like the girl – actually like both lovers – the author and reader of the literary text risk disappointed expectations because of a problematic relationship between them. The author's text will not be read as he conceived it; he will inevitably consider all readings of his text to be misreadings, even those that are appreciative, because no one else can share completely what he had in mind as he composed his text. Hence he will think of himself as victimized, misused by his readers. And in a way the author of narrative deserves the 'misunderstanding' he gets because he intensifies the dissimulating quality of the literary text by plotting against the reader: by withholding information, trailing red herrings, employing unreliable narrators, devising twists of plot and offering surprise endings. To write narrative is to indulge in trickery, and it is therefore no wonder that the author as trickster provokes animosity in his readers, for we are sometimes charmed by being fooled but more often antagonized by it. Yet the author who deceives must also court; he needs his readers (no matter how he protests otherwise) and thus must somehow accommodate them, with the result that he builds a resentment against these creatures who are both his reason for writing and an obstacle to his art.

'You, dogged, uninsultable print-oriented bastard', the narrator of John Barth's 'Life-Story' addresses the reader, in one of fiction's more provocative epithets, and it is a phrase that catches the ambivalence an author feels toward his readers.[18] Yet this exasperated love-hate is just as strong on the other side. The reader feels at the mercy of the dissembling writer, not only because she is toyed with but also and perhaps above all because she is required to be the passive partner, is given no voice, no opportunity to respond. This is, of course, in an important sense the way it should be: the artist speaks through his art and should not be obliged to defend his creation – not least because no one is forced to read him in the first place. On the other hand, the reader who makes the effort, who engages the text and is challenged, vexed, instructed, pleasured by it, desires more, wishes for the immediate human contact that the narrative dramatizes, seems to promise but never can deliver. Thus reading is experienced as an eternal foreplay, without ultimate fulfilment, and the reader, for her part, develops a resentment as strong as the writer's.[19]

Writing and reading as risks, it seems, do not pay off but leave author and reader with disappointed expectations. Why then keep on? A compelling reason is that the author-text-reader relationship, including its fundamental and uncorrectable frustrations, embodies instructively the 'problematics' of human relationships, so that to write and to read narrative is to trace these relationships, exercise them in an arena of free play, in a kind of neutral zone where the mistakes will not have lethal consequences. One thinks of flight simulators as an analogy.[20] The airline pilots logging fictional flight time in them are both playing and developing reflexes, learning how to respond to emergencies, living out potential crises that they hope will never take place. This activity is representational, obviously, in much the same way that literature remains representational – incidentally so. The represented here is the context, the given of the movable cockpit and the filmed or computer-simulated 'outside', but the pilot-trainee does not believe in their reality as *being* the external physical world, any more than the thoughtful author or reader believes that the fictions she writes or reads are actually happening. Both play with their respective fictions and take them very seriously *as fictions* to the degree that these fictions do not represent so much as they substitute for reality.

But what is the difference between representation and substitution? That which represents 'takes the part of' its referent but not so powerfully as to obscure it and cause the observer to forget the referent. That which substitutes takes the part (could we say 'takes the whole'?) of its referent so effectively that it effaces it and causes the observer to lose sight of it. An analogy would be a defence lawyer who represents his client skilfully in the courtroom and who portrays him in ways that the client by himself cannot, so as to let the complexities of the defendant and his actions come to light, versus the lawyer who by the strength of personality or rhetorical brilliance presents a picture – a fiction – of his client so aligned to the lawyer's own self-projection that the jury, its attention transferred to him, forgets to form its own judgement of the defendant. Representation at its most forceful stage, in other words, becomes substitutionary, just as metaphor at its most efficacious 'carries over', transfers so significantly that it generates a new perspective on or a new arrangement of reality. Metaphor or the literary text in this sense substitutes for reality by creating a new version of it, and for this reason writing and reading fictions pose a risk: they can lead us to change our minds and therefore our behaviour. As the speaker says in the last line of Rilke's poem 'Archaic Torso of Apollo', stunned by the sculpture's force: 'You must change your life.'[21] One stands to become a different person, to gain a different identity. The resentments and frustrations of writer and reader directed against each other come to focus on this fearful anticipation of change, and it is hardly a lesser threat for the author than for the reader, for the author sooner or later reacts to her interpreters and is thus brought by her fictions to an altered identity.

This third alternative of understanding literary language as a placing of everything at risk, rather than understanding it as merely representational, is connected, finally, to the matter of power. It creates a situation in which power relationships replace mimetic ones. One observes how this works on the way to the climax of 'The Hitchhiking Game'. The young man, after he and the girl retire to the hotel room, not only refuses to let her drop her role of temptress; he demands that she intensify it into one that places her wholly under his control. 'He longed to humiliate her. Not the hitchhiker but his own girl. The game merged with life. The game of humiliating the hitchhiker became only a pretext for humiliating the girl. The young man had forgotten he was playing a game. He simply hated the woman standing in front of him. He stared at her and took a fifty-crown bill from his wallet. He offered it to the girl. "Is that enough?" ' (88)

He pays her to perform a striptease for him, which she does anxiously but still in the spirit of this risky and now frightening game. Then, when she tries to stop the game and call forth both of their familiar selves, he will not relinquish his role – which has somehow joined reality – and takes her sexually as if she were a whore. At this point, for the young man the full substitutionary

power of metaphor exerts itself: 'The game merged with life.' The
girl for him *becomes* a whore, and she feels herself as one.

None of this lasts, obviously; the couple do not remain in a
literal liaison of prostitute and client. Yet a new relational reality
is established between them, or an old, hitherto unarticulated one
is confirmed, that is based on power, and in a way in which power
overcomes mimesis. One sees how it may work by addressing the
question, why does the young man abruptly hate the girl and
wish to humiliate her? Psychiatrist Robert Stoller in his book
Observing the Erotic Imagination offers a disturbing and complicated
answer:

> In the daydreams of perverse people, especially those stories
> concretized in pornography, I can make out the construction of
> a script, the principal purpose of which is to undo childhood
> traumas, conflicts, and frustrations by converting these earlier
> painful experiences to present (fantasized) triumphs. To build
> these daydreams, the patients also make use of mystery, secrets,
> risk running, revenge, and dehumanizing (fetishizing) of their
> objects. In all these qualities, hatred is a manifest or latent
> presence. But having found these factors in perversions and
> their pornographies, I realized that the same dynamics were
> present in the pornographies of everyday life and in the erotic
> excitement of the nonperverse patients I had treated for years.
> So I was now studying normative erotic excitement. I found that
> what makes excitement out of boredom for most people is the
> introducing of hostility into the fantasy.[22]

If Stoller is right, Kundera's young man is hostile because of his
problem of identity, and what I have described as role-playing is
a part of Stoller's scripting that, he says, we all follow in our
attempts to resolve who and what we are. Our scripts are both,
and simultaneously, fictions and reality, and we find ourselves
driven, for reasons of overcoming trauma, finding security,
relieving boredom and so on, to convert the fictions into reality
via power manipulations such as the young man indulges in.

Leo Bersani writes at the end of an essay on 'The Subject of
Power' (the title's pun is intentional): 'As I have attempted to
suggest with the model of realistic fiction, the modes of excitement
in the exercise of power may even include an explosive end to the
frictions of confrontation and the suicidal apotheosis of the subject

beyond the conditions of life itself. Literature is the conjunction of a purely coercive aim with bizarre forms of *jouissance* [erotic action, sexual fulfilment] for which the vocabulary of coercion may finally be inadequate.'[23] Bersani's first sentence sounds like an interpretation of 'The Hitchhiking Game', while the second suggests that fiction may teach us to plot something beyond our hostile scripting.

Such power-play, at any rate, need not be the goal of risk-taking as the third alternative to understanding literary language as representational, as mainly and merely imitating some larger and other real life. Power relationships can be dissolved into collegial relationships, even if it rarely happens, and I propose to describe in the next chapter how the most positive and productive result of the narrative experience is not in persuading readers to accept a particular interpretation – not in overpowering them with a superior reading – but rather in provoking a compassionate reaction of mutual care and concern. Literary language as a mode of knowing ought to expand into a mode of *trustful* interacting, in which the risk-taking is made to pay off – unlike what it does for the Czech lovers, and unlike what it usually does for writers and readers today – by creating a community of response.

Notes

1. The first quotation is from John Updike, 'The Importance of Fiction', *Esquire*, vol. 104/2 (August, 1985) p. 62. The second quotation is from Wallace Stevens, 'Notes Toward a Supreme Fiction', in Holly Stevens (ed.), *The Palm at the End of the Mind: Selected Poems and a Play by Wallace Stevens* (New York: Vintage, 1972), p. 234. The third quotation is from Milan Kundera, 'Edward and God', in *Laughable Loves*, tr. Suzanne Rappaport (New York: Penguin Books, 1975) p. 229. Page numbers of sources from which quotations are taken are given in parentheses following the citation.
2. Milan Kundera, 'The Hitchhiking Game', in *Laughable Loves*, pp. 67–91.
3. Peter Brooks, *Reading for the Plot: Design and Intention in Narrative* (New York: Vintage Books, 1985) p. 37.
4. Max Frisch, *Mein Name sei Gantenbein* (Frankfurt/Main: Suhrkamp Verlag, 1964) p. 30. To my knowledge, this novel has not been translated into English. The sentence in German reads, 'Ich probiere Geschichten an wie Kleider!'
5. Annis Pratt, *Archetypal Patterns in Women's Fiction* (Bloomington: Indiana University Press, 1981) p. 178.

6. Kaja Silverman, *The Subject of Semiotics* (New York: Oxford University Press, 1983) p. 45.

7. Howard Gardner, *Frames of Mind; The Theory of Multiple Intelligences* (New York: Basic Books, 1985) pp. 252–3.

8. Emile Benveniste, *Problems in General Linguistics*, tr. Mary Elizabeth Meek (Coral Gables: University of Miami Press, 1971) p. 227. Quoted by Silverman, p. 45. The quotation immediately following from Silverman herself (p. 52) refers to the contribution of Jacques Lacan's psychoanalytic theory to Benveniste's work.

9. Cf. Gilles Deleuze, *Différence et répétition* (Paris: PUF, 1969), and *Logique du sens* (Paris: Editions de Minuit, 1969). Other texts helpful to me in understanding the concept of the aggregate self are these: James Ogilvy, *Many Dimensional Man: Decentralizing Self, Society, and the Sacred* (New York: Oxford University Press, 1977), in which Ogilvy attempts a theory of how a 'plurality of selves' or what he calls 'intrapersonal selves' function; Jeremy Hawthorne, *Multiple Personality and the Disintegration of Literary Character* (New York: St. Martin's Press, 1983); Bradd Shore, *Sala'ilua: A Samoan Mystery* (New York: Columbia University Press, 1982), especially Chapter 8 on 'persons', in which Shore gives a stimulating account of the many facets of selfhood and the importance of relationships in Samoan society, as well as a provocative description of naming in that culture; William James' *The Principles of Psychology*, vol. 1 (Cambridge, Mass.: Harvard University Press, 1981), especially Chapter X on 'The Consciousness of Self', in which James distinguishes among the material self, social self, spiritual self, and pure ego; Erving Goffman, *The Presentation of Self in Everyday Life* (Garden City, New York: Doubleday & Company, 1959); and Geoffrey M. White and John Kirkpatrick (eds), *Person, Self, and Experience: Exploring Pacific Ethnopsychologies* (Berkeley: University of California Press, 1985).

10. Walter J. Ong, *Orality and Literacy: The Technologizing of the Word* (London and New York: Methuen, 1982) p. 24.

11. The quotation is from Fredric Jameson in his Foreword to Jean-François Lyotard, *The Postmodern Condition: A Report on Knowledge*, tr. Geoff Bennington and Brian Massumi (Minneapolis: University of Minnesota Press, 1984) p. xviii. Deleuze (cf. Note 9) offers a similar perspective.

12. In Suzanne Gearhart, 'Philosophy before Literature: Deconstruction, Historicity, and the Work of Paul de Man', *Diacritics*, vol. 13/4 (Winter 1983) p. 70.

13. Owen Miller, Preface to *Identity of the Literary Text*, Mario J. Valdes and Owen Miller (eds) (Toronto: University of Toronto Press, 1985) p. xiii.

14. Kenneth Burke, *Language as Symbolic Action: Essays on Life, Literature, and Method* (Berkeley: University of California Press, 1966).

15. John Updike, *Hugging the Shore* (New York: Alfred A. Knopf, 1983) p. xv.

16. Although as Brooks points out in *Reading for the Plot*, 'Plot . . . must

use metaphor as the trope of its achieved interrelations, and it must *be* metaphoric insofar as it is totalizing. Yet it is equally apparent that the key figure of narrative must in some sense be not metaphor but metonymy: the figure of contiguity and combination, of the syntagmatic relation' (91). The essays in Sheldon Sacks (ed.), *On Metaphor* (University of Chicago Press, 1979) present a number of representative positions in the ongoing discussion on metaphor, and I have been helped considerably by Sallie McFague's Chapter 2, 'Metaphor, Parable, and Scripture', in her *Metaphorical Theology: Models of God in Religious Language* (Philadelphia: Fortress Press, 1982), and by Chapter 2, 'Metaphorical Theology', in her *Models of God: Theology for an Ecological, Nuclear Age* (Philadelphia: Fortress Press, 1987).

17. Jacques Derrida, 'La Pharmacie de Platon', in *La Dissemination* (Paris: Seuil, 1972) p. 71. I have used the translation by Steven Randall that appears in Mihai Spariosu, 'Mimesis and Contemporary French Theory', in Mihai Spariosu (ed.), *Mimesis and Contemporary Theory: The Literary and Philosophical Debate* (Amsterdam and Philadelphia: John Benjamins Publishing Co., 1984) p. 71.

18. John Barth, 'Life-Story', in *Lost in the Funhouse* (New York: Bantam Books, 1969) p. 123.

19. Brooks uses similar sexual imagery in his discussion of proper and improper endings in narrative: 'it is characteristic of textual energy in narrative that it should always be on the verge of premature discharge, of short-circuit' (109).

20. A flight simulator is a module mounted on hydraulic rods that can move the module in virtually any direction that an airplane in flight can take. The instrument panel in the cockpit that constitutes the inside of the module is 'real', but its use extends, of course, only to the capacity to move the module and change the simulated image of the outside world. This image is projected via film or computer on a screen that replaces the outside.

21. Rainer Maria Rilke, 'Archaischer Torso Apollos', in *Gedichte: Dritter Teil* (Leipzig: Insel Verlag, 1927) p. 117. The final line and a half read in German: 'denn da ist keine Stelle,/die dich nicht sieht. Du musst dein Leben ändern.'

22. Robert J. Stoller, *Observing the Erotic Imagination* (New Haven: Yale University Press, 1985) p. vii.

23. Leo Bersani, 'The Subject of Power', *Diacritics*, vol. 7/3 (Fall, 1977) p. 21.

2
What is Reading Religiously?

And when the cock crows, and the thief abandons his traps, and the sun lights up, and we are in every way called back to God by the well-meaning admonition of this bird, here the very blindnesses of religion become the deepest truths of art.[1]

RELIGIOUS READING: TOWARD COMMUNITIES OF PLAY

To suggest that an activity called 'religious reading' is possible, or is a concept worth taking seriously, is itself a risk that inspires all sorts of presuppositions and prejudices. Objections to the value of discussing such a venture can range from the conservative argument that the issue has already been decided (religious reading is what believers do with their sacred texts) to the liberal assertion (any 'existential' reading of any text that addresses matters of 'ultimate concern' is religious) to the radical rejection (in a world in which religious belief is no longer plausible it is pointless to speak of religious readings unless to describe objectively the phenomenon of what believers do) to the deconstructive position that in a world without authoritative 'presence' religious discourse, including reading, must be redefined along with all other modes.[2] I would like to *play* with the possibility of religious reading precisely because it appears to be such a pointless and undecidable issue. Its very perceived gratuitousness hints at the likelihood that a most significant complex of irresolutions and anxieties is hidden in the dismissal of the question.

I begin with the premise that writing and reading fiction are activities (not the only ones) through which we seek to replace whatever satisfactions were provided by intact storytelling communities. To posit the existence of such communities some-

time in the long-ago comes close, of course, to evoking an originary presence that, as Jacques Derrida reminds us, never was.[3]
One should not romanticize narrative into something more foundational than it has ever been; the fact that certain communities
were (or are) non-literate and aligned only to an oral tradition does
not mean that their use of narrative was either more pristine or less
subtle than ours – only that it was different. Hence our question is
not, what was the ideal storytelling context that we have lost and
that modern narrative fiction seeks to replace, but what
deficiencies do the history and substance of fiction seem to
address? Or, what lacks and absences in our social and individual
lives lead to the writing and reading of fiction? We can observe
first that the rise of the novel coincided more or less with the
incipient privatizing of society in the 1700s, a social phenomenon
that Peter Gay has described as 'that remarkable discovery that
became a realistic possibility in the eighteenth century only to
sweep all before it, rapidly establishing itself as a necessity for the
affluent and an aspiration for the poor'.[4]

The growth of chirographic fiction was part of this movement
toward the separation of society into smaller units, toward a stress
on the individual and toward the increased withdrawal of persons
into times and places where they could live unobserved and undis-
turbed by their fellows – a phenomenon made possible by the
increase of middle-class wealth that allowed the acquistion of time
and space for privacy. Steven Mintz in *A Prison of Expectations: The
Family in Victorian Culture,* for example, calls attention to Orson
Fowler, a nineteenth-century 'American phrenologist and
writer . . . [who] regarded private bedrooms for children as an
extension of the principle of specialization of space that had been
discovered by merchants'.[5]

Literary fiction both celebrates this new condition and tries to
compensate for its lacks. It gives persons in their state of privacy
something substantial to do, and it offers a replacement, to the
individual imagination, for the richer configurations of the waning
more public and communal life. In this sense also narrative fiction
substitutes rather than represents. It takes the place of the very
activity it dramatizes, permitting its practitioners, its writers and
readers, to participate, via a version of Burke's symbolic action, in
an imagined experience of social life in privacy, at their leisure
and without exertion. Not all fiction portrays social life, of course;
some of it depicts persons in various degrees and stages of

isolation, and some recent psychological fiction especially 'forgets' the 'theatre' of public life in its stress on turning the mind's intro-spections inside out and thus making them public. Such attempts to expose the mind's intimacies are really extensions of fiction's effort at drawing the public realm into the private and making it accessible there to persons who want the semblance of shared lives, of fellowship, without paying its price. The escape that fiction provides is an escape from social responsibility, a flight sometimes necessary for emotional equilibrium but at other times a replacement for genuine participation. Those religious bodies that forbade the reading of novels sensed the displacing power of fiction: it can indeed distract one from communal involvement. That is, in fact, one of its functions as an activity of the privatizing middle-class culture. Thus fiction supplies the medium for what we could call para-voyeuristic engagement that takes the place of the literal one. As John Updike expressed it, 'no doubt fiction is also a mode of spying: we read it as we look in windows or listen to gossip, to learn what other people *do*'.[6] The unspoken assumption in Updike's conjecture is that such spying is necessary, or at least understandable, because people do not interact sufficiently in other ways: voyeurism, like reading fiction, becomes needful when the establishment of privacy as a major desideratum curtails the adequate measure of communal intimacy. A simpler way of saying this is that we tend to become specialists in prurient curiosity because we have feared an eroticized culture.

The evolution of privacy connected to the growth of the novel has also abetted the problematic accent on individuation and self-hood. Ian Watt summarizes the situation brilliantly in *The Rise of the Novel*:

> The development of the novel's concentration on private experi-ence and personal relationships is associated with a series of paradoxes. It is paradoxical that the most powerful vicarious identification of readers with the feelings of fictional characters that literature had seen should have been produced by exploi-ting the qualities of print, the most impersonal, objective and public of the media of communication. It is further paradoxical that the process of urbanisation should, in the suburb, have led to a way of life that was more secluded and less social than ever before, and at the same time, helped to bring about a literary form which was less concerned with the public and more with

the private side of life than any previous one. And finally, it is also paradoxical that these two tendencies should have combined to assist the most apparently realistic of literary genres to become capable of a more thorough subversion of psychological and social reality than any previous one.[7]

Against such knowledge the escape *from* the self depicted in Kundera's 'The Hitchhiking Game' becomes predictable, suggesting that what was once desirable – the retreat into singularity – becomes burdensome; and the deployment of a once-felt solid selfhood into multiple selves in fiction and lived existence appears as a way of seeking both to maintain privacy and to enjoy the company of 'others'. One tries to find community in the proliferation of selves rather than in the actual public sphere that always threatens one's privacy. That such attempts must end in failure goes without saying; that they are undertaken at all attests to the tenacity of the double pull of the private and public upon us.

What could a religious reading consist of in a society that sets great store by individuality and privacy, that is attracted to *fictions* of communality which substitute for actual shared public life, that nurtures with some nostalgia the myth of the ideal storytelling culture but does little to realize it? One possibility is to read in a way that counters the privatizing nature of writing and reading with participatory interpretations. The act of reading is necessarily an individual experience that is also always an act of interpretation, but this encounter with the text in private need not detract from, or take the place of, a communal response. Virtually all of our interpretation is aggressive and confrontational, if not outright belligerent. It depends on the marshalling of so-called evidence to support the rightness of one's analysis, and it employs devices of persuasion intended to sway others emotionally toward one's 'position'. It is common nowadays to repeat Paul Ricoeur's phrase, 'the conflict of interpretations', as a description of our hermeneutical condition: this is what we have come to and what we have learned to survive – even flourish – in.[8]

Samuel Weber is a critic who sees this domination coming to an end and argues, 'Perhaps the Humanities, which have traditionally been concerned with values, have become the arena in which the logic of opposition that has determined the value of values is being replaced – that is, relocated, not merely eliminated – by something else.'[9] A religious reading (and religion surely belongs to the humanities) might recall what is virtually forgotten in the 'logic of opposition': not only that texts do not demand *the* correct interpretation but that interpretation itself is not always the response that the text seeks. Texts, in fact, do not demand or seek anything, contrary to what the animating metaphors of the language of hermeneutics have led us to accept. Texts are, finally, the vehicles of human expression and have no life of their own, in spite of the extravagant claims made for them by a culture with strong bibliolatrous tendencies. It is true that language 'speaks' us in the sense that we are involved in vast networks of communication that we do not control, and that language constructs the grammar of the ego, but the old structuralist assertion that texts exist without humankind should by now be demythologized.

At any rate, as critics such as Gaston Bachelard and Roland Barthes have shown us, one can learn a variety of reactions to a text, of which interpretation is only one.[10] Sometimes texts need to be absorbed, taken in and then offered up not to a relentlessly analytical readership but rather to a contemplative fellowship. One can learn to relax with texts, play with them, take them less than seriously and thereby employ them as a means of escaping our privacies on occasion and of indulging the *conversation* that we claim to value but seldom make time for. Heidegger's assertion, borrowed from Hölderlin, that 'we have been a conversation' is not plausible so long as our interchanges consist largely of monologues and long silences (silences not of the sort that Heidegger praised);[11] a ludic interactive response to our texts might recuperate our conversations and remind us of the pleasures of trustful exchange based on principles of friendship rather than power. Literary texts for the most part elicit such a response; they are themselves playful, purposeless structures that we insist on reworking into units of meaning, and perhaps little is more difficult for *Homo interpretans* than letting the text be its multifold articulation that is the object of our communal curiosity. To call for such a relaxed reading is by no means a new suggestion, merely a revived one. Maud Bodkin in her influential *Archetypal Patterns in Poetry* (first published 1934), for example, described her approach to a poem as 'akin to that method proposed by Keats – that one should read a page of poetry, or distilled prose, and wander with it, reflect, and prophesy, and dream upon it.'[12]

A religious reading, therefore, might be one that finds a group of persons engaged in gestures of friendship with each other across the erotic space of the text that draws them out of their privacy and its stress on meaning and power. Sallie McFague's elaborate proposal in *Models of God* that one consider God as mother, lover and friend, as theological models to replace paternalistic and sexist models, strikes me as very conducive to such a reading. It would be religious in its very openness to others; its willingness to accommodate and adapt; its readiness to entertain the new, the invention, while honouring the old, the convention; its celebration of the text's possibilities rather than a delimiting of them. These are characteristics contrary to what most religious institutions have championed. These tend to be closed, restrictive, defensive and prescriptive – in short, what the dominant interpretive tradition has also been. Two German terms not easily translatable suggest what both religious and interpretive communities could strive for: *Gelassenheit* and *Geselligkeit*. *Gelassenheit*, a term already used by the fourteenth-century German mystic Meister Eckhart and developed by Heidegger, is sometimes rendered as 'releasement' or 'abandonment', but it also conveys relaxation, serenity and nonchalance, a condition of acceptance that is neither nihilistic nor fatalistic but the ability – and it may be a gift – to move gracefully through life's fortunes and accidents, or to wait out its calamities.[13] *Geselligkeit* can be translated as 'sociability', but the German term manages to impart a sense of closeness that is not cloying.[14] If 'togetherness' had not been ruined by encounter group psychology, it would be appropriate. 'Communality' is also fitting. Religious reading might be *gelassen* and *gesellig*, balancing our dogged insistence on interpretation with a pleasurable interchange made valuable precisely by a refusal to simplify and manipulate the text into something else, another statement.

Kundera's lovers, attempting simultaneously to enact and interpret an unfamiliar script, do not manage either *Gelassenheit* or *Geselligkeit*. The first becomes, instead, *Ausgelassenheit*, a state of abandon with touches of hysteria and frenzy, while their comradeship slips into perverted desire, a visceral lustfulness that causes its victim to forget the other as person and to gain control over him. Their playfulness, in other words, does not lead to an expansive understanding of one's selves through exposure to the possibilities of difference. Rather, the playfulness stops, even though the game goes on, as the couple find themselves swept up in a compulsion that is not playful at all. It is a compulsion to work through this game of assumed identities, to learn how it will come out, to get a meaning from it, and as such is not unlike the compulsion to interpret texts and arrive at final, unequivocal meanings – just what the playful attitude wishes to counteract. The young man in his obsessively lustful state needs to find a single designation for his lover and determines – destructively – that she is a whore, an interpretation that he forces upon her, that simplifies her drastically and renders her his victim. The girl as the young man's text is violated by his interpretation, an interpretation guided by his privatizing, voyeuristic imagination. It is play gone astray in the subjugation to the drive to analyse.

RELIGIOUS READING: TOWARD BELIEF AND THE INTENSITY OF FORM

But human beings cannot *not* attempt to create meaning, so that our playfulness as the purposelessness of friendship is constantly subverted by the drive to make meaning, to control, to draw into the private sphere, and hence to turn friends into victims. A religious reading designed to tame this tendency would not only nurture an attitude of communality marked by *Gelassenheit* and *Geselligkeit;* it would also aid the reading community's participation in the construction of myths and rituals against chaos. If the play impulse of the reading community inspires an occasional escape from the goal-mindedness of interpretation, the myth and ritual impulse probes the nature of hermeneutics and checks the drive to interpret, not head-on but obliquely, via the elaboration of narrative, festival and belief. Four scholars who are helpful in the articulation of this impulse are Clifford Geertz, Mikhail Bakhtin, Stanley Fish and Kenneth Burke.

Geertz's influential 1965 essay 'Religion as a Cultural System' argues from an anthropologist's point of view that

> Sacred symbols funtion to synthesize a people's ethos – the tone, character and quality of their life, its moral and aesthetic style and mood – and their world-view – the picture they have of the way things in sheer actuality are, their most comprehensive ideas of order. In religious belief and practice a group's ethos is rendered intellectually reasonable by being shown to represent a way of life ideally adapted to the actual state of affairs the world-view describes, while the world-view is ren-

dered emotionally convincing by being presented as an image of an actual state of affairs particularly well-arranged to accommodate such a way of life.[15]

A culture's religion, in effect, takes over where the 'rational', objectivizing mind can find no resolution to the possibility of chaos as the fundamental reality, and provides a myth (a narrative of sacred acts) and rituals (the symbolic acting-out of these acts) to create (not represent) a more tolerable view of existence. This narrative 'sanctifies' a particular ethos in the process of embodying and expressing it, and its rituals as 'consecrated behaviour' (86) selectively enact the ethos to inspire and confirm belief in it.

The narrative and rituals are necessary above all to defend against the threat of chaos, which Geertz defines hermeneutically as a fear that the world is finally not interpretable, that the symbols might not be manipulable toward providing coherence and meaning. This threat is not limited to believers, according to Geertz:

> A man, even large groups of men, may be aesthetically insensitive, religiously unconcerned and unequipped to pursue scientific analysis, but he cannot be completely lacking in commonsense and survive. The dispositions which religious rituals induce thus have their most important impact – from a human point of view – outside the boundaries of the ritual itself as they reflect back to color the individual's conception of the established world of bare fact. (87)

Although Geertz does not continue this line of argument in terms of non-believers, we could add that since no one exists outside of some framework of belief, separate from some posture of acceptance of a world view, all persons adopt some narrative and indulge in certain repetitive actions that assure them of the world's intelligibility and assuage the threat of chaos. And indeed, culture critics such as Jean-François Lyotard now refer to the 'grand narratives' that have permeated civilization for centuries, many of which cut across the traditional religious narratives but which, by their existence, testify to the need of humans for *some* sort of 'story' and for participatory action in that story to shape their view of the 'really real' (as Geertz puts it) and of their behaviour in relation to that ultimate reality.

A religious reading of literary texts nowadays thus would be one in which a reader understands herself as part of a community engaged in simultaneously recognizing, criticizing and reshaping the myths and rituals it lives by. This effort is playful in a double sense – in so far as the refashioning of one's script, one's life narrative, is a probing and testing of what both feels and 'thinks' right, and in so far as ritual behaviour is a kind of play-acting – and therefore *more* than the nonchalance and communality out of which it is generated.

What distinguishes any reading geared to ultimate concern from a religious one? One trait of a religious reading is that it joins the play of story and ritual in an atmosphere of festival. The storytelling and story-listening community that we hearken back to is the one in which tellers and hearers are joined in reciting and responding to their life-narrations, their culture's master narratives. We hear the echoes of these events in the moments when, for example, a Christian congregation recites the creed of the church as part of the liturgy. Such texts as the Nicene Creed ('I believe in God the Father Almighty . . .'), which is a skilfully concentrated summary of the grand narrative of Christianity (its myth), barely suggest the festive, celebratory atmosphere that we think should permeate the story-enactment event (and this may be the case with the Christian story because its telling was shaped in a context of, often, secrecy and martyrdom, in which writing and written documents were already strong influences). It is an atmosphere even further removed from the privatizing experience of modern chirographic cultures – individual readers reading texts by themselves and responding to them only in further texts (read in private) or in academic and intellectual discussion.

A religious reading could seek to regain the group-celebratory nature of story enactment by transferring it to the reading experience. Something of such storytelling and response, with a celebratory atmosphere, can of course appear, and does, in theatre; yet drama, which evolved out of religious ritual and retains the power to engage our sense of sacred ceremony, is not the best model for a religious invigoration of the reading experience. An obvious reason why it is not is that it consists of a different medium: drama takes place on the stage, not in the book, and although drama employs narrative, it cannot offer the variety of time, space, action, character, perspective and so on that the novel can. But more importantly it is not drama, nor theatre, to which the project of reading aspires. Reading is, after all, reading and not viewing, and in so far as it can be communal it has to be a sharing of the written text and not of a staged spectacle.[16]

Thus a religious reading is one that celebrates the text for the individual reader *and* for groups. The celebration can take place via more of a communal listening to texts: at services of worship, in the classroom, at professional meetings where research on texts is presented, in religious and secular discussion groups, in small circles of friends. We insistently speak and write *about* our texts, assuming them to be our hermeneutical foundation, but seldom is the text itself shared. It is as if we are confident that we know the text and can forego the hearing of it, as it is read aloud, whereas in fact our private readings are often hasty and slipshod. The occasional (at least) utterance of our texts to each other, in attitudes of attentive appreciation, is an intensification and stylization of our *gelassen* and *gesellig* playing with the text that gestures toward the festive, helps to fulfil the longing for ritual that technological societies provide for only clumsily, and reminds the individual reader, when she is by herself, also to meet the text ceremoniously before, and sometimes instead of, analysing it.

Why make such ado about a festive encounter with the text? Is this not a still greater bibliolatry? Such reading is, for one, a way of reacting to the challenge of the surplus of meaning that reading supplies. The surplus of meaning, a concept treated in detail by Ricoeur, refers to our awareness that a text always offers more than the mind can absorb and make signify.[17] The text in this view is seen as an incredibly rich cache of meaning from which we are able to grasp and project only small portions at a time. Yet because we sense that there is much more there than we can receive and channel, we remain always frustrated and dissatisfied with our knowledge and interpretation of the text: in a crucial way it remains hidden and uninterpreted. The analogous Freudian concept is that the unconscious itself is a vast reservoir of drives, impulses, memories, images seeking to come to awareness, but since our conscious minds are capable of processing only relatively small amounts of 'information', we know much less, consciously, than what we know unconsciously. And the Platonic version of this 'surplus', revived by the Romantic poets such as Wordsworth, was that the grand totality of experience rests in the mind of God, to which humans in childish innocence, through 'memory' of our pre-natal abode there, have access but which we lose as our growing absorption with the world blocks the channel and makes us ignorant of what we once knew naturally.

Less fancifully, we advance metaphoric language as a way of dealing with the surplus: in its capacity for joining discrete entities and making them mean more, and something else, than they did by themselves, metaphor economizes the surplus, joins meanings together – although in the process it also adds to the excess. Nevertheless, the excess of language meaning that metaphor both orders and perpetrates contains an element of festivity that the Russian critic M. Bakhtin examined over forty years ago.[18] Bakhtin stresses the carnivalesque dimension of festivals, the holiday-from-the-norm that permits indulgence, breaks the rules and ridicules authority, that for a brief – and set – period of time inverts the normal order and turns it into frolic. It fosters bodily excess, especially of eating, drinking and sex, and through masks and costumes allows the participants to hide their indulgence and to play at being other selves. This sort of festivity functions as release, as the letting-go of energies and tensions accumulated by one's ordinarily more or less proper behaviour – as if behind or beneath this behaviour great repressed forces were seeking to escape.[19] Freud even earlier argued in *Totem and Taboo* (1913) that religion itself developed out of excess and a festival-ritual that sought to domesticate it: primitive man gradually transcended patricide (the sons killing the father, who controlled all the females) and the cannibalizing of the father's body by substituting totemic animals for his, and at a later stage of civilization even these became merely symbolic figures in religious systems.[20] One of Freud's theories that never found strong support, it nonetheless reinforces the view – which I take seriously – that ritual and festival (which are sometimes identical and sometimes not but always connected) *like metaphorical language* try to control excess but in doing so participate in it and sometimes increase it.

A religious reading will recognize that, while metaphor attempts to deal with a surplus of meaning, it shares aspects of the efforts of ritual and festival to encounter or order the human excesses that are more emotionally and viscerally inspired (although the Freudians would claim that excessive linguistic meaning is also generated by our biological needs). Hence such a reading will uncover the elements of excess in the texts it addresses and see them in their double role. First, it will show them as witness to the great ineffability of existence in the face of its richness of meaning. Second, it will disclose them as a reminder that the practice of religion, for all of its sublime moments, always remains close to humanity's most primitive impulses – and even more that the sublime is possible only because the primal underlies and invigorates it.

Thus in our Kundera story one can perceive in the *Ausgelassenheit* of the lovers the excess that is at first merely festive, then slides into the carnivalesque, and becomes finally an action that seems both a total loss of control and a ritual-like inevitability. Their indulgence in food, alcohol and erotic teasing, all in the guise of assumed personae, places them in the context of carnival (although they do not actually wear masks and costumes, of course), an atmosphere in which they find themselves, at last, in the grip of sheer lust, an excess both beyond meaning and, as a primitive force, prior to it. Their behaviour even follows the pattern implied in the etymology of *carnival:* it is the time of riotous conduct before the abstemiousness and austerity of Lent, and the sobering return to ordinary reality that the couple undergo at the end of the story suggests a penitential mood replacing the transgressive one. The concluding scene is given mainly through the young man's perspective: 'The young man . . . was aware of the sad emptiness of the girl's assertion ["I am me"], in which the unknown was defined in terms of the same unknown quantity. . . . The young man began to call compassion to his aid (he had to call it from afar, because it was nowhere near at hand), so as to be able to calm the girl. There were still thirteen days' vacation before them' (91).

Geertz claims that humans construct myths and rituals to believe in as a reaction to the fear that the world may be finally uninterpretable, that it makes no sense. Stanley Fish argues that humans have no choice but to interpret, that one never exists outside of some framework of interpretation that constitutes our belief system, and that even when we think we are interpreting objectively, merely explicating 'what is there' (Fish calls it interpretation as demonstration), we are actually engaging in persuasion, for we can interpret only from a position of belief.[21] One must, in other words, always believe in something, and if that something is radical scepticism or undecidability, it is still a position of belief. To be part of an interpretive community is thus to be part of a community of shared belief (even though what is shared may be broad and general and allow for much diversity), so that one inevitably interprets what one believes to be true, although one may wish to practise objectivity (judging from beyond any position) or may realize that one is caught in an endless relativism. As Lyotard puts it, 'there is nothing but perspectives; one can invent new ones. The statement that there are only perspectives includes itself among them'.[22] And even though everything *is* relative, Fish says, because there are only the competing activities of interpretive communities, and even though our beliefs change frequently, in lesser or greater degrees, as we try out different versions of the hermeneutical game, there is no way of abandoning the game. We continue to play it and we consider it worthwhile, because we can do no other than believe, and believe in the value of, whatever our present position is.

Fish is not arguing about belief as a theologian or philosopher of religion but as a literary critic, and he does not therefore treat 'belief' and 'community' in religious terms. Belief does not mean faith, and community here does not mean *koinonia*.[23] Yet his comments guide us in understanding that when, following Geertz, we examine myth and ritual as hedges against chaos, we are not referring to myth as 'dead religion' or somebody else's religious story that we do not accept, nor are we treating ritual as a mere 'going through the motions' of some ceremony that has lost its force. Fish helps us to see that belief is at the centre of *all* reading, not just of religious reading, and that we must discover what a religious reading does differently with the matter of belief. I will turn to an argument of Kenneth Burke to guide me toward expressing this difference.

I said earlier that the myth and ritual impulse deals with the human need to interpret via belief (along with narrative and festival). Myths are narrative histories of an interpretive community's shaping of a belief system – one could also say of such a community's history of struggle with its beliefs – and ritual is the community's expression of solidarity regarding its beliefs that provides continuity and support as the community undergoes its incessant alteration of its interpretation of its beliefs. What may distinguish this mythic belief from the sort that Fish treats is what Kenneth Burke over fifty years ago called 'eloquence' or 'intensity of form'. Burke inquires at one point in *Counter-Statement* why readers (or viewers of drama) return to classic works again and again though they already know the plot, and replies that it has less to do with the release of suspense and much more with an appreciation of *how* the suspense is released through the artist's skill.[24] The artist provokes in the reader a desire that seeks fulfilment, but that fulfilment must occur through the puzzling-through of a structure of frustration that is the plot, the characterization, the image patterns and so on; or it can be thought of as the resolution of a dissonance through a recognition of a deeper or more complicated harmony (Burke employs the analogy of music). Artistic form creates a desire to interpret and to find pleasure in the act/art of interpretation, and the more intricate the form, if it is well-crafted, the greater the desire for and pleasure of interpretation.

But this is not to say that interpretation is rendered valuable only because it involves invested and expended effort. Rather, the effort must be guided by the reader's sense of the rightness, the proper fit of the work's components; it involves, in Burke's terms, 'the exercise of human propriety' (42). We become intrigued by and then committed to a good work of art (in our case a good text) both by the degree of work/play it leads us to expend – the putting-forth of the pleasurable effort – and by the text's reciprocity – its rewarding us with a feeling of satisfaction and consummation through our experiencing 'the formulation of symbols which rigidify our sense of poise and rhythm' (42). Burke is clearly struggling here at the end of his essay to articulate what is virtually inexpressible – why we are drawn so powerfully to certain art works. Yet he assumes the organic integrity of good art, and one needs to ask, in our age of discontinuity, what the basis of that assumption is. Surely we respond to the 'propriety' of well-crafted texts because, as Geertz says about the function of religious beliefs, such texts reinforce our hope that the world's seeming chaos is fathomable, and in this sense the texts become models of clarity and order.

But what if the clarity and order are the products of our imagination? Then the organic unity of the work/text is a non-representational fiction offered by the artist and accepted (and developed) by the reader. Burke seems to recognize this and thus calls on the 'psychology of form' to explain the appeal of good art: something in the human mind demands it and enjoys locating or making it, whether or not any ultimate or absolute order exists. Burke's theory is not representational but rather psychological-functional. It transfers the organic unity of the art work to the mind of the artist and viewer/reader.

A religious reading should venture one step beyond Burke to explore an 'intensity of form' that depends neither on the text's organic unity (which appears increasingly less plausible) nor the psychological need for order, and that relates belief to the *irreducibility* of form. Even the aesthetic sensibility of twentieth-century criticism (formalism, the New Criticism, Neo-Aristotelianism) has viewed form as problematic rather than salutary, as something needing translation, categorization and simplification. We have not finally in any sense believed in form but in the abstractions of atomizing and quantifying, operations that seek to transform form, domesticate it and render it less threatening. A religious reading could, by the process of playing with form, become the only approach to take it seriously. Christian myth and ritual, in celebrating the Incarnation and Resurrection, hint at a far stronger commitment to form than Christian theology has seemed to recognize. Whereas these have been co-opted by a specific soteriology, a programme for a particular kind of personal salvation, they could be comprehended just as well as powerful metaphors of form, so that to 'believe' in Incarnation and Resurrection is to believe in the reality of form and in its fundamental mystery. Christian myth attempts to answer Heidegger's question, 'why is there not nothing?', by narrating a case of a god born into human form, dying in that form and resurrected in a more exalted form.[25] It is a typical mythic theme, yet the Judeo-Christian tradition is one of the few to grapple with the concept of form by relating it to a myth-history and suggesting both that nothingness is not necessarily the primal condition and that it need not be the condition of an ending. Unlike comparable cosmogonies, Yahveh is already present, in the Genesis narrative, *Bereshith*, in the beginning; he does not need to be created, is not one of a number of deities who emerge at the start.[26] Although the 'earth' is formless and a void, Yahveh's controlling presence counteracts nothingness, and Yahveh creates form through language: the celestial bodies, the dry land and so on. Hebrew mythology is little interested in formlessness and stresses instead the articulating of the world in a manner whereby form and text are immediately joined and whereby the world is in fact textualized. This is an emphasis that marks early Christianity: Jesus is textualized as the incarnate *word* and is replaced, following death and resurrection, by a text. Finally, Christian apocalypse is thoroughly 'texted' in Revelation, as the reading of the great book precipitates cataclysmic action and as the action involves the literal devouring of texts.

There is thus not *nothing* in the Judeo-Christian tradition because we cannot imagine it. As soon as we try, the very effort creates form, and thus we find ourselves, as Heidegger says, speaking being even as we say nothing. This is the irreducibility of form that a religious reading confesses and that inspires what we might call 'deep play' with a text, an experience of the intensity of form that does not expect a transcendence of form, not a working through it to a purer state or a non-state, but that anticipates the infinite interplay of its discontinuities and differences. Religious reading, moreover, is the deep play that reminds us how the text can never *really* be completed, no more than can the author or reader. It is an effort that requires belief because we are always on the verge of being seduced by the (non-)vision of nothingness, the ultimate abstraction and the final goal of interpretation, and we need to recall, against that nihilism, the enduring inexpressibility of form that incessantly inspires our desire.

Much of what I have been saying has overtones of Søren Kierkegaard's depiction over a century ago in *Concluding Unscientific Postscript* of the three spheres of existence: the aesthetic, ethical and religious, with the aesthetic and ethical connected (or separated) by the 'boundary zone' of irony and the ethical and religious meeting at the 'boundary zone' of humour.[27] Indeed Kierkegaard, ahead of his time in so many ways, had a far stronger sense of the discontinuity of existence than most of his fellows, and it is tempting to consider developing the remainder of my discussion in terms of a Kierkegaardian argument. Instead of doing that, however, I will think of Kierkegaard's treatment of the three spheres and their boundaries as a sub-text and construct upon it a description of three other kinds of texts that provoke religious reading.

RELIGIOUS READING AND TEXTS OF PAIN

All such belief as I have discussed it in the previous section can be construed as a probe (as I used that term in the first chapter). It becomes a dare or a risk when the multifold self, challenged by a community, rewrites sacred texts or identifies new ones. There can be many kinds of these. Three are: those written on the body in/as pain, those exchanged between bodies as pleasure, and those circulated among bodies as worship. The prepositional pun 'on the body' is intentional. I mean it to suggest the literal body as a text inscribed by instruments of pain to render it immediately and directly meaningful, in ways that collapse representation, and I mean it also to refer to literary texts that narrate such painful corporeal inscriptions. Such inscription, often in the form (note: the irreducibility of form) of mutilation, has been a part of religious ritual (and of its mythic-narrative conterpart) for millenia and persists in Western society today, for example, in the still wide-spread practice of infant male circumcision. Most males in the West, however secularized our civilization may be, are inscribed in this manner: it figures as a portentous lack, the foreskin's gratui-tous absence setting off a chain of signifying interchanges that find no resolution as we attempt to create new narrations (medical, anthropological, sociological, aesthetic) that 'explain' this ritual's survival.[28]

Far more influential are the inscriptions of modern surgery in which the intricacies of the body's organs, and their diseases and traumas, are construed as a text to be interpreted by the surgical team and, via scalpel, rewritten. No profession is more highly regarded than the surgeon's. It is the technological sacred vocation, controlling life and death, and its rituals are precisely prescribed, practised by the select few, and incomprehensible even to the laity who suffer them and benefit from them. It is so highly esteemed because it valorizes our myths concerning the priority of individual survival at all costs, and of the value of attractive appearance, so that we accept pain as the price of extended and enhanced existence. Rather the suffering of major surgery that may provide extra months or years than death; rather the suffering of cosmetic surgery than too great a deviation from the aesthetic or erotic bodily norm.

The high valuation that our culture assigns to bodily pain in the cause of health and beauty, longer and (perhaps) better lives, is not surprising in light of the stress on it in the Christian tradition. Close to the centre of Christian myth and ritual is the passion of Christ, the mutilation, pain and suffering inflicted on his body in our stead, according to our theology of atonement: an inscription that we still read, Christian believers or not, in attitudes of guilt and awe. The pain of the crucifixion retains its power to affect us emotionally and is still at the heart of the Western sense of the sacred. And as Heidegger shows in his essay on the Austrian Georg Trakl's poetry, the Western sensibility abandoning Christianity for a Romantic alienation and self-absorption continues to focus on pain as mysterious provider of meaning.[29]

But as Elaine Scarry points out in *The Body in Pain*, it is the painful inscriptions on the body by the machinations of torture and war that particularly mark contemporary economies of suffering.[30] Whether twentieth-century humankind has progressed or regressed in its attitudes of humaneness (and the assumption that we have progressed may be another of our myths), we have indeed become vastly more efficient in the maiming and killing of each other, in ways that concentrate both on ever more refined ways of producing pain in individuals and on methods for effecting mass death. We have tended to look away from the intense and massive intentional infliction of pain in our time – perhaps increasingly so. The torture of political prisoners in many nations as a regular practice is not, in spite of efforts of protesting groups such as Amnesty International, highly publicized; the genocide of millions of Cambodians in the late 1970s seems not to have reached the awareness of many Westerners; we appear resigned (perhaps we have no choice) to increasing terrorist mayhem as a fact of modern life.

Pain renders us dumb, incapable. Its inscriptions on the body erase the intentions of consciousness and cause us to lose interest, will-power and even comprehension. By itself and in its way it can do what threatens us most: make the world uninterpretable. It can unite our multifold selves into a single concentration of traumatic sensation. It takes us out of ourselves and at the same time makes us focus intently on the field of pain. Many gradations and variations of pain must occur, from discomfort to agony, but we have not developed an efficient lexicon to label them, for pain exceeds our capacity for articulating it. The body in pain at the very least distracts the mind; in serious pain it absorbs the mind, demands its total concentration and reminds the mind that its separation from the body is after all a fool's paradise, a fiction. Pain recalls the mind from its reflective holiday back to its corporeal locus and nature and challenges the efficacy of language. It generates an experience of the intensity of form but at the same time the experience of non-interpretability and chaos. We can convey where it hurts, to a degree how it hurts (it aches, throbs, sears; it is sharp, dull, gnawing, etc.) and often why it hurts, but

we cannot convey, in language, the essence of the sensation. If
pain constitutes a metalanguage, it is one that we speak without
understanding. As anthropologist Michael Herzfeld puts it,
'physical pain expresses the incomprehensible experiences of
injury and rejection, organic and social alike'.[31]

This very inexpressibility is a mystery that inspires sacred texts.
The mind up against its limits in pain, consciousness unable to
reflect in pain and reduced – or expanded – to sheer sensation,
are threatened and intrigued and, when sufficiently relieved of
pain, return to it to metaphorize and valorize it. Herzfeld in a
discussion of pain and illness says that 'Pain, though felt as an
immediate experience, is localized; yet it means something else,
something vaster than itself or distanced from it.' And a paragraph
later: 'illness is above all an *interpretation* and as such constitutes
a *text* (although not a primarily linguistic one) upon which the
cure – a *reading* of the text and, as such, a further interpretation –
is performed' (108).[32] One could understand Herzfeld's view of
illness and pain as comprising a kind of physiological hermeneutic,
and the sacred texts of pain I have just mentioned as a still deeper
reading of the mystery of the traumatized body. There may be
many of these texts among us in the form of diary entries, letters,
prayers, last words, warnings. Most of these will never become
public, or will become so only in intimate circles. It is the task of
the literary artists, those sufficiently moved and committed, to
compose narratives worthy of these private and intimate texts born
out of pain. These literary narratives will not be sacred texts but
will function as metaphors of witness: they will attempt to image
forth the private texts sanctified by pain, for which pain is the
pre-text but which are too close to the painful events to do other
than cry them forth. It is no surprise, given the Jewish Holocaust
of the second world war, that our few prominent fictions that
metaphorize these holy hidden texts of pain are composed mainly
by Jews. One thinks of Elie Wiesel's novels or of André Schwarz-
Bart's *The Last of the Just* as fictive elaborations of such fugitive
texts.

A religious reading will seek to identify and celebrate such
fiction that provides these private, sanctified texts a public voice,
that offers these witnessed events in metaphors which transform
the witness into language that does not profane it but that also
makes it bearable. Such reading will also distinguish between such
fiction and the sort that merely sensationalizes the witness and the

pain behind it, for such discernment is necessary in our societies dominated by entertainment media and profit motive, in which all events, no matter how private or horrific, are processed and sold to the prurient consumer. One suspects that such private texts of pain are generated daily in Lebanon, Iran, Northern Ireland, South Africa, the American ghettoes, the Amazon Valley; in middle-class families, penitentiaries, mental institutions, hospices and in places we cannot imagine, and that literary fictions seeking to amplify these witnesses already exist, unknown to the literary establishment. It is a task of the religiously-reading community to locate, disseminate and thus complete these narratives.

RELIGIOUS READING AND TEXTS OF LOVE

The pain inflicted by the torturer on his victim is, among other things, a perverted language of love (although we shall see that it is more problematic than this). An intimacy is forced, through the violation of the other's body, through the reduction of him to total vulnerability and will-lessness, so that the torturer renders his victim 'open' to him as if he were a lover. The lovers in Kundera's tale in the violent consummation of their game are driven by a measure of sado-masochistic attraction whereby pain produces pleasure (although the encounter is not depicted as involving physical pain), and the girl at least seems to be aghast at the discovery that she has the capacity within her for absorbing such pleasure. They both experience the excitement of transgression, of going 'too far' with the other person by allowing and being allowed the violation that causes pain and humiliation. Participation in this violation, paradoxically, effects an intense intimacy – a knowing of the other beyond conventional and normal relationships – through transforming the free play of love (one could say interpreting that free play) into the acting out of sado-masochistic roles. In this sense the fiction and the acting-out of it take the couple into a new depth of 'real' experience.

The sado-masochism of the couple is, however, also attractive because it makes the 'exchanges' of love more tangible and longer-lasting; it responds to the human compulsion to regulate experience, makes it definite and predictable, and this too is an interpretation and thus a channelling of the playfulness of lovers' liaisons.

The fact that the couple transcend their normal relationship by transgressing it – moving into the arena of the hitherto erotically forbidden – where their action generates both shame and arousal, only to find themselves at last merely enacting a mildly sado-masochistic scenario, suggests how the search for the new, the unfamiliar, seldom relaxes into play but tends rather to rigidify into the repetition of established patterns.

A kind of text with sacred propensities that embraces both the desire of lovers for perpetual playfulness and, at the same time, for resolution – and that thus illustrates the fundamental tension of the hermeneutical condition – is the love letter. It is a text exchanged between the 'bodies' of lovers in the sense that it is written almost exclusively when the lovers are separated, so that the letter substitutes for the absent erotic body; but it also suspends (in the sense of *aufheben*, meaning both to cancel and fulfil) the text inscribed on the body in/as pain, acting as a civilizing agent against the human tendency to conduct erotic encounters aggressively. For if Robert Stoller is right, 'normal' sexual relations have an undertone of hostility and violence, a hypothesis confirmed by our knowledge of the ease with which many – perhaps most – partnerships settle into patterns of dominant-submissive and even victimizer-victim.[33] The love letter resists this natural sado-masochism by encouraging the partners, absent from each other, to reflect on the nature of their desire as an interdependency that should mature beyond mere mutual exploitation. The very composing of the *billet-doux* consists of a reflective extravagance, of creating metaphors of overvaluation of the other that help to relieve the underlying hostility of sexual excitement.

One would not wish to argue, of course, that the love letter by and of itself domesticates violent sexuality and thus mitigates the aggressiveness of intimate relations. It is, however, a kind of text with redemptive potential, in so far as it shows how writing that imagines and addresses the other can elevate passion (which includes suffering and desire) into *com*passion. One could think of love letters as the shorthand of our erotic scripts, of those scenarios that take shape in our conscious and unconscious minds as to how we would like our love lives to evolve. And since little is more important to us, beyond our health (beyond pain), than the constitution of our loves, we can comprehend these letters as marking certain sacred moments or passages of our existences, when we are deeply involved in establishing, nurturing or even ending a union with someone who has come to represent virtually another one – a crucially significant one – of our orchestrated, incorporated selves. Or, as William Kraft puts it, 'The authentic lover always participates explicitly or implicitly in the sacredness of the Other', and surely the love letter can help to authenticate the lover.[34]

At the same time the love letter tends to dissemble, for even as it engages in the play of extravagance it carries as a sub-text the lover's insecurity, his lack of assurance that he is truly loved by the absent other (so that even in his *dis*closure of himself he holds something back), and that makes him want closure – or interpretations of the relationship that then can take the form of victimization. Love letters thus can be pre-texts either for the maturation of partnerships or for regression into sexual power relationships.

That some of the determinative works in the evolution of the novel in the West have been epistolary narratives comprised in part of love letters (for example, Richardson's *Clarissa*, Goethe's *The Sorrows of the Young Werther*) should not surprise us, for this is the period in which realistic literature, represented above all by the novel, was taking shape, and love letters *in* novels and constituting whole novels were appropriate forms of writing to convey the varieties and complexities of actual middle- (and lower-) class love relationships – which had been hitherto largely ignored in favour of attention to the liaisons of the privileged classes in the 'high' genres such as romance, tragedy and the epithalamion. It was also the era in which middle-class persons, better off, realizing the opportunities for greater privacy and increasingly better equipped with literacy, employed the novel, as a privatizing genre, to explore the nature of intimacy *alone*, without the obligation of commitment or even relationship to another person as a focus of intimacy. Peter Gay in *The Bourgeois Experience* describes the curious popularity of the diary or private journal (no doubt evolved out of the great tradition of letter writing) as this mood came to fruition a century later, in the 1800s, when persons wrote to and in their diaries, confessing intimacies that they would not, by and large, tell even to the closest of friends (446ff). Such love letters to the self, solipsistic fictions of shared intimacy, can be viewed as an amateur effort that parallels the nineteenth-century novelists' fascination with creating public depictions of intimacy from their own positions of nurtured privacy.

Terry Eagleton argues that 'letters can be no more than "supplementary" sexual intercourse, eternally standing in for the real thing. Letters concede yet withhold physical intimacy in a kind of artfully prolonged teasing, a courtship which is never consummated; like Derrida's "hymen", they join and divide at a stroke.'[35] Eagleton's reliance here on Derrida's vocabulary causes him to undervalue the love letter. The ambivalence of the love letter makes it an ideal purveyor and conveyor of desire: marking its author as open to the other, addressing her with longing and compassion in her absence, but also as dissembling, using the letter as indulgence, as a way of finding pleasure in the lover's absence and thus focusing longing and compassion as self-pity back on the self. As such the love letter also reveals a sacred propensity, resembling the desire of the believer for the consummation of his hope and faith through the appearance of a redeemer, the advent of an eschaton, the transformation of the body and so on, yet literally creating and maintaining that faith and hope and enjoying them (even exulting in them) *because* the deliverer, new age and transfigured body remain absent. There is thus an irony at work in the dynamic of the absence that motivates both the love letter and religious faith.

A religious reading would regard the love letter as a text that takes us out of ourselves and into a concern for the other, teaching us compassion over selfishness, but also as a text that teaches us how to deal valuably with absence, how to translate desire into productive equanimity, living nonchalantly, *gelassen* (or with what Brooks calls 'lucid repose' [61]), with the possiblity that the lover may never return.

Like the texts of pain, love letters are for the most part private, and perhaps even more closely guarded. Unlike the texts of pain, they are more commonly composed, sent and received by most of us, so that we can recall, re-read or write love letters as pretexts to a playing with and interpretation of literature that stresses lovers' unions. Since such liaisons have been the central theme of fiction at least in the Western world, and we are thus overwhelmed by the sheer wealth of it, we can employ the love letter in our religious reading as a highly concentrated model (I called it a shorthand earlier) of our narratives of *eros* and affection, and we can view much fiction not only as transformed and expanded versions of the love letter but also as the authors' 'love letters' to their readers. This is not as fanciful as it sounds, particularly in the context of the self-conscious, 'metafictional' strategies displayed by contemporary authors toward their craft and their readers. Apart from significant fiction of recent years that employs letters with erotic and sometimes religious implications (Saul Bellow's *Herzog*, D. M. Thomas's *The White Hotel*, John Barth's *Letters: A Novel*, Alice Walker's *The Color Purple*, John Updike's *A Month of Sundays*, in which the pastor's writing assignments are a variation on such letters), one thinks of novels such as Margaret Atwood's *The Handmaid's Tale* and Russell Hoban's *Riddley Walker*, in which the narrators relate the stories in which they act (and which constitute these novels) and address them to both a specified (in Atwood's case) and an unspecified (in Hoban's case) readership.[36]

The very nature of these narratives as inscribed, and as seeking readers, signals their authors' use of fiction as an elaborate device – like the love letter – both to maintain privacy while writing intimately and to make significant contact with a readership. A religious reading will recall that the world of literature is, after all, the world of 'letters' and will be especially alert to the authors' desire to communicate their own coming to terms with absence through the pleasure of the text. Brooks says that

> Narratives portray the motors of desire that drive and consume their plots, and they also lay bare their nature as a form of human desire: the need to tell as a primary human drive that seeks to seduce and to subjugate the listener, to implicate him in the thrust of a desire that never can quite speak its name – never can quite come to the point – but that insists on speaking over and over again its movement toward that name. (61)

This desire of desire to speak its name is particularly strong in the 'lettered' fiction I alluded to, where it borrows the name of the absent loved one (Riddley Walker's dead father; the handmaid's missing husband and daughter in Atwood's novel) to articulate a greater absence inciting true existential longing that has no name, yet finds existential pleasure in its *imagined* 'movement toward that name'.

Yet another aspect of the love letter, as a kind of text directing secular persons toward the sacred, which requires commentary is its significance for women's writing. Ian Watt in *The Rise of the Novel*, referring to Samuel Richardson's appropriation of the epistolary novel sub-genre (in *Pamela* and *Clarissa*), describes him as

borrowing from 'an essentially feminine . . . tradition of letter-
writing . . . [which] helped him to break with the traditional deco-
rums of prose' (193–4). And a page later: 'The letter form, then,
offered Richardson a short-cut, as it were, to the heart' (195). That
this tradition is 'essentially feminine' is debatable, yet to raise the
argument is to introduce the critical issue of gender difference in
writing in relation to religious reading. Terry Eagleton, also writing
on Richardson, observes: 'It has been claimed that men and
women under patriarchy relate differently to the act of writing.
Men, more deeply marked by the "transcendental signifier" of the
phallus, tend to view signs as stable and whole, ideal entities
external to the body; women will tend to have a more inward,
bodily· relationship to script' (52). If this is so, then Western
societies gradually overcoming patriarchy may look to women's
texts as *embodying* what is nothing less than an extended sacred
moment in our history: our passage from the violence of male
domination in our sexual politics to the equanimity of compassion
that can come through authentic female – male partnership. It is
a sacred moment I will study in detail in my treatment of writing
and the body in Chapter 5. If this partnership is something still
more hoped-for than realized, it is nevertheless the sort of absence
that is not merely endured and valorized in women's texts; rather,
some of these texts – and women's love letters in fiction in
particular – anticipate and project and thus help to realize an era
of sexual equality and thereby a greater measure of erotic fulfilment. Linda Kauffman argues persuasively in her provocative
Discourses of Desire that a tradition of women's love letters persists
in Western fiction that resists the discourse of patriarchy and
insists instead on celebrating the body.[37] Such celebration, as we
shall see in the pages ahead, contributes to a foundational mystery
that both underlies and is the result of religious reading.

RELIGIOUS READING AND TEXTS OF WORSHIP

The *maranatha* passage at the end of The Book of Revelation (22:20)
– 'come, Lord Jesus' – is like a plea for the absent lover to return
and reminds us of a third kind of sacred text, apart from those
of suffering and of pleasure, rewritten by the multifold self in
community: those circulated among bodies as worship. What is
there to worship in a discontinuous, non-representational

universe? Mystery remains. But why worship mystery, if that is a name for what is unknown and hence uncontrolled, in a world that, thanks to the capriciousness of language, we perceive as out of control? To put it like that is to remind ourselves that mystery is not the same as chaos: mystery has a content, a focus; chaos has neither. To sense mystery rather than chaos is not a matter of choice, for it is not possible for us, for very long, to imagine chaos. Whatever mythological world we are enveloped in, even if it is that of late capitalism, high technology and/or post-Einsteinian physics, it is one that compels us to avoid chaos by substituting for it visions of order, and·these are always visions which we only partially understand but must, nonetheless, believe in. Thus mystery remains, and humankind is inevitably, one way or another, *Homo religiosus* – and perhaps never more so than when it attempts to get beyond the vision, outside the system, to dispel mystery and find certainty, truth, ultimate reality.

To be aware of mystery is not necessarily to wish to worship it, however, and thus humans have in fact regularly provided mystery with enough of an identity to be able to worship it and to want to: hence our sacred stories. But in a culture which denies the plausibility of the sacred and then proceeds to valorize the secular, the energies of worship are transferred to the techniques and methods by which – always unsuccessfully – we seek to *de*mystify existence: the various enterprises of science and technology.[38] A religious reading for such a culture might involve the exploration of texts that redirect these energies to the myths – the powerful fictions we choose to play with – that demystify not existence but rather our most prominent demystifiers, science and technology, and guide us toward saving the sacred. Our myths and rituals of liminality appear well-suited for this task.

The immensely helpful and by now familiar concept of liminality was developed by Victor Turner beyond its original use by Arnold van Gennep to label the middle or transitional stage of rites of passage, those rituals marking important changes that all societies, however overtly or unconsciously, practise.[39] Barbara Myerhoff, summarizing Turner, says that he 'describes liminality as occurring during transitional periods of history. . . . Play, imagination, and paradox with all its possibilities come to the fore, and along with them an attitude of mind that is interpretative, self-reflexive, self-conscious. Criticism and awareness are almost inevitable in liminal circumstances.' Beneath the characteristics of the liminal experience such as innocence, vulnerability, disorder, 'are a lurking sacrality and power that accompany movement toward the borders of the uncharted and unpredicted. The edges of categories, as Mary Douglas (1966) has also stated, are charged with power and mystery.'[40]

It would appear that our society is remarkably liminal, according to Turner's use of the term, yet also sufficiently unliminal for us to employ the concept to criticize our self-identity. We see liminality, for example, in our drive toward intense introspection and in our obsession with change itself; yet we also see in liminality the antithesis of our faith in progress, of our faith in our increasing human self-sufficiency and of our belief that virtually all kinds of growth and expansion are somehow good, or at least necessary. Although it accompanies and articulates change, liminality is more concerned with the process of change than with its product; it stresses the *difference* that constitutes change, and encourages cultures to celebrate that difference rather than making it the object of anxiety or idolatry. What depresses the young lover at the end of 'The Hitchhiking Game' is the liminal interlude in which he is trapped, those thirteen days ahead with the girl whom he has used and, by his standards, expended. Because he has abused the difference of their relationship, forcing her and it toward a quickly gratifying (for him) resolution, he is unable to envision a deepening and maturing of anything between them; he has nothing left to contribute toward a pleasurable exploration of the more subtle and rewarding differences between them. The mystery totally eludes him, for he has violated its time and its space.

Both the Jewish and Christian traditions (and surely others) have a familiar language of worship that is liminal, that celebrates mystery, and that could serve as a third kind of model – although a badly flawed one – for those wishing to understand and undertake religious readings of contemporary fiction. This is the language of liturgy, consisting of texts that function as *sacra* even as they communicate the myth-history of a religious heritage. Turner defines sacra as holy things, 'objects and activities believed to be charged with supernatural power, which are presented for worshipful attention in religious celebrations'.[41] A problem with both Judaism and Christianity is that they have severely limited the range of sacra permitted for worship. As Herbert Schneidau argues in *Sacred Discontent*, the Yahvists were already possessed of a demythologizing consciousness that caused them to avoid much of the idol-mongering of their polytheistic Canaanite neighbours and concentrate on the holiness of the emerging texts.[42] This focus came to mark Christianity definitively, especially Protestantism, and as Turner declares, 'The early Americans . . . rejected the visible symbolic system which gave expression to the political and religious *anciens régimes*. Sacredness was interiorized; . . . the individual rather than the corporate group was the basic unit of worship. The Word was to be heard, not the icon or image seen. . . . The *sacra* of other cultures . . . have always fascinated the Western public. Perhaps this is because they make visible what Westerners have thrust from conscious awareness in order to effect their rational conquest of the material world.' (13)

One might argue that Westerners, in purifying their religion of idolatrous holy objects and leaving themselves only with certain texts on which to confer sacrality, have come to overvalue textuality itself and, in the secular era, used textuality *per se* as the substitute for sacred scripture, the text 'charged with supernatural power'. A dominant aspect of the mythology that surrounds and encloses us (in spite of our demythologizing), along with the components of technology and science, is the language of texts.

There is no way we can escape this mythology. Even as we try, we find ourselves using the reflexes of scripting and texting by which we identify ourselves. But we can turn to liturgy as a kind of liminal text that guides us beyond mere bibliolatry. For in the words of the liturgy, whether they consist of quotations from sacred scripture (Torah or Bible), prayer, confession or instructions for the sacraments, is a stress on language apart from its role as communication. It is a stress on the form of language unlike that of poetic/literary form, in that the exact words, the precise arrangement of words, the sequence of phrases, the timing and the rhythm all matter, in a different way, as the beauty of form thickens into the mystery of form. This awareness, however inarticulate, of the fundamental mystery of form in liturgical language is why congregations, synods and dioceses come into conflict over whether to use the 'proper' Hebrew and Latin or modern translations, over which translations should be privileged, over what may or may not be said in a service and who may say it. This language is regarded as sacrum, holy *object* in a way that collapses representation: the holy is not merely reflected in or by this language; it is not merely the referent of this language; it *is* this language, and while liturgical language is in operation, read and spoken from memory, it effects sacred time and space, blocking out the profane. Its performance suspends the normal communicational role of language. Thus the New Testament metaphors of God as *logos*, of Jesus and the Spirit as the word, are not always only metaphors; they have a liturgical function in which the Christian names of God, signifying the holy, become identical with the quiddity, even the palpability, of language.[43]

The Western mind is not easy with this description of religious language, for we have inherited demythologizing tendencies from both the Judaic and Greek traditions that cause us to want a language in control of the holy rather than as an uncontrollable part of it.[44] It is an irony of our age that the fairly recent view of the capriciousness and unreliability of language, considered to be a profound secular insight, provides an avenue toward uncovering a sacredness of language always present in liturgies but largely suppressed in the reference-orientation of our worship.

Secular persons who wish to know what it is to read religiously, yet who cannot imagine what the language of liturgy means when it projects the names of divinity, may nonetheless be able to respond to liturgy if it embodies holy language as mystery. It can be made accessible, for example, via the route of Burke's 'intensity of form' that I treated briefly earlier. Liturgy offers a text that in the very thereness of its language provides no resolution – that is its mystery – but that leaves the celebrant not with a fear of chaos but rather with a sense of satisfaction and fulfilment.[45] Mystery embodied in the liminal language of liturgy appears as an ultimate, as a formal inexpressibility of form, that serves paradoxically as a resting point, as a foundation for *Gelassenheit*. This is a different kind of satisfaction from that produced by the pattern of anticipation and fulfilment experienced by the student of the art work according to Burke's 'psychology of form'. The satisfaction generated by the confrontation with the intensity and inexpressibility of form in the liturgical text is based on the faith that discontinuity and the failure of representation are complicit with a mystery that encompasses chaos itself. This may be a faith that even secular humankind can entertain seriously.

To 'entertain seriously' suggests deep play, and I want to consider finally how an intense playing with narrative texts shapes the interpreters. Victor and Edith Turner describe 'ludic recombination' and *communitas* as two features of liminality (along with communication of the sacra as a third) (204–6). These can be borrowed to examine the relationship of liturgy to modern fiction, to show how each can respond to the strengths and weaknesses of the other. A problem with using liturgy to convey the power of mystery to secular persons is its relentlessly verbal nature even as a 'holy' object. Because Western religions have largely limited their sacra to what can be expressed in language, most of the immediacy of the holy is inevitably lost. A problem with using narrative fiction, including contemporary writing, to do any more than reflect the privatizing and alienating tendencies of modern life is its necessarily non-liminal structure. Because the novel and story have traditionally been patterned on situations of conflict that demand resolution, that drive author and reader to seek closure, the expanded and suspended time that marks the liminal experience has difficulty in taking hold.[46]

Nurturers of liturgy, however, can still learn from narrative fiction how to practise playful experimentation, or 'ludic recombination'. This is, according to the Turners, 'The analysis of culture into factors and their free, playful ("ludic") recombination in any and every possible pattern, however deviant, grotesque, unconventional, or outrageous. This process is quintessentially liminal. . . . In solemn, initiatory ritual, such exaggerations or distortions of reality may be regarded as religious mysteries. . . . The cake of custom is broken and reflective speculation liberated' (204–5). One sees why fiction can instigate an enlivening of liturgy; although it is also obviously a verbal medium and cannot escape the wilderness of its linguisticality, its capacity for unrestrained imagining can lead to suggestions as to how liturgy can be 'objectified' into dance, music, costuming, architecture, holography and so on to reinvest more of life, via such playfulness, with mystery. There is much in the novels and stories of Jorge Luis Borges, John Fowles, Cynthia Ozick, Darcy Ribeiro and Patrick White, for example, to inspire reincursions of the holy through liturgy and beyond it.

One does not expect that an openness to the possibility of mystery will come easily in a world deadened by the substitutions manufactured by the entertainment and consumption industries: our sophisticated amusement parks, stunning shopping malls, sports extravaganzas, ever more spectacular cinema and pharmaceutical intoxications. Yet all of these evince the dilemma of the privatizing force: persons become isolated parts of the mass without finding community, and a profound longing for the other, and others, eventually occurs. To fill this void gestures toward *communitas* can be offered. The Turners define *communitas* as the fellowship of neophytes or initiates, those brought together by some deeply significant shared liminal event that cuts across social differentiations such as class, wealth and profession. It is not a traditional power group. Rather, 'the secular powerlessness may be compensated for by sacred power, the power of the weak' (205).[47]

Religious readers will not limit their texts to those 'authenticated' by formal publication, those printed and distributed by publishing houses. Although our literature is largely written in private and then sold to a publisher who in turn sells it to readers, who read it in private, this is not the only possibility for the performances of reading and writing. One alternative in operation is the *samizdat* of the Soviet Union, an underground of writers, amateur publishers and readers of literary (and other) texts that are ideologically unfit for state-approved publication and thus distributed illegally. One imagines that the *samizdat* authors and readers (by no means a homogeneous group) function in some ways as a *communitas*.[48] The Western scene of writing and reading is not politically repressive (or only minimally so), yet subtle forces determine what is available to read and, therefore, what is written: editors' concerns with what sells, critics' and reviewers' biases, the momentum of tastes and trends. There is no reason to believe that the economy and cultural politics of publishing will change – and there is no compelling reason why they should change: no one knows what a more equitable kind of publishing, perhaps with more attention paid to unknown authors and the interests of minority readerships, would look like, how it would be financed and what kind of pressures and constraints it might impose. Yet the conditions as they are challenge religious readers to form their own 'underground' that supplements and constructively criticizes the writing and reading establishment. Such persons could meet regularly in small groups to share and interpret their own writing and that of other 'unknowns', in addition to studying conventionally published literature. Especially nowadays, in the era of quick and inexpensive publication and duplication processes, it should be easy to produce a group's own texts.

This is hardly a revolutionary concept, yet it has to my knowledge not been extensively tried, possibly because we are inhibited by the relative prestige of published literature and also used to the private writing and reading of narrative, apart from formal attention paid to it in university classrooms. Nevertheless, I believe that groups committed to an intensive play with literature, engaging each other in search – and sometimes in the creation – of texts that, wherever they originate, take them against the grain of conventional reading, may discover themselves as *communitas*, powerless against the literary establishment and indeed uninterested in challenging it. It is not that they will attempt to propagate some new doctrine of religious reading but rather, in the shared process of reading for the mystery, marking the traces of liminality even in secular and fugitive texts – and celebrating those discoveries – will find themselves constantly learning anew what religious reading is. Such a *communitas* will, to be sure, try to fix those celebratory moments in language and gesture adapted from liturgy and thus will function, however tentatively, as a contemporary approximation of the old storytelling cultures.[49]

Such an effort to respond to mystery through the narrative community both agrees and conflicts with Lyotard's concluding vision in 'What Is Postmodernism?' 'The postmodern', he writes, 'would be that which, in the modern, puts forward the unpresentable in presentation itself.'[50] Yet he does not view this endeavour as communal but describes post-modernism further as 'that which denies itself the solace of good forms, the consensus of a taste which would make it possible to share collectively the nostalgia for the unattainable; that which searches for new presentations, not in order to enjoy them but in order to impart a stronger sense of the unpresentable'. I find little difference between what I call mystery, approached via an intensity of form, and what Lyotard calls the unpresentable, and indeed, Lyotard's discussion in these pages has religious echoes: for example, '. . . work and text have the characters of an event'; '*Post modern* would have to be understood according to the paradox of the future (*post*) anterior (*modo*).' But Lyotard denies the efficacy of both community (a reaction against his German rival Jürgen Habermas) and narrativity in the task of presenting the unpresentable and thus forfeits a valuable context and a *modus*, out of an exaggerated fear of a false 'totality' and 'reconciliation'. It is truly 'our business', as he states, 'not to supply reality but to invent allusions to the conceivable which cannot be presented' – and this is precisely what religious writing and reading as I have sought to redescribe them can do: the *communitas* is drawn together by the need to celebrate the conceivable but unpresentable, and its narratives act as the allusions that Lyotard calls for.[51]

In the chapters that follow I will offer four religious readings, addressed to texts involving various combinations of pain, love, mystery and worship, that a *communitas* might draw upon to plot its own allusions to the unpresentable.

Notes

1. Kenneth Burke, 'Psychology and Form', in *Counter-Statement* (University of Chicago Press, 1957) p. 44.
2. For a discussion of deconstruction not unsympathetic to religious readings cf. Geoffrey H. Hartman, *Criticism in the Wilderness: The Study of Literature Today* (New Haven: Yale University Press, 1980).
3. Jacques Derrida, 'From/Of the Supplement to the Source: The Theory of Writing', in *Of Grammatology*, tr. Gayatri Chakravorty Spivak (Baltimore: Johns Hopkins University Press, 1976).
4. Peter Gay, *The Bourgeois Experience, Vol. I: Education of the Senses* (New York: Oxford University Press, 1984) p. 439.
5. Steven Mintz, *A Prison of Expectations: The Family in Victorian Culture* (New York University Press, 1985) p. 35. For a bleak and very provocative view of what our electronic society is doing to both our public and private spheres, cf. Jean Baudrillard, 'The Ecstasy of Communication', tr. John Johnston, in Hall Foster (ed.), *The Anti-Aesthetic: Essays on Postmodern Culture* (Port Townsend, Washington: Bay Press, 1983). Baudrillard writes: 'In a subtle way, this loss of public space occurs simultaneously with the loss of private space. The one is no longer a spectacle, the other no longer a secret. Their distinctive opposition, the clear difference of an exterior and an interior exactly described the domestic *scene* of objects, with its rules of play and limits, and the sovereignty of a symbolic space which was also that of the subject. Now this opposition is effaced in a sort of *obscenity*, where the most intimate processes of our life become the virtual feeding ground of the media' (130).
6. John Updike, 'One Big Interview', in *Picked-up Pieces* (Greenwich, Conn.: Fawcett Books, 1975) p. 497.
7. Ian Watt, *The Rise of the Novel* (Berkeley: University of California Press, 1962) p. 206.
8. Paul Ricoeur, *The Conflict of Interpretations*, ed. Don Ihde (Evanston: Northwestern University Press, 1974) p. 206.
9. Samuel Weber, 'Ambivalence, the Humanities and the Study of Literature', *Diacritics*, vol. 15/2 (Summer, 1985) p. 13.
10. Cf. for example Gaston Bachelard, *The Poetics of Space*, tr. Maria Jolas (Boston: Beacon Press, 1969), and Roland Barthes, *The Pleasure of the Text*, tr. Richard Miller (New York: Hill and Wang, 1975).

11. Martin Heidegger, 'Hölderlin and the Essence of Poetry', tr. Douglas Scott, in *Existence and Being* (Chicago: Henry Regnery, 1949) pp. 277–8.
12. Maud Bodkin, *Archetypal Patterns in Poetry: Psychological Studies of Imagination* (New York: Vintage Books, 1958) p. 28.
13. Cf. John D. Caputo, *The Mystical Element in Heidegger's Thought* (Athens, Ohio: Ohio University Press, 1978) pp. 173–83, on *Gelassenheit*.
14. Cf. Weber, 'Ambivalence, the Humanities and the Study of Literature', p. 19, on *Geselligkeit* in Kant's writings.
15. Clifford Geertz, 'Religion as a Cultural System', in William A. Lessa and Evon Z. Vogt (eds), *Reader in Comparative Religion: An Anthropological Approach*, 4th edn (New York: Harper & Row, 1979) p. 79.
16. Cf. Derrida, 'The Theater of Cruelty and the Closure of Representation', in *Writing and Difference*, tr. Alan Bass (University of Chicago Press, 1978), on staged drama, texts and the sacred.
17. Paul Ricoeur, *Interpretation Theory: Discourse and the Surplus of Meaning* (Fort Worth: Texas Christian University Press, 1976).
18. Mikhail Bakhtin, *Rabelais and His World*, tr. H. Iswolsky (Cambridge, Mass: MIT Press, 1968). I have also used a German translation of Bakhtin: Michail Bachtin, *Literatur und Karneval: Zur Romantheorie und Lachkultur*, tr. Alexander Kaempfe (Munich: Carl Hanser Verlag, 1969).
19. Mark C. Taylor's treatment of carnival in *Erring: A Postmodern A/theology* (University of Chicago Press, 1984) has been helpful to me.
20. Sigmund Freud, *Totem and Taboo*, tr. J. Strachey (New York: W. W. Norton, 1950). Cf. also Volney P. Gay, *Freud on Ritual: Reconstruction and Critique* (Missoula, Montana: Scholars Press, 1979).
21. Stanley Fish, *Is There a Text in this Class? The Authority of Interpretive Communities* (Cambridge, Mass.: Harvard University Press, 1980) pp. 356–71.
22. Jean-François Lyotard, 'The Unconscious as Mise-en-scène', in Michel Benamou and Charles Caramello (eds), *Performance in Postmodern Culture* (Madison, Wisconsin: Coda Press, 1977) p. 96.
23. *Koinonia* in the New Testament is the voluntary gathering together of those sharing the new Christian identity. *Ecclesia* refers to the assembly summoned for worship.
24. Cf. the chapter on 'Psychology and Form' in *Counter-Statement*.
25. What Heidegger actually asks in 'What is Meta-Physics?' (tr. R. F. C. Hull and Alan Crick, in *Existence and Being*, p. 349) is, 'Why is there any Being at all – why not far rather Nothing?' Cf. also Heidegger's powerful discussions of nihilism and nothingness in his *Nietzsche, Vol. IV: Nihilism*, tr. Frank A. Capuzzi (San Francisco: Harper & Row, 1982).

I have not attempted in this discussion to distinguish between form and matter and do not think that it is necessary for my purposes to do so. For a literary treatment of the distinction, cf.

64 Breaking the Fall

William K. Wimsatt, Jr. and Cleanth Brooks, *Literary Criticism: A Short History* (New York: Vintage Books, 1957) pp. 742ff.

26. Although there is evidence from archaeological sites in Egypt and more recently in what was Palestine that the Hebrew Yahveh had a female consort. Cf. André Lemaire, 'Who or What Was Yahveh's Asherah?', *Biblical Archaeological Review*, vol. 10/6 (November/December, 1984).

27. Søren Kierkegaard, *Concluding Unscientific Postscript*, tr. D. F. Swenson and W. Lowrie (Princeton University Press, 1941). *I was reminded of this connection while reading John Dominic Crossan, Raid on the Articulate: Comic Eschatology in Jesus and Borges* (New York: Harper & Row, 1976) p. 47. As will become evident, my use of the concept of 'deep play' is not the same as that of Clifford Geertz, who borrowed it from Jeremy Bentham's *The Theory of Legislation*. 'By it [Bentham] means play in which the stakes are so high that it is, from his utilitarian standpoint, irrational for men to engage in it at all.' Clifford Geertz, 'Deep Play: Notes on the Balinese Cockfight', in Geertz (ed.), *Myth, Symbol, and Culture* (New York: W. W. Norton, 1971) p. 15.

28. Jewish colleagues in religious studies assure me, however, that the old theological narrative of the reasons for circumcision remains meaningful to them. Mircea Eliade in his study of the initiation rituals of the Australian Karadjeri that involve torture and mutilation as part of an initiatory death symbolism offers a striking example of the uses of pain in a non-Western religion. Cf. Eliade, 'Mysteries and Spiritual Regeneration', in his *Myths, Dreams, and Mysteries: The Encounter between Contemporary Faiths and Archaic Realities*, tr. Philip Mairet (New York: Harper & Row, 1967).

29. Martin Heidegger, 'Language in the Poem: A Discussion on Georg Trakl's Poetic Work', tr. Peter D. Hertz, in his *On the Way to Language* (New York: Harper & Row, 1971).

30. Elaine Scarry, *The Body in Pain: The Making and Unmaking of the World* (New York: Oxford University Press, 1985).

31. Michael Herzfeld, 'Closure as Cure: Tropes in the Exploration of Bodily and Social Disorder', *Current Anthropology*, vol. 27/2 (April, 1986) p.108.

32. Herzfeld goes on in his article to describe how cases of *thiarmos* (being cursed by an evil eye) are 'cured' in a Cretan village in a ceremony invoking Christ and the Virgin. It is an example of how a traumatized body is interpreted by elements of a traditional sacred text. His analysis, however, does not confront directly the phenomenon of physical pain.

33. Robert J. Stoller, *Sexual Excitement* (New York: Pantheon, 1979).

34. William Kraft, *The Search for the Holy* (Philadelphia: Westminster Press, 1971) p. 52.

35. Terry Eagleton, *The Rape of Clarissa: Writing, Sexuality and Class Struggle in Samuel Richardson* (Minneapolis: University of Minnesota Press, 1982) p. 45.

36. Offred, the enslaved handmaid in Atwood's novel, cannot write

her story because she is not allowed writing instruments. After her escape she records her story onto tape cassettes, reconstructing it in part in the historical present, and these approximately thirty tapes are transcribed, and the story arranged sequentially, by scholars around the year 2195. Cf. Chapter 6 for a full treatment of *The Handmaid's Tale* and *Riddley Walker*.

37. Linda Kauffman, *Discourses of Desire: Gender, Genre and Epistolary Fictions* (Ithaca: Cornell University Press, 1986). Cf. also Annie Leclerc, 'La lettre d'amour', in *La venue à l'écriture* (Paris: Union Générale d'Editions, 1977). It is worth pointing out that a text that has been a focal point of recent literary criticism, Edgar Allan Poe's 'The Purloined Letter', has to do with a love letter, and that Poe's plot displays much of the duplicity and dissembling of the love letter itself. For an essay that criticizes two earlier prominent readings of the Poe story, by Jacques Lacan and Jacques Derrida, cf. Barbara Johnson's 'The Frame of Reference: Poe, Lacan, Derrida', in Geoffrey Hartman (ed.), *Psychoanalysis and the Question of the Text* (Baltimore: Johns Hopkins University Press, 1978) pp. 149–71.

38. For a fine discussion of Heidegger's concerns about the demystifying nature of technology expressed in essays such as 'Die Frage nach der Technik', cf. Gregory Tropea, *Religion, Ideology, and Heidegger's Concept of Falling* (Atlanta: Scholars Press, 1987).

39. Victor Turner, *The Ritual Process* (Chicago: Aldine, 1969), and *Dramas, Fields, and Metaphors: Symbolic Action in Human Society* (Ithaca: Cornell University Press, 1974).

40. Barbara Myerhoff, 'Rites of Passage: Process and Paradox', in Victor Turner (ed.), *Celebration: Studies in Festivity and Ritual* (Washington: Smithsonian Institution Press, 1982) p. 117.

41. Victor Turner, Introduction, *Celebration*, p. 13.

42. Herbert N. Schneidau, *Sacred Discontent: The Bible and Western Tradition* (Baton Rouge: Louisiana State University Press, 1976).

43. I appreciate the effort of David Michael Levin to express this sense of quiddity in liturgical texts, especially as they inspire our response of embodiment, in *The Body's Recollection of Being: Phenomenological Psychology and the Deconstruction of Nihilism* (London: Routledge & Kegan Paul, 1983). He writes, for example: 'The liturgical texts which lay claim to our embodiment in such a way that we are helped to *focus* on *our bodily felt sense* of their textual meaning are texts which have been written with the very deepest kind of wisdom. For they appreciate that there are dimensions of meaning (*Sinn*) which are such that it is only with my body, i.e., only through the process of actually incarnating those dimensions of sense in a disciplined and eventually skillful way, that I may ever come to understand them' (214).

44. For a representative expression of this position, cf. Ernst Cassirer, *Language and Myth*, tr. Susanne K. Langer (New York: Dover, 1946). A recent work by a German philosopher that challenges Cassirer is Hans Blumenberg, *Work on Myth*, tr. Robert M. Wallace (Cambridge, Mass.: MIT Press, 1985).

45.   The Jewish practice of 'rejoicing in the Torah' as part of the worship
       service is an example of a confident, communal response to the
       mystery of form. William Scott Green in 'Romancing the Tome:
       Rabbinic Hermeneutics and the Theory of Literature' (in Charles E.
       Winquist [ed.], *Text and Textuality* [*Semeia 40*] [1987]) calls attention
       to the centrality of form in rabbinic use of scripture: 'the writing
       we would call "scripture" was conceived by rabbinic culture as a
       holy object. . . . As an artifact, the Torah scroll, with its holy and
       allegedly unchanged and changeless writing, formed the requisite
       stable center for rabbinism's system of piety' (158). And: 'The sanc-
       tity of scripture gave its writing an intrinsic efficacy, an almost
       totemic quality' (160). I do not think that such stress on the mystery
       of form revives what J. Hillis Miller refers to as 'Cratylism, the
       stubborn belief that the phenomenality of words somehow naturally
       corresponds to the essence of things.' Cf. J. Hillis Miller, 'The
       Triumph of Theory, the Resistance to Reading, and the Question
       of the Material Base', *Publication of the Modern Language Association*,
       vol. 102/3 (May, 1987) p. 282.
46.   Cf. Brooks, *Reading for the Plot*, pp. 90ff., and Frank Kermode, *The
       Sense of an Ending* (New York, Oxford University Press, 1967), on
       resolution and closure in the novel.
47.   Wayne A. Meeks, *The First Urban Christians: The Social World of the
       Apostle Paul* (New Haven: Yale University Press, 1983) pp. 88ff.,
       discusses the relationship of Turner's concept of *communitas* to the
       early Christian communities.
48.   Turner would probably consider the *samizdat* writers examples of a
       marginal rather than a liminal group, since they represent a perma-
       nent form of 'outsiderhood'. Cf. *Dramas, Fields, and Metaphors*, pp.
       232–3.
49.   Cf. James F. Hopewell, *Congregation: Stories and Structures* (Philadel-
       phia: Fortress Press, 1987), for an excellent discussion of how Chris-
       tian congregations can make use of their narrative capacities. As
       Barbara G. Wheeler points out in her editor's foreword to Hopew-
       ell's book, he contended that 'congregational culture is not an acci-
       dental accumulation of symbolic elements but a coherent system
       whose structural logic is *narrative*' (p. xii). It is a pleasure to acknowl-
       edge the influence of my late colleague (Hopewell died in 1984) on
       my study.
50.   Jean-François Lyotard's 'Answering the Question: What Is Post-
       modernism?', tr. Regis Durand, is the Appendix to *The Postmodern
       Condition*. All quotations given here are from p. 81 of this essay.
51.   I am also intrigued by the relationship between mystery and what
       Peter Brooks (inspired by Freud's *Beyond the Pleasure Principle*) calls
       'nonnarratability'. Brooks relates the nonnarratable to 'ends', to
       death and quiescence (*Reading for the Plot*, p. 107). I would argue
       that the nonnarratable – that which canot be told or plotted – is not
       always a component of the death instinct but sometimes also a
       reaction to a sense of the overwhelming richness of life, which
       sense is part of our sense of mystery.

3

Braking the Fall
Walker Percy and the Diagnostic Novel

We all fall. This hand here falls.
And look at others: it's in everyone.

And yet there's one who holds this falling
infinitely gently in his hands.[1]

WRITING OFF-CENTRE

Early in Walker Percy's 1980 novel *The Second Coming*, one of the
two main characters, a young woman named Allison, starts to
recover her identity by reading notes to herself.[2] This is not only
a metaphoric looking for the self; Allison has just escaped from a
mental institution following her latest electro-shock treatment and
she sits on a bench on the main street of a North Carolina town,
literally not knowing who she is, as a result of the jolts to her
brain cells. But she has prepared for this situation, just as she
prepared for her flight, by writing a series of elaborate instructions
to herself. For example: 'Go down the hill to K-Mart and Good's
Variety. Buy clothes and articles (see list below). Go back up hill
to Gulf station. Change clothes in restroom. Check into Mitchell's
Triple-A motel one block east. Don't worry about not having car
or suitcase. You will have knapsack and they're used to it. Pay in
advance. Check your driver's license to be sure you remember
your name. Sometimes I, you, forget after a buzz' (38).

This is a daring and ingenious way of beginning the description
of a character's development in a novel. One accompanies an
adult's dawning perception of herself virtually out of nothingness,

as her written messages start to bring back her stunned recollections of who she is, and within a few paragraphs, in a concentrated and accelerated fashion, one experiences with her her personal history returning to her.

Such tactics have helped to make Walker Percy one of our more highly regarded English-language authors. After a relatively late start as a novelist – a career for which he was, by his confession, 'singularly unqualified' – Percy has published six well-wrought novels that comprise a both comic and despairing vision of persons trying to find, or maintain, sanity in a world that is at the least absurd and often mad.[3] All of Percy's protagonists have a perspective on life that is askew, off-centre, but they are that way in part because the crazy world has made them so. Their perception is off-centre because the world is out of kilter, yet they are not mad in any standard way, although sometimes recognizably mad enough for society to want to lock them up. Rather, their creative craziness establishes a distance from the world that allows them and the reader to see its madness more clearly and persuasively. As Percy puts it, 'the common thread that runs through all of my novels is of a man, or a woman, who finds himself/herself outside of society, maybe even in a state of neurosis, psychosis, or derangement. . . . What I try to do is always pose the question, "Is this man or woman more abnormal than the 'normal society' around them?" I want the reader to be poised between these two values, and I want the question always to be raised as to who's crazy, whether the protagonist is crazy, or the outside person.'[4]

This strategy of creating characters whose madness refracts rather than reflects a mad world suggests that Percy's own authorial vision is off-centre, and indeed it is. He is, of course, not alone in his nurturing of such a perspective. It is a dominant one among late twentieth-century writers (one thinks of Günter Grass, John Cheever, Kurt Vonnegut, Mordecai Richler, for example), but Percy extends a more specific tradition, one represented by such diverse authors as Evelyn Waugh, Graham Greene, Flannery O'Connor and to a degree François Mauriac: the Roman Catholic writer intensely critical of his/her corrupt world, who chastizes it through a humour of exaggeration and grotesquerie. Indeed, Percy thinks of himself as 'by nature a satirist' as well as a committed Catholic.[5] He differs from his confessional predecessors, however, in displaying a greater empathy with his strange protagonists, a willingness to give up the protective distance between himself and them that a Waugh, Greene and O'Connor seldom risked. One reason for this is that Percy is more familiar with the aberrations of selfhood, recognizes their relative normality and is less afraid of them. He was at one point 'a medical student undergoing psychoanalysis with the intention of going into pshychiatry' and he discusses knowledgeably in both his fiction and his essays the contemporary 'malaise' in psychological/psychoanalytic terms.[6]

Such empathy does not mean identification. 'Given that life in the modern world is deranged,' he says, 'it does not follow that the novelist should in the exercise of his vocation write deranged novels.'[7] Rather Percy manages, much like the adept and experienced psychiatrist, to imagine in depth the psychotic and neurotic personality without, finally, permitting them to determine his own. His fiction shows him more powerfully in dialogue with madness than most other novelists writing today (Patrick White would be one exception). Thus in his first novel *The Moviegoer* Percy puts himself inside the head of Binx Bolling, his neurotic protagonist who feels more at home in the fantasy world of cinema than in his own historical life; in *The Last Gentleman* he introduces the young Will Barrett, who is afflicted with spells of amnesia and attacks of *déjà vu*; in *Love in the Ruins* he takes the voice of Dr Thomas More, a bizarre alcoholic and libidinous physician who has invented a lapsometer, a device for measuring the condition of human souls in the apocalyptic era that the novel inhabits; in *Lancelot* he adopts the personality of a wealthy mental institution inmate who has blown up his adulterous wife and their mansion; in *The Second Coming* he speaks through both the brain-shocked Allison and the ageing Will Barrett, who is subject to seizures and who believes, when his chemical imbalance is severe, that the world is ending because the Jews are leaving North Carolina; and in *The Thanatos Syndrome* he returns to Dr Thomas More, who fights a cabal of abortionists and euthanasists, and introduces an old priest, Father Smith, who preaches a powerful concluding sermon against this megalomanic death-dealing.

All of these novels are, at the same time, centrally concerned with the religious condition of their characters – a condition that interacts with but is not identical with their psychological health. Although the psychological vocabulary is the dominant signifier for expressing the spiritual condition, it is not for Percy a privileged language. Rather, he employs it provisionally as the lexicon that is becoming more familiar in order to interpret the Judeo-Christian

tradition whose language is less and less resonant. Although the
language of psychiatry in good part replaces the language of
religious belief and of theology, it is not foundational, but is in
fact the language of what we experience as lack and absence: the
lack of faith and the absence of meaning that are spoken because
nothing else makes sense.

Percy (who has also published essays in professional journals
such as *Psychiatry*) thus addresses squarely the phenomenon, a
main trait of twentieth-century life, of a psychological world-view
overtaking the religious one, and uses the language in his novels
diagnostically and self-diagnostically to analyse what is wrong
with humanity that can no longer be articulated meaningfully in
the old religious terms, but also to undermine this very language
of diagnosis through the structures of narrative. He describes quite
specifically what he is about in his 1986 essay 'The Diagnostic
Novel: On the Uses of Modern Fiction'. Here he argues like
Foucault (whom he does not cite) that persons nowadays afflicted
with a deep sense of crisis and predicament, of the world and
themselves in it gone wrong, turn to the specialists, such as the
psychiatrists, who can type them according to certain theories but
never treat their individuality. '*Only* the writer, the existentialist
philosopher or the novelist' is equipped not only to portray the
psychological/spritual dilemma but above all to explore it for 'the
possibility or non-possibility of a search for signs and meanings'.[8]
This is a kind of writing that wishes to venture well beyond
traditional representation. It has to, Percy thinks, because the
older, more or less unified worlds to be reflected are fast
vanishing, and because merely to represent the confusion and
chaos in their place (as the anti-novel does, according to Percy) is
a nihilistic exercise. Rather, the author of the diagnostic novel is
also an epistemologist, someone who in his writing has to describe
how his characters think and feel even as he portrays the substance
of their thought and experience, and thereby suggests to his
readers, in the absence of other credible models, how their own
cognitions and affective faculties function and can be made to
create meaning.

The Second Coming is such a diagnostic-epistemological novel,
and Allison's shock-induced amnesia that I described is part of
Percy's exploration of the current pathology of thinking and
feeling. In the remainder of this chapter I will discuss three aspects
of the novel that Percy develops 'diagnostically', to disclose what

is wrong in 'an age when both the Judeo-Christian consensus and rational humanism have broken down' and to project how the disoriented inhabitants of this age might regain identity and direction.[9] The three aspects are the imagery of falling, the novel's patterns of intimacy and its stress on messages. My approach will consist of a conventional close reading of the text combined with an informal use of phenomenology that attempts an openness both to Percy's orientation to existentialism and phenomenology and to his growing awareness of – and wariness regarding – postmodern critical modes such as deconstruction. Not least, I will be concerned to show the significance of Percy's literary art for religious reading at a time when his increasing (or at least more outspoken) conservatism, especially since the publication of *The Thanatos Syndrome* in 1987, threatens to weaken his impact.

FALLING GRACEFULLY

Allison's coming to consciousness following the blankness of shock therapy and her whole off-beat manner constitute one of two crucial instances of an askance perspective in the novel. *The Second Coming* actually begins with an account of a literally skewed angle of vision experienced by Will Barrett, the other protagonist. Barrett is a middle-aged millionaire originally from Mississippi, now a respected figure in the business and country club circle of Linton, North Carolina, who married a wealthy northern woman but has been recently widowed, bereaved through the demise of his wife, who virtually ate herself to death. Barrett has a minor brain lesion or a mild form of epilepsy, called Hausmann's Syndrome (345), that precipitates *'wahnsinnige Sehnsucht'* (translated misleadingly on page 346 as 'inappropriate longing') and his suspicions that the apocalypse is at hand because the Jews are departing North Carolina and returning to Jerusalem as predicted in the Book of Revelation.[10] The novel begins with an account of Barrett collapsing on the golf course, an act that introduces the imagery of falling as well as the off-balance view of the world: 'One moment he was standing in the bunker with his sand iron appraising the lie of his ball. The next he was lying flat on the ground. Lying there, his cheek pressed against the earth, he noticed that things looked different from this unaccustomed position' (3). But a psychological reason also exists for Barrett's tumbles. As an adolescent Barrett was shot by his father, a suicidal depressive; that trauma, in which he lay wounded on the forest floor, was a shock that he has never overcome and a moment that his unconscious returns him to repeatedly, making him re-enact it involuntarily in an effort to resolve it. This reversal of the Oedipal drama, in which the father tries to kill the son (characteristic of Percy's refreshingly perverse use of psychoanalytic theory in his fiction), is repressed in Barrett's mind, too grim for him to acknowledge, yet helps to explain why he is also obsessed with death and the question of the existence of God, the final authority figure, and determines to force God's hand. Here is one of the many instances in *The Second Coming* in which the psychological and the religious interact. Barrett is intermittently crazy, prone to deep depression, suicidal impulses and what we used to call existential despair. Life lacks meaning for this man so well-off materially and socially, and he makes this lack a religious matter. It is significant that he has to be at least semi-mad before he becomes uninhibited enough to see the problem of meaningless-ness clearly as a religious one, connected to the question of whether or not there is a God who could provide sense and order. Barrett devises a scheme whereby he will prove whether or not God exists (acting out Pascal's familiar wager) and makes prep-arations to descend into an isolated cave, determined to stay there and die unless somehow miraculously rescued. This rescue would be the sign forced from God that he exists.

This descent into the cave is an elemental manoeuvre a good deal like Allison's escape from the hospital. Undertaking some-thing like a physical version of a phenomenological reduction, Barrett strips away as many trappings as he can and tries to reduce his identity to a fundamental living or dying. Yet like Allison's situation his effort is not elemental but strongly influenced by the technology that always worries Percy and his characters. In her case it is the electro-shock therapy that alters her personality and her sense of identity. In Barrett's case it takes the form of ninety-six Placidyl capsules that he takes into the cave with him – tranquil-lizers that will ease the pain as he slowly starves to death – unless God rescues him. But the drugs instead cause him to hallucinate during most of the time, the days he spends underground. Unable to listen intently for a redemptive message, he finds his mind drifting aimlessly and erratically along many tracks. More than that, his life-and-death effort to call God's hand fails for a very prosaic reason. He awakens in the cave from one of his drugged states with an incredible toothache, one so bad that the pain and nausea force him to crawl back out of the cave, a difficult task for him in his weakened state, and to fall *downward*, out of another exit, through the roof of an isolated greenhouse in which Allison meanwhile has hidden herself.

This passage invites all sorts of second-level interpretations. It can be read variously as Barrett's return to the womb from which he emerges, painfully, into a new life; as his venture into his uncharted unconscious; as his death, burial and resurrection; as his descent into hell; as his dark night of the soul – all archetypal patterns with combined psychological and religious import. Common to the imagery of all of them is the downward movement from control to loss of control. This fall is a climactic, transforming moment of the narrative, for what happens afterwards is marked by grace and healing. Barrett crashing ludicrously through the greenhouse roof falls literally into Allison's life, an accident that precipitates their falling in love (even, appropriately, in the fall of the year).

Yet their journey toward intimacy and health does not produce an optimistic novel. It remains a grim comedy, for the falling as a loss of control is emphasized. Barrett is a wealthy man whose material needs are all met, who has good breeding and who enjoys the respect of his community and profession. Yet he has experienced the suicide of his father and the death of his wife, who could not curb her appetite and died through overeating. He himself is deeply depressed and wants, at times, to kill himself. Barrett, with the rest of Percy's technologized, wealthy America, is out of control. He, and it, live post-lapsarian life, life after the Fall, with a vengeance. Describing this existence is what Percy does best. He excels in depicting the chaos, confusion and disarray of American lives, along with the attendant violence, senselessness and corruption in what he has Will Barrett call, sarcastically, the most Christian nation in the world. The irony is incisive, for the point of technological development is to achieve greater control over existence, to overcome the vagaries of nature, disease, ignorance and crime.

The failure of technology, which is the failure of control, in Percy's view is not primarily an indictment of technology. 'The real pathology', he says, 'lies elsewhere – not in the station wagon or the all-electric kitchen' but in what he defines as idolatry, a false worship of scientific method that seduces individuals into giving over control of their lives to 'experts' who by their very method cannot deal with individuality.[11] This false worship is prominent in the plot of *The Thanatos Syndrome*, where the experts are a secret society of doctors who control the population through drugs and decide life and death situations. Thus the new version of the Fall is still the temptation toward a specious self-reliance that is actually the disintegration of selfhood, as we discover ourselves incapable of a disinterested, objective knowledge of the self, since the self and its orchestrations are always already constituted by the individual and her relations to others. The world is thus fundamentally 'fallen', flawed by the individual's recognition of difference that at the same time both creates the conditions for meaning and frustrates the project of science to create objective, generalizing knowledge.

Because things are basically wrong in Percy's fictional world, a healing interaction such as Allison and Will Barrett come to experience is not modelled on some vision of originary wholeness or on an anticipation of some cosmic perfection to come. It happens out of the world's brokenness, and in spite of it. They fumble toward health and wholeness of mind and body, step by step, as individuals erring together, without a master pattern, as if they were the first to encounter the possibility of wholeness. It is a good deal like Ricoeur's description of the 'fault' in his *Fallible Man*, where the Fall is presented as a paradoxical condition in which consciousness and self-consciousness generate the gap that the individual feels between the self and what is other – namely, nature and the others – and that even hinders the individual from knowing the self, for this self has no effective point of orientation for exploiting the difference, the sense of otherness it feels.[12] Percy's sensitive characters, made neurotic and psychotic by the inability of the self to comprehend itself in isolation, in formal relationships with others or in technological relationships with nature, fall into a lovers' liaison, the mystery of which encourages them to clearer and firmer identities. That it is a process without distinct models (even though Barrett was married for many years) Percy shows by emphasizing its novelty for them. Yet it is a vigorously metaphoric process in which their differences collide and then merge to form a new selfhood for them, individually and together. The process is also, one might add, non-representational, in that the couple

do not base their behaviour on cultural custom but on experimentation and discovery.

I will return to the matter of the lovers gaining a stronger sense
of self through each other in my discussion of patterns of intimacy.
For now, I wish to treat the novel's imagery of falling further by
reviewing our century's most original explication of the subject in
Heidegger's *Being and Time*.[13] Heidegger's complicated analysis of
falling deals with it in philosophical terms that can also illuminate
its symbolic use in Percy's narrative. Falling informs Heidegger's
examination of *Dasein* (Being-there, existence, in contrast to Being)
as that which of necessity leads *Dasein* astray, in its struggle for
authenticity, by tempting it to accept the judgements of the public
as its own. *Dasein* is above all tempted to avoid contemplating
death, as the most authentic realization of existence, by assuming
the opinions of the group. *Dasein* thus fallen is driven by anxiety to
attempt authentic choice but is able only to recognize its alienated
individuality, its involvement in *Unheimlichkeit* or 'not-at-home-
ness'. The sciences in particular demonstrate fallen *Dasein* in operation. They show how the intolerability of constantly facing authenticity, especially the authenticity of death, gives way to the
solidifying of public judgement into what is construed as objective
knowledge, in which operation ideology masquerades as truth.
Dasein, recognizing this dilemma, cannot therefore simply with-
draw from the world, however. Rather, it practises 'resoluteness',
a term used in *Being and Time* for what Heidegger later comes to call
Gelassenheit. It is always a *'Gelassenheit zu den Dingen'*, a 'relaxation
toward things' that both admits to the value of the technological
but refuses to be dominated by it. For Heidegger technology is the
expression of scientific ideology and is thus a danger to authentic
revelation, and until such a time as technology can be employed
judiciously, in accord with ontological thinking, it needs to be met
in an attitude of *Gelassenheit* and *Sorge* or care, care meaning both
concern and compassionate involvement.

One sees in this sketch of Heidegger's treatment of falling an
articulation of the ways in which Percy presents falling as a narrative trope, and one can allow the philosophy and fiction to
comment on each other by focusing on the concept of *Unheimlichkeit* emphasized by Heidegger in *Being and Time*. *Unheimlich*, literally 'not at home' or (less literally) 'unfamiliar', is usually translated
as 'uncanny', and catches the sense of strangeness, unfamiliarity
with the self, that Allison and Barrett feel and that registers in

their off-balance perspectives. Their lives are also *unheimlich* in
their inability to feel at home where they have dwelt, Allison an
alien in her parents' home and in the mental institution and Barrett
ill at ease wherever he is, 'a placeless person in a placeless place'
(385). When Allison takes refuge in the abandoned greenhouse
(that is actually on her own inherited property) and Barrett crashes
in on her, this unlikely spot becomes their temporary home, the
locale of both their incipient convalescences that substitutes
mystery for the uncanny as their love takes hold and deepens
there. It is there too that an authentic technology, in the service
of the individual rather than dominating her, is initiated. Allison
constructs an intricate arrangement of ropes and pulleys to
position a heavy stove that she will use against the autumn cold,
and later she uses the same contraption to lift the unconscious,
crippled Barrett onto a table/bed after he has fallen through her
glass roof – her hoisting is the response to his falling! This use of
technology in the spirit of care is carried on by Barrett when he
hires two old men from the nursing home to build log cabins 'at
a price young couples, singles, and retired couples can afford'
(395) and a third elderly man to turn the abandoned greenhouse
into a modest commercial venture.

All this is in contrast to the high-tech hospital and the love-and-
faith community that Barrett's daughter, an enthusiastic convert
to charismatic Christianity, wants to build with funds from her
mother's (Barrett's dead wife's) estate, examples of a merely
fashionable cause, linked to technology rather than to care, that
Percy satirizes. Barrett, as well as Allison in her plan to be
productive after their marriage, authenticates technology, raises it
from its fallen state as the slave of scientific ideology, by releasing
it to individual and communal compassionate endeavours. Or one
could say that the lovers attempt to domesticate technology, to
make it less *unheimlich*, by placing it at the service of the vulnerable
in a *communitas* rather than of the powerful.

Percy presents Barrett as struggling with religious belief, so that
his encounters with falling, literal and metaphoric, are understood
at last not only in terms of *Gelassenheit* but also in the corres-
ponding Christian theological terminology of grace. Yet this
traditional terminology is itself enlivened by the characters' growth
– especially their growth toward each other – and made to embrace
the corporeal as well as the spritual. Will Barrett's falling down,
the result both of a brain lesion and of a riddle hidden in his

unconscious, is connected to death: what his memory has hidden from him all these years is that his father tried to make him part of a double death, the son's murder and the father's suicide. This terrible paternal act, too awful for the son to face for much of his life and lying buried in his unconscious, becomes at last a good part of his revelatory movement away from his own suicide (death as inauthenticity) and toward an authentic living toward death that makes the living valuable, even precious. In two critical instances he leaves Allison in order to face death. In the first of these he leaves her in her greenhouse, after he has recovered enough from his fall to manage, thinking to reorder his own life and help Allison re-emerge into the world, but instead of returning home he spends the night in his Mercedes in a mad, ecstatic state during which he recites a death litany, learns 'all the names of death', then falls asleep to portentous and reconciliatory dreams. In the second, some weeks later after he has moved into a motel with Allison, he lies next to her in the dark as she sleeps, argues with himself a final time about suicide, then leaves the motel, takes his guns from the trunk of his car and throws them over a cliff. In both of these a grace connected to the bodily prevents him from yielding to a false kind of death, and allows him to face ageing and old age that may well 'close you out with the drools and the shakes and your mouth fallen open, head nodding away and both hands rolling pills' (386). Allison's vitality and vulnerability motivate him to wish to live, and she becomes, eventually, quite overtly an expression of grace for him – the unexpected gift who fills and quickens his life and inspires him toward usefulness.

After his fall, then, comes the grace that points toward wholeness, but even before that the agony underground, in the cave, is fraught with grace. The Placidyl tablets, first, are his technological substitute for grace, the painkillers designed to get him through the worst as he starves or is rescued by God. They are his *pharmakon*, both medicine and poison, that will make his death bearable. But grace intercedes, ironically, in the form of intense pain that forces him to crawl out of his chamber in a search for relief – causes him to lose his will to draw out God or die, to lose his way and fall into Allison's refuge.

Barrett's fortunate fall, then, is encompassed by a grace in touch with the significant corporeal: with the erotic, whereby sexual energy generates pleasurable abundance, and with the painful, whereby the assault on the visceral produces an economy of choice. Pleasure and pain, fullness and deprivation constitute the rhythms of mortality wherein one has to articulate meaning. In stressing these as elements of grace, Percy is doing no more – or less – than recovering the old eschatology of Christianity and giving it immanent meaning. Heaven with its pleasures and Hell with its torments, important to aspects of Christian mythology that twentieth-century theology treats as awkwardly – if it treats them at all – as it does the life of the body, are transferred by Percy to the everyday and are transformed from their role as results of divine grace to the components of grace. Graceful living is the gift of those who have learned how to balance pleasure and pain, in whatever measures they receive them, in the long fall to death. It is *Gelassenheit zu den Dingen*, a response toward things that enables one, like Barrett, to throw away the guns and get back to love and work. And, it should not be forgot, grace works here at the physical level through technology: Barrett's *petit-mal* epilepsy and/or brain lesion can be controlled. if not healed, by the use of a simple drug, so that he can live a fairly normal life.

INTIMACY AND THE APOCALYPSE

Percy may domesticate technology, but he does not try to tame eschatology. When Barrett crashes through the greenhouse roof, the last thing he sees before unconsciousness is 'the great black beast of the apocalypse roaring down at him, eyes red, jaws open and ravening' (262). Although this monster turns out to be merely Allison's dog in the path of Barrett's fall, such description typifies the latter-days vision of Percy's characters and an outlook that seems to be a persistent dimension of Percy's own personality. He remarks in the 1986 *America* interview,

> It's hard for a novelist not to be concerned with the apocalypse these days, isn't it? . . . So, if by 'apocalypse' you mean the Last Days, the novelist has reasonable grounds for exploring this territory. It is also good novelistic practice. Characters behave more interestingly both before the ultimate catastrophe and after. . . . If the Bomb is going to fall any minute, all things become possible, even love. A novelist is always interested in boy-meets-girl, but not the greatest novelist, not even Shakespeare, could contrive to have boy meeting girl and falling in

love on the regular 5:30 P.M. commuter train to Hackensack. But if the Bomb is going to vaporize New Jersey any minute and the boy knows how to get the girl to Delaware in time – we're suddenly in the realm of the old master Hitchcock, if not the Bard.[14]

One might challenge Percy's assertion that commuter eros is not an attractive subject for writers and readers – it has been depicted credibly often enough – but his comments otherwise indicate his interest in blending the erotic with the apocalyptic and the eschatological. I want to examine that blending, first by studying the patterns of twoness in the novel and then by looking again to Heidegger, this time to his discussion of intimacy.

Most fiction operates on some principle of twoness. One has protagonists and antagonists, double plots, alternation of diegesis and mimesis (or telling and showing) and so on. But this novel moves beyond these standard strategies to develop a doubling and replication that are indicated in the title itself. All readers recognize 'the Second Coming' as referring to the return of Christ, the Parousia, the Last Judgement, and that eschatological flavour permeates the narrative. Will Barrett during his periods of imbalance thinks that he is living in the so-called latter days, one bit of evidence being his conviction that the Jews are leaving North Carolina for Jerusalem and thus fulfilling a biblical prophecy on signs that advertise the end of the world. Percy has used this setting more literally in his semi-futuristic third novel *Love in the Ruins*, in which the era truly is the latter days and an apocalypse of sorts occurs in the late twentieth century, followed by an age of tranquillity in which the protagonist and his lover, who have survived, live quietly and simply in a domestic seclusion.

But in *The Second Coming* Percy's stress on twoness causes the reader to think of personal relationships and emotional/spiritual growth in apocalyptic terms – something one does not generally do. He accomplishes this mainly by shifting the usual cosmic focus of apocalyptic writing, the replacement of the old world with the new, to a focus on consciousness, personality and relationships. Allison's old, damaged ego-structure is replaced by a new one; she becomes capable of facing people, taking responsibility, fending for herself. Will Barrett exchanges his depressive, suicidal nature for one of relative equilibrium, joy and the desire to work productively. In each of their lives an individual 'apocalypse' has

happened that precedes the new self. For Allison it is the debili-
tating mental illness and that final shock treatment that obliterate
her personality; for Barrett it is the suicidal depression that leads
him to the voluntary burial alive and its painful climax. For both
of them the 'second coming' happens through the other person:
their new, second personalities or egos take shape in interaction
with each other. They are redeemed and renewed by each other,
and in a process replete with twoness. Even their histories double
and replicate each other. Each gets into a dangerous position; each
has reached a personal dead end, a stage of dysfunction. Each has
developed a behaviour so at odds with the patterns of others that
they no longer interact. Their askew perspectives have become
nearly total distortion. Each, especially Allison, speaks a disjunc-
tive language that does not communicate. The condition of each
provides the reader with a diagnosis of both: they are two of a
kind.

Yet they are also conducive opposites. He is old; she is young.
He is a 'bad' father; she a 'bad' daughter. He is a veteran; she is
a neophyte. Each is at some time the patient and the other the
nurse. Their love, when it becomes known, creates a scandal – not
least because many years earlier Barrett was the lover of Allison's
mother, and in fact certain overtones of incest are heard in the
narrative – yet the two of them fit. Their lives not only double
and replicate each other, sometimes as mirror images; they are
also disparate parts who find unexpected completion through each
other. Percy conveys this through the imagery of their physical
closeness: 'He nested her, and circled her as if he were her cold
dead planet and she his sun's warmth' (293); 'She was . . .
enclosing him, wrapping her arms and legs around him, as if her
body had at last found the center of itself outside itself' (295).
Those are very elaborate similes, both erotic and 'metaphysical' in
the sense of John Donne's conceits, and Percy employs them, as
did Donne, to insinuate cosmic meaning into physical embrace. It
is an instructively old-fashioned concept revived here. The new is
not merely a replacement of the old, as our era, having substituted
technology for history, tends to think. Rather, the new results
from a reconfiguration of the old, from a rejoining of the broken
parts. Thus the lovers come together, attracted by a sameness of
damaged personality and history of misfortune, but manage to
turn their fragmentation into a dyadic wholeness.

David Halliburton in a phenomenological analysis of Edgar

Allan Poe's 'The Fall of the House of Usher' (surely a tale that merges the cosmic and personal apocalypse) offers a helpful contrast in terms of twoness and doubling to my treatment of *The Second Coming*.[15] He shows how Roderick and Madeleine Usher, the doomed brother and sister, are fatally similar and further each other's destruction in a series of doubling events until at the end she emerges from her coffin and falls over him in deadly embrace as the great house collapses. Percy's novel provides a sort of healthy alternative to Poe's Gothic horror. His characters do not yield to madness and the paralysis of despair but use the strength of their twoness to overcome the curse they feel upon their lives. Literally and metaphorically, they save their houses and plan, through marriage and childbirth, to carry on the lineage.

The Second Coming quite obviously also displays Christian redemption imagery – even though Percy claims, disingenuously, that he 'had not thought of Will's experience as a paradigm of the Christian experience'.[16] Its connection between cosmic and personal apocalypse is anticipated by the biblical metaphors of the old and the new Adam: the old creation must be replaced by a new, but it occurs through a catastrophe, a radical break with the old structure, symbolized by the apocalyptic imagery (darkness, earthquakes, graves opening, the rending of the temple veil) attending the crucifixion of Jesus. The new being (we could say the new ego-structure) that emerges results from a relationship with a loving being, who is Christ.

The analogy of the lovers using each other to find wholeness and the despairing individual finding new life through Christ breaks down instructively, however, in the area of reciprocal relations. Most Christian theologians would find offensive the proposition that Christ needs the 'broken' individual in the same way that these lovers need each other. It is not the same sort of 'fit', not the same kind of twoness called for. The Judeo-Christian tradition has in fact largely avoided the figures of sexual interaction – unlike many other religions – in its theologies of redemption, apart from such innocuous ones as the metaphor of the church as the bride of Christ. It is mainly the Christian mystics such as St John of the Cross and the modern fiction writers who have eroti-cized these theologies; one thinks of D. H. Lawrence's parody *The Man Who Died*, where Christ is portrayed as a thoroughly sexual being whose redemptive message emerges through his coupling with a fertility goddess. The breakdown of the analogy, at any rate, suggests that Percy is not simply dramatizing the healing of human brokenness through human love, for Barrett constantly evokes an awareness of God and the need for God in his life and thus keeps before the reader the question of how, in fact, the healing of two persons through each other relates to God. The answer arrives with clarity only in the final paragraph of the novel, where Will Barrett discerns Allison at last as a gift, a sign of God's grace, the incarnation of the message (ironically) that he has been looking for all along. *His* task then, at the end of the novel, becomes to theologize from the fact of this grace, its mystery, and to learn what it means to be blessed in this way.

The novel's conclusion, in fact, is a comic and profound passage on grace, love and physical intimacy that nearly lapses into overt theologizing.[17] At this point Barrett has cornered an old and frail Episcopal priest, Father Weatherbee, and asks him to perform the wedding ceremony for him and Allison. But Barrett's bodily chemicals are acting up again and lead him to ravings about the Jews returning to Jerusalem and other signs of the latter days. All this alarms the old priest and makes him want to flee this crazy man, but Barrett holds on to him. This is how the novel ends:

> What do I want of him, mused Will Barrett, and suddenly real-ized he had gripped the old man's wrists as if he were a child. The bones were like dry sticks. He let go and fell back. For some reason the old man did not move but looked at him with a new odd expression. Will Barrett thought about Allie in her greenhouse, her wide grey eyes, her lean-muscled boy's arms, her strong quick hands. His heart leapt with a secret joy. What is it I want from her and him, he wondered, not only want but must have? Is she a gift and therefore a sign of a giver? Could it be that the Lord is here, masquerading behind this simple silly holy face? Am I crazy to want both, her and Him? No, not want, must have. And will have. (411)

Barrett considers the eros of his relationship with Allison as a sign for and part of the gift of grace to him. The language stresses desire: 'No, not want, must have. And will have.' This is the language of possession – must *have*, will *have* – that indulges a concluding pun: *Will* have. Here, the language of possession is used ironically by Percy against the backdrop of America's immature attitude toward desire, love and intimacy, for Barrett and Allison have learned far better than most that intimacy does not consist of possession.

Inhabitants of the Western world, living off the relatively young tradition of romantic love and exploiting it commercially and technologically, tend to make little distinction among desire, love and intimacy. Desire, in our mythology of romance, is supposed to result quickly in intimacy – the sooner the better – and this then constitutes love. One finds a contrast to this superficiality, and a sense of the quality of love that Percy strives to convey, in Heidegger's reflections on intimacy, which are based on interpretation of poets such as Hölderlin and Trakl.[18] 'Intimacy' in Heidegger's German (borrowed from Hölderlin) is *Innigkeit*, which could be translated just as well as 'inwardness'. This inwardness does not lead to a mystical oneness or unity but is characterized by difference. Persons can become truly intimate only by maintaining their distinctiveness, and the object of friendship or love relationships is not to merge personalities, as if that were possible, but to find oneself defined and complemented by the other's difference. Intimacy opens the lovers' minds to their individual potential and what they can accomplish by sharing that potential. It is a maturation that the lovers exemplify in *The Second Coming*. The celebration of their passion quickly turns to a desire to become useful, productive, socially responsible. These intentions become erotically charged and thus motors of passionate engagement. The lovers' intimacy turns outward. They wish to serve out of the power of love.

Intimacy, Heidegger says, is also marked by pain and silence. In our popular love culture pain has been subverted into romantic agony, which, reinforced by media technology, serves as the stuff of thousands of songs, stories and dramas. That is, of course, not what Heidegger has in mind. He regards pain as basic to intimacy because maintaining the self in the process of sharing is always a rending, a separating act. The self in intimacy is vulnerable to hurtful acts of the other and perpetrates those acts on the other. There is no other way of creating intimacy. *The Second Coming* is an extremely painful novel marked by such traumatic things as Allison's electro-shock treatments and Barrett's memory of the wound to his face and head long ago from his father's shotgun blast. Their love relationship begins in pain, physical and mental,

and progresses toward a healing intimacy that will never be
entirely pain-free – as it indeed should not.

Heidegger's kind of intimacy, finally, involves silence. It is the
state of abiding, in trust of the other, and in offering the other
one's trust, that allows one to maintain the fullness of the self
without defences, without explanation. It is (although Heidegger
does not put it like this) living in an attitude of *Gelassenheit* in
relation to the other. The lovers in Percy's novel have not yet
learned the silence of intimacy. In fact, as they explore their deepening love they chatter incessantly. Each of them has been enveloped too long in the silence of isolation, so that their conversation
is a bursting-forth of words to another who, at last, understands.
But one can imagine, in projecting the fiction further, that these
two are on the way to intimate silence, the state in which the
sharing of difference takes place beyond language.

Barrett's and Allison's experience with intimacy as difference
and pain, and toward silence, is what pushes him toward the
possibility of faith. This love affair is not a substitute for the
experience of faith. Rather, Barrett learns that his difference of
self, his pain, and perhaps above all the silence of God, are
conditions for an intimacy more intense and encompassing than
he has been able to imagine. 'Could it be that the Lord is here,
masquerading behind this simple silly holy face?' Heidegger
remarks, 'What is strange in the thinking of Being is its simplicity.
Precisely this keeps us from it.'[19] One could say the same things
about grace, and *The Second Coming*, in many ways a profane
novel, is excellent 'religious' fiction, for it dramatizes the paradox
of the simplicity of grace.

DISCERNING MESSAGES

I introduced this chapter with an arresting example of a fictional
character's attempt to decipher a critical message. Allison, still
literally shocked out of self-recognition, reads her instructions to
herself to re-learn who she is and how to behave. What she does
is a radically pared-down, elemental version of more standard
reflexive and tacit human attempts at signifying. Humans are
meaning-seeking and meaning-producing creatures, but we do not
as a rule start with the need to recover basic information about
ourselves such as name, family relationships, habits, profession,

strengths and weaknesses. We take these things for granted and presume to build on them in our search for and generation of meaning. Percy cuts through such presumption in his description of Allison and suggests that meaning-making is always at heart a fundamental identity exercise: we do not build more and more securely upon an increasingly solid sense of selfhood but constantly try to reach back and discover who we are. Our efforts to make meaning out of anything, however complicated, may be, in a way, a grand attempt to name ourselves.

Allison's ordeal is, indeed, not all that alien to those of us who have not suffered emotional breakdown. We all fall into situations of vulnerability, wherein we are surprised by a new sense of who we are. Herbert Spiegelberg has referred to this as the I-am-me experience.[20] According to Spiegelberg, some of us, at least every now and then, find ourselves in a condition where we experience our I-ness, our selfhood, with a special intensity and face the mystery of what it means to be this particular aggregate of mind, body and lived history named, fairly arbitrarily, Allison or Will or whatever it may be. It seems to me that we experience this usually when the comfortable balance of selfhood is threatened: in those frozen seconds of drifting toward impact in a car accident, in the immediate aftermath of some great disappointment, for example. At these times we sense how fragile and vulnerable is the structure of the I, that it is nothing substantial but more of a construct, a lived story that we develop and learn to call the self.

It is because the situation of the self is so precarious in Percy's fiction that his characters constantly look for reinforcing messages and that they look in places and according to tactics that are both typical and unusual. Binx Bolling in *The Moviegoer* hopes to find directions on how to live from watching the fictions of cinema. Lancelot in the novel of that name hires a surveillance expert to film his wife betraying him with her lovers, so that he gains proof of her infidelity and impetus to kill her. Percy's preoccupation with getting signs and directions is illustrated especially well by the title of his collection of essays called *The Message in a Bottle*.[21] In traditional adventure fiction such messages are cast into the water, often by someone marooned somewhere, in the hope that the bottle will be picked up and rescue will follow. Such a desperate trusting to luck, because nothing else is available, stresses what Percy's plots regularly emphasize. His people, in

mental, spiritual and sometimes social distress, wait for messages
that may somehow save them.

The *Message in a Bottle* essays illustrate well how communication
for Percy is always involved with technology. Communications
technology figures strongly in his writing. But the technology,
typically, in Percy's plots comes to obscure the openness to the
potentially redemptive messages and turns into a preoccupation
and an end in itself. In all of his novels his characters virtually
preach on how the modern age idolizes its technology and has
lost its capacity to hear and receive messages about value, meaning
and deep relationships. In many ways secularization and the
triumph of technology are synonymous for Percy's protagonists,
who ponder how both to accommodate the technology of a secular
age and still be open to the news of ultimate things. It is not that
messages do not come through but that they come through in
such volume and confusion that the capacity for absorbing them
and differentiating among them is overwhelmed. The prison-
house of language is now like a communications centre with too
many phones and screens operating all at once.

In his repeated dramatization of this problem, Percy continues
the tradition of Kafka and Beckett but also complicates it. Like the
character K in Kafka's *The Castle*, who spends a lifetime waiting
in vain for a word from the inhabitant of the building inside the
walls and beyond the gate, and like the two tramps waiting for
Godot to appear in Beckett's drama, Percy's people long for that
all-clarifying, all-resolving message to reach them (they suffer
wahnsinnige Sehnsucht), yet they also are distracted by a steady
noise that makes any deep message almost impossible to hear.
Their lives are lived, as a result, in a state of agitated suspense and
anticipation, a condition of private marginality that has, instead of
communal support, the loud rumours of communications
enterprise.

That support is missing because there is no genuine *communitas*
to supply it. In *The Second Coming* both the established church and
sectarianism are lampooned, made to seem inept, insincere or
both. And because institutionalized religion as well as its alternatives have failed, the characters in need and in isolation seek
communitas in intimate relations. Percy is very serious about the
novelist's responsibility for portraying actions that can show
persons how to move from the merely marginal to the liminal:

Then what is the task of serious fiction in an age when both the Judeo-Christian consensus and rational humanism have broken down? I suggest that it is more than a documentation of the loneliness and the varieties of sexual encounters of so much modern fiction. I suggest that it is nothing less than an explor- ation of the options of post-modern man. . . . The contemporary novelist, in other words, must be an epistemologist of sorts. He must know how to send messages and how to decipher them. The messages may not come in bottles, but rather in the halting and muted dialogue between strangers, between lovers and friends. One speaks, the other tries to fathom his meaning – or indeed to determine if the message has any meaning. . . . The challenge now is nothing less than the exploration of a new world and the re-creation or rediscovery of language and meanings.[22]

One observes Percy here, himself a transitional figure between the modern and the post-modern, struggling to span the gap. His solution is for the literary artist to assume a philosopher's perspec- tive, yet to do so with the resources of literary language – an effort just the obverse of what Geoffrey Hartman describes as the contemporary literary critic's challenge to think and write creatively (that is, more metaphorically than has been the custom) yet within the framework of critical discourse.[23]

   Allison and Barrett themselves come to function with each other as 'epistemologists', and help each other to re-create 'language and meanings' in ways that form the nucleus of a real *communitas*. Their messages to the outside world are often misunderstood. It happens to Barrett when he becomes periodically unhinged and raves about the signs of the apocalypse. It happens more often to Allison because, as a result of her illness, she no longer uses normal phrasing but speaks instead a bizarre private idiom that is at once highly metonymic and metaphoric. Thus she utters phrases like 'Moreover a continuity is beginning for the first time but is not climbing on me' (376) and 'One plus one equals one and oh boy almond joy' (301). These expressions of her unin- hibited manner others take as evidence of her persisting mental illness, but Barrett actually listens to her and learns *her* language. It becomes their lovers' dialogue, the 'halting and muted' message that, in its strangeness, communicates *more* than ordinary talk and thus radiates its own meaning. Because it evokes so forcefully –

and playfully – the mystery of their growing intimacy, it even serves as the liturgy of their erotic faith. This fragile two-person *communitas* is the most tangible creation of Percy's 'off-centre' diagnostic and epistemological novel, in which the psychological and the religious are subsumed in the erotic. The lovers' erotic liaison is offered as the articulation of one possibility of being in the postmodern world.[24]

Notes

1. From Rainer Maria Rilke, 'Herbst', in *Das Buch der Bilder, Sämtliche Werke*, I (Wiesbaden: Insel Verlag, 1955), p. 400. The translation is my own.
    Wir alle fallen. Diese Hand da fällt.
    Und sieh dir andre an: es ist in allen.
    Und doch ist Einer, welcher dieses Fallen
    unendlich sanft in seinen Händen hält.
2. Walker Percy, *The Second Coming* (New York: Farrar, Straus and Giroux, 1980). Page numbers of the text from which quotations are taken are given in parentheses following the citation. Percy's other novels published to date are *The Moviegoer* (1960), *The Last Gentleman* (1966), *Love in the Ruins* (1971), *Lancelot* (1977), and *The Thanatos Syndrome* (1987). Williston Bibb 'Will' Barrett is the young protagonist of *The Last Gentleman*, and his lover there is Kitty Vaught, the woman who would become, in the plot of *The Second Coming*, Allison's mother. But *The Second Coming* is in no significant way a sequel to *The Last Gentleman*.
3. Walker Percy, 'The Diagnostic Novel: On the Uses of Modern Fiction', *Harper's*, vol. 272/1633 (June, 1986) p. 43.
4. John Griffith Jones, 'A Conversation with Walker Percy', *The Critic* (Spring, 1986) pp. 30–1.
5. Patrick H. Samway, 'An Interview with Walker Percy', *America*, vol. 154/5 (15 February, 1986) p. 122.
6. Percy, 'The Diagnostic Novel', p. 42.
7. Ibid., p. 39.
8. Ibid., pp. 43, 45.
9. Ibid., p. 44.
10. '*Wahnsinnige Sehnsucht*' is better rendered in English, both semantically and for purposes of the plot, as 'mad longing' or 'untempered longing'. Both the symptom and the name of the illness are Percy's invention, although the symptoms match those of temporal lobe epilepsy.
11. Percy, op. cit., pp. 41–2.
12. Paul Ricoeur, *Fallible Man*, tr. Charles Kelbley (Chicago: Henry Regnery, 1965).

13.	Martin Heidegger, *Being and Time*, trs John Macquarrie and Edward
	Robinson (New York: Harper & Row, 1962). I am indebted to
	Gregory Tropea's fine study, *Religion, Ideology, and Heidegger's
	Concept of Falling* (Atlanta: Scholars Press, 1986), for guidance
	through Heidegger's writing on falling.
14.	Samway, 'An Interview with Walker Percy', p. 122.
15.	David Halliburton, *Edgar Allan Poe: A Phenomenological View* (Prin-
	ceton University Press, 1973).
16.	Samway, op. cit., p. 123.
17.	Although Percy is aware of this danger and works to avoid it. As
	he says, 'That's why the main criticism of my novels is that they
	all end indecisively, which is very deliberate. They'd be in big
	trouble if they ended decisively.' Quoted in Jones, 'A Conversation
	with Walker Percy', p. 29.
18.	Cf. Martin Heidegger, 'Language in the Poem: A Discussion on
	Georg Trakl's Work', in his *On the Way to Language*, tr. Peter D.
	Hertz (New York: Harper & Row, 1971). I do not mean to suggest
	that Heidegger himself necessarily exemplified a matured intimacy
	in his personal relationships. As Elisabeth Young-Bruehl describes
	it in *Hannah Arendt: For Love of the World* (New Haven: Yale Univer-
	sity Press, 1982), Heidegger's affair with Hannah Arendt when
	she was his eighteen-year-old student in Marburg reveals him as
	vulnerable to the romantic clichés that typify the kind of infatuation
	he criticizes. Thus Heidegger in 1949 could confess to his wife
	that 'Hannah Arendt had been the "passion of his life" and the
	inspiration of his work' (Young-Bruehl, p. 247).
19.	Martin Heidegger, 'Letter on Humanism', trs Frank A. Capuzzi and
	J. Glenn Gray, in *Basic Writings*, ed. David Farrell Krell (New York:
	Harper & Row, 1977) p. 240. I am grateful to James D. Tichenor for
	pointing out this quotation to me and for the guidance of his
	doctoral dissertation, *The Wave of Transcendence in Faulkner's Narra-
	tives: A Heideggerian Interpretation* (Emory University, 1984), for my
	comments on intimacy in Heidegger's thought.
20.	Herbert Spiegelberg, 'On the "I-am-me" Experience in Childhood
	and Adolescence', *Review of Existential Psychology and Psychiatry*,
	vol. 4/1 (Winter, 1964) pp. 3–21. Richard M. Zaner has a valuable
	discussion of this experience in 'Awakening: Towards a Phenomen-
	ology of the Self', in F. J. Smith (ed.), *Phenomenology in Perspective*
	(The Hague: Martinus Nijhoff, 1970) pp. 174ff. Percy himself, not
	incidentally, has contributed essays to journals such as *Philosophy
	and Phenomenological Research*.
21.	Walker Percy, *The Message in a Bottle* (New York: Farrar, Straus and
	Giroux, 1975).
22.	Percy, 'The Diagnostic Novel', pp. 44–5.
23.	Geoffrey H. Hartman, *Criticism in the Wilderness: The Study of Litera-
	ture Today* (New Haven: Yale University Press, 1980).
24.	Since Barrett's perspective dominates *The Second Coming* and some-
	times produces a patronizing attitude toward Allison, the naive
	young woman, it should be stressed that Barrett learns at least as

much from her, and has his life changed by her, as she learns from and is transformed by him. Something of what he experiences is explained by Carol Gilligan at the end of *In a Different Voice*, where in arguing 'the need to delineate *in women's own terms* the experience of their adult life', she says:

> My own work in that direction indicates that the inclusion of women's experience brings to developmental understanding a new perspective on relationships that changes the basic constructs of interpretation. The concept of identity expands to include the experience of interconnection. The moral domain is similarly enlarged by the inclusion of responsibility and care in relationships. And the underlying epistemology correspondingly shifts from the Greek ideal of knowledge as a correspondence between mind and form to the Biblical conception of knowing as a process of human relationship. (173)

Barrett indeed learns to live according to such interconnection, responsibility and care, and comes to *know* 'as a process of human relationship'. Whether or not Percy would recognize these traits as 'feminine', he has been able to portray them in action as transforming agents of Barrett's character. Carol Gilligan, *In a Different Voice: Psychological Theory and Women's Development* (Cambridge, Mass.: Harvard University Press, 1982).

4

John Updike's Sermons

In every act of genuine faith the body participates,
because genuine faith is a passionate act.

Disintegration of the Word has taken place.[1]

TEXTS OF SEX AND RELIGION

At one point in his youth John Updike is supposed to have thought
of studying theology and preparing for a career in the ministry.
Instead, he majored in English at Harvard as prelude to a vocation
as literary artist, yet his interest in theological and religious matters
has never flagged, as is evidenced by his attention paid to figures
such as Kierkegaard, Barth and Tillich in his reviews and essays
as well as in his fiction.[2] His narratives are frequently inhabited
by clergy and contain a large number of church services and other
fictionalized religious discourse. Many of his other, non-clerical
characters are more or less earnest believers and churchgoers, and
the religious sanctuary still plays a fairly prominent role in the
towns that constitute the settings of his narrations.

Since Updike himself has reported on his Barthian-style conversion that saved him from existential despair as a young man, one
is not really surprised at the frequency of religious moments in his
art. More remarkable is that this religious concern has apparently
caused or helped to cause him to play, repeatedly, with a non-
fictional genre in his fiction: the sermon. No fewer than nine
sermons and sermon fragments can be found in his narratives
published to date, not counting the long theological discourse in
his first novel *The Poorhouse Fair* (1958), the theological disputation
on the existence of God that permeates *Roger's Version* (1986), or
the scriptural passages and liturgies that mark a funeral in *Rabbit,
Run* (1960) and a wedding in *Rabbit Is Rich* (1981). A sermon

fragment is preached in *Rabbit, Run* and another in *Couples*. The short story 'Lifeguard' is composed as a complete sermon, one full sermon is delivered in *Of the Farm*, in *A Month of Sundays* the pastor-narrator writes four complete homilies, and *The Witches of Eastwick* contains one partial and one complete sermon.[3] Updike's fascination with preachers and preaching has thus spanned his artistic career.

This phenomenon is worth further attention for several reasons. First, it suggests that the sermon genre holds a special attraction for Updike and that one might do well, therefore, to examine the sermons in his fiction in order to learn if they are somehow paradigmatic of his art as a whole. The fact that they appear so regularly and at strategic points indicates that they are. Second, one discovers here more evidence of a trend in post-modern fiction identified by a number of critics; namely, that the boundary between fiction and non-fiction is blurring increasingly and especially that various types of non-fiction (for example, auto-biography, journalistic essay, scientific data, legal protocol, computer printouts) are being blended into narrative. The sermon represents another such use of non-fiction in recent narrative that deserves our notice. Third, our attention to Updike's borrowing of the sermon genre for his fiction prompts the recognition that other authors are employing the same strategy. American exam-ples are James Baldwin (*Go Tell It on the Mountain*), Frederick Buechner (*The Final Beast*), John Gardner (*The Sunlight Dialogues*), William H. Gass (*Omensetter's Luck*), A. J. Langguth (*Jesus Christs*), Walker Percy (*The Thanatos Syndrome*), William Styron (*The Confessions of Nat Turner*) and Peter De Vries (*The Mackerel Plaza*).

Yet the use of the sermon in recent *American* fiction, at least, represents not so much the introduction of an alien genre into narrative as the reappearance of it, for some of the best American fiction of the nineteenth and earlier twentieth centuries contains prominent sermons. One thinks of the Reverend Dimmesdale's dramatic confession before the crowd of townspeople at the end of Hawthorne's *The Scarlet Letter* (1850), of Father Mapple's famous address in Melville's *Moby-Dick* (1851), of Harriet Beecher Stowe's *Uncle Tom's Cabin* (1852) which is *all* homily, of the hero's hypocritical homilies in Sinclair Lewis' *Elmer Gantry* (1927), of the black preacher's passionate sermon on the recollection and the blood in the fourth section of Faulkner's *The Sound and the Fury* (1929). These and scores of other preachers expounding their way through lesser novels, especially in the nineteenth century, recall for us that the sermon was, after all, for generations the most prominent form of discourse – religious, cultural and even literary – in America, that a very strong tradition of the sermon and a great respect for it existed in American life that made it natural for the sermon to be borrowed by the literary artists as material for their writing.

This tradition died down, but not out, during the years of increasing secularization in our century. Certainly the sermon lost much of its attraction for the literary artist and the readers of fiction in the modern era, but it did not disappear altogether, and its mode of survival is illustrated in the two examples of important twentieth-century fiction sermons that I just mentioned. Either it was integrated into the narrative action in ways that would give the theme the special, positively intended impact of religious proclamation, as in *The Sound and the Fury*, or it was handled satirically, as a way of criticizing the quality of American religiosity, as in *Elmer Gantry*.

Updike's sermons continue these two tactics in a manner that seems to reveal his own ambivalence about religion in contemporary American life but that also reflects secularized Americans' uncertain and conflicting attitudes toward religion. An analysis of the sermon fragments in two of his best-known novels exemplifies such ambivalence and Updike's attempt, at the same time, to convey the complexity of the American religious mood. A sermon fragment is introduced at a critical point in the novel *Rabbit, Run*. Actually better described as a sermon summary (presented largely via the novelist's use of free indirect discourse), it is preached by the Episcopalian Reverend Eccles on a Sunday morning with Harry 'Rabbit' Angstrom, the novel's luckless protagonist, in attendance. It is brief enough to be quoted in full:

It concerns the forty days in the Wilderness and Christ's conversation with the Devil. Does this story have any relevance to *us*, here, now? In the Twentieth Century, in the United States of America. Yes. There exists a sense in which *all* Christians must have conversations with the Devil, must learn his ways, must hear his voice. The tradition behind this legend is very ancient, was passed from mouth to mouth among the early Christians. Its larger significance, its greater meaning, Eccles takes to be this: suffering, deprivation, barrenness, hardship, lack are all an indispensable part of the education, the initiation, as it were, of any of those who would follow Jesus Christ. (197)

The passage is a gentle parody of sermon rhetoric, imitating the stylized question-and-answer format learned in seminaries and the hermeneutical leap, the imaginative but rather artificial attempt to make the New Testament account 'relevant' to the current situation, and it may even be a mild parody of European Protestant crisis theology that became popular in the United States during and after the second world war. Yet it is in no sense satirical but serves rather as a serious reinforcement to plot and theme. Angstrom at this point in the novel has abandoned his girlfriend, a prostitute, and returned to his wife, who has recently given birth to a baby girl, and he comes to the church service out of a sense both of gratitude to God (vaguely felt) and of obligation to the priest, who has been instrumental in reconciling him to his wife.

But the sermon and its aftermath, instead of confirming Angstrom in his new start, ironically lead him astray. He rejects what he hears of the sermon, not bothering to listen attentively: 'Harry has no taste for the dark, tangled, visceral aspect of Christianity, the *going through* quality of it, the passage *into* death and suffering that redeems and inverts these things, like an umbrella blowing inside out. He lacks the mindful will to walk the straight line of a paradox' (197). After the service, then, Angstrom meets the pastor's young wife, who arouses him sexually, but when his own wife rejects his sexual advances back home (she is recovering from childbirth) he runs off again; she drinks herself into a stupor and accidentally drowns the baby. The irony, of course, is that the weak-willed protagonist who rejects the suffering aspect of Christianity, 'the passage into death', has to experience these things anyhow, and has to struggle through them with his impoverished and even childish religiosity because he won't, or can't, consider a matured view, embodied in the sermon, that tries to deal with suffering and death.

This is the background for the funeral and burial in *Rabbit, Run,* which is presented in a climactic moment in which Angstrom breaks down. It involves no sermon but rather formal services, the services for the dead baby at the funeral parlour and then at the cemetery, performed again by the Reverend Eccles and comprised only of biblical quotations and liturgical prayers. These affect Angstrom deeply but in a perverse way. The words of intended comfort, metaphors of shepherds and sheep, of little children and heaven, touch him sentimentally and then provoke bizarre behaviour. He publicly accuses his grieving wife, at the graveside, of killing the baby, then tries to comfort her, then runs away in confusion and panic in reaction to the shock of the mourners. This is essentially the way the novel ends, with everything unsolved and Angstrom running again, mindlessly, through the night, away from responsibility and from himself. These scriptural passages and the prayers at the funeral services also produce irony. They provoke a strange response from the protagonist that condemns him in the eyes of the others, and thus the religious word here, even though constituted only of recited scripture and prayer, has the effect that preaching, according to Christian theology, is supposed to have; it ought to lead to grace or judgement, and here it is judgement.

In this early Updike novel, then, the sermon has an operative role both in the construction of the narrative and in the lives of the people it deals with, and the author has integrated the sermon genre skilfully into his art and embodied world view. Eight years later in his novel *Couples* (1968) Updike offers a sermon fragment much less subtle in intention and impact and more reminiscent of the satiric strategy of Sinclair Lewis. The scene here, early in the 480-page text, takes place in the Congregational Church of Tarbox, Massachusetts, on a Palm Sunday. The pastor is the Reverend Horace Pedrick, 'a skeletal ignorant man of sixty' (25). Updike is merciless in his derision of the clergy type that Pedrick represents, the minister who adapts himself so easily and completely to what he imagines his congregation's milieu to be that he forfeits his true pastoral and prophetic duty. Pedrick perceives his parishioners as predominantly businessmen and unctuously struggles to 'transpose the desiccated forms of Christianity into financial terms' (26). His sermon, as a result, is an appalling example of hermeneutical clumsiness: 'The man Jesus does not ask us to play a long shot. He does not come to us and say, "Here is a stock for speculation. Buy at eight-and-one-eighth, and in the Promised Land you can sell at one hundred". No, he offers us *present security*, four-and-a-half per cent compounded every quarter!' (26). It is important for Updike to mock the ineffectiveness of the church in this fashion early in the novel, for one of the main efforts of the five middle-class married couples whom the narrative depicts is to create a kind of substitute church, out of the erotic fellowship they

obsessively nurture, to take the place of the inadequate real
church. The group engages in games and conversations that
displace the rituals and language of worship. It is a self-serving,
sometimes ingenuous and sometimes desperate endeavour that
eventually disintegrates, but its very existence is an expression of
the literal church's impotence, and when the edifice burns down
late in the novel one has no sense of loss but of deserved fate.

Updike does not often indulge in such transparent satire as he
composes through Reverend Pedrick's sermon fragment in
Couples, and his sermons in four other works reveal a much more
complex attitude and intention. The earliest of these is the short
story 'Lifeguard' from the *Pigeon Feathers* collection (1962), which
consists *in toto* of the first-person musing of a divinity student as
he performs his summer holiday job of lifeguard on a New
England beach and watches over a Sunday morning crowd there.
Although the monologue is an 'interior' one and not preached to
an actual listening congregation, it is definitely composed, for the
most part, according to the conventional sermon format, with an
introduction, a 'text', exposition, illustrations and final exhortation, all done in a formal and stilted style that recalls a pulpit
address rather than a casual meditation from a lifeguard's tower.
It is, however, also a confession and a parody – added forms that
complicate its design and its impact on the reader. The confession
focuses on the novice theologian's admission that he is as much
attracted to the flesh as to the spirit, a tendency exacerbated by
the sight of bare bodies before and beneath him, and that he not
only has trouble with attaining to a genuine religious belief but,
finally, that he is preparing for the Christian ministry without any
sense of calling. As a result, the sermon he preaches to himself is
a deeper parody than the stylistic imitation would produce; it is a
parody that thickens, in this fine character study, into a self-ironic
display of emptiness. It is a conventional parody of a serious
sermon, first, in its exaggerated analogues, comparisons between
physical and spiritual of the sort usually employed to illustrate the
spiritual, the realm of faith, but taken here to quasi-allegorical
extremes: the sunners and bathers are a church congregation, the
young man in his tower (which has, appropriately, a Red Cross
symbol on it) is the pastor in his pulpit, and the Sunday morning
hour suggests the time for worship.

Above all, the parallel that the divinity student sees between
himself as potential rescuer of drowning swimmers and as a saver

of souls seems absurd, because he does not possess a religious faith himself but exhibits instead a cocky theological sophistry and a precocious intellectual self-absorption that make him incapable of belief. Here the parody becomes irony. The immature narrator's immense self-confidence and pride cause him to criticize and condemn much of modern theology for its excesses and distortions in trying to accommodate modern scepticism, yet his own arguments are even more tortuous. His effort to establish his thesis, therefore, and his resultant exhortation ring false. His thesis, 'that the texts of the flesh complement those of the mind' (147), might well be defensible, were it not that he immediately turns it into an excuse for his sexual appetite – and even this could be tolerated, except that he tries so hard, and so offensively, to present his lust in a profound context. 'To desire a woman is to desire to save her' (149), he intones, misappropriating Augustinian thought, and further, 'Every seduction is a conversion' (150). Likewise, his final 'command' to his beachside congregation to enjoy their sensuality, because he is there self-sacrificially to protect them, is hollow, for it inspires no trust. He has overestimated his cleverness and exposed himself as thoroughly egotistic; hence his attempted manipulation of the theological word revenges itself. The final irony is that he is judged by his own words and appears in their light as a foolish and presumptuous figure.

The blend of sex and theology in 'Lifeguard' figures strongly in the narrative context of Updike's later fictional homilies. The protagonists who listen to the sermons and react to them in *Rabbit, Run, Of the Farm* and *Couples* are all adulterers yet are also all Christian believers of more or less conservative religious background, and all of them make vague connections between sex and religion. For Piet Hanema, the Dutch Calvinist-reared church worshipper in *Couples*, for example, 'prayer and masturbation' have 'long been mingled' (27), and the benediction at the end of the service leads him to think of his naked mistress. Similarly, Harry Angstrom in *Rabbit Redux* masturbates lying on his stomach because he is uneasy about God watching him from above. Such characterizations lead one to recall Updike's longstanding dual interest in Freudian psychology and neo-orthodox (Barthian) theology, what seems like a strange combination until one recognizes the relationship: both are a blend of lively imagination and sternly rational thought.

The naive associations between sex and religion that Updike's people nurture are explored further theologically and given sophistication in a Lutheran sermon preached within the narrative framework of Updike's fourth novel, *Of the Farm* (1965). The sermon is spoken by a young pastor to a sparse Sunday morning congregation in a Lutheran church in rural eastern Pennsylvania. In attendance are the protagonist Joey Robinson, visiting from Manhattan, and his mother, a widow living on a local farm. Joey has brought his second wife along to Pennsylvania to become better acquainted with his mother, who has disapproved of her son's divorce and remarriage, and against the background tension of the weekend visit the pastor's choice of a text is apt even if too neat a coincidence. He preaches on Genesis 2:18: '*And the Lord God said, It is not good that the man should be alone; I will make him an help meet for him*' (149–50). What follows is a serious, non-satirical, learned exposition of the story of Eve's creation from Adam's rib. The essence of the mildly sexist (male-biased) sermon is that woman as second in creation is slightly inferior to the man but also a more successfully realized created being ('Think of God as a workman who learns as he goes' – 152) who causes the male to contemplate his own imperfection especially as revealed in his awareness of death. Particularly, woman as created *from* man inspires him to consider the mystery of himself imaged in another but also – and the preacher invokes Karl Barth here – appeals to the man to respond to her in faith and compassion, for the very act of 'reaching out' to a woman implies an act of faith and thus demands kindness as well.

Unlike the facile argument of 'Lifeguard', the thought here is genuinely enlightening, whether or not one ultimately agrees with it, and one discovers that an authentic sermon even within the confines of fiction can have a kerygmatic quality: one feels addressed, in a fairly direct way that collapses in part the illusions of fiction. Updike is able here to fix a receptive mood in which the reader is led to respond to the message as well as to the fictive situation. In fact, one responds to the sermon, among other reasons, because it is appropriate to the narrator-protagonist's situation. Joey Robinson is pulled in many directions by the women in his life: by his ailing but strong-willed mother, with whom he suffers an Oedipal relationship; by his first wife, toward whom he feels guilty; and by his present wife, through whose earthy qualities he is learning to be himself. The three points in the pastor's sermon regarding women are illustrated in the three women who influence Joey's life. His mother recalls to him his flaws and mortality; his first wife, now in far-off Canada, inspires nostalgia for the old mystery of an innocent relationship; and his second wife, for whom he has cut off the past and made a new start, impels compassion and faith. Not surprisingly, Joey likes the sermon; it helps him to reorder his life.

The sermon in *Of the Farm* may well epitomize Updike's own attitude on the interaction of sex and religion to which he returns so often in his art. He has treated the subject discursively in a review of Denis de Rougemont's *Love in the Western World* and *Love Declared* that has many similarities to this sermon.[4] There, while condemning the Gnostic and Romantic misconceptions of women and *eros*, on which de Rougemont reports, Updike also acknowledges the value of the female mystery for male identity, for protection against the fear of death, and as the force that produces a compassion that must be grounded finally on an incarnational theology – one that takes into account the realities of the flesh. It is worthwhile knowing that this roughly constitutes Updike's opinion, for one recognizes then that much of his fiction has been an exploration of what goes wrong, sexually and religiously, between men and women in their search for something to live for and live by.

A MONTH OF SUNDAYS: PREACHING AS THERAPY

This is not to say that Updike is merely illustrating, in his novels and stories, an otherwise discursively articulated opinion. Rather, he continues to worry at the problems of sexuality and religious belief through his narratives, and in *A Month of Sundays* (1975) he confronts the themes again through the sermon format, this time interspersing the book at crucial points with four complete sermons. This is Updike's most substantial effort of fictional sermonizing and deserves expansive treatment. The situation of this narrative differs from the others in which Updike presents sermons (except 'Lifeguard') in that here the preacher himself is the protagonist and not some hearer in the audience. He is a preacher in considerable distress whose misfortune has also a ludicrous side: the Reverend Thomas Marshfield, pastor of a midwestern American Protestant (not further identified) congregation, whose adulterous affair with the church organist and liaisons with various other women in his spiritual care have been exposed. Instead of firing him his congregation has sent him, in November of 1973, for a month of enforced meditation and recuperation to a spa for 'fallen' clergy in the southwestern desert. There, instead of a hot and barren place befitting a repentant, he has a cooled and comfortable motel room in which he is supposed to compose a daily quota of confessional prose as his therapy. His outpourings are read by the large and inscrutable Ms Prynne, who manages the desert retreat and oversees the other daily activities of Marshfield and his culpable colleagues. But although Marshfield is co-operative in doing his writing, he remains sexually irrepressible and in fact uses his compositions late in his stay to try to seduce Ms Prynne, even though upon his arrival she struck him as unattractive. One could, in fact, construe Marshfield's prose, after he learns who his reader is, as a series of elaborate but dishonest 'love letters' designed to bring his keeper under his control. By the end of his visit he has succeeded. Ms Prynne makes love with him shortly before his return home, and one is left wondering what he has learned during his thirty-one days in the air-conditioned wilderness.

This is the setting for the four sermons which Marshfield writes faithfully, one on each of his four Sundays in exile. As he says, he is a preacher, and when Sunday comes he must preach, even though he is not permitted to have a Bible during this month of so-called cure. He preaches, successively, on Jesus' encounter with the woman caught in adultery, on the miracles of Jesus, on the subject of the desert and on the resurrection. Marshfield himself, writing on the twenty-eighth day of his desert sojourn, describes the first three of these sermons as containing 'neurotic and mocking fire' (213) in contrast to the fourth which, as Ms Prynne judges and Marshfield agrees, could actually be preached to a congregation. The first two of these sermons are very clever, erratic and occasionally hysterical, reflecting the emotional stress their composer labours under at the time, but the third is calmer and conciliatory, and the final one is indeed an address that might be well received by an intellectual liberal audience. The third and fourth are, in fact, addressed to Marshfield's fellow clergymen at the retreat, whereas the first two project, in Marshfield's imagination, his parishioners at home as his listeners. This shift of focus in itself suggests a healing progression. Marshfield after the second sermon abandons the imaginary bullying of his congregation –

which has sent him into the desert – and turns his attention constructively to his erring colleagues close at hand.

The first sermon, however, is in its obsessiveness and confused argument a good deal like 'Lifeguard'. Focusing on the passage describing Jesus' reaction to the woman whom the Pharisees surprised in an adulterous situation, Marshfield immediately presents his scholarly credentials, showing that he is acquainted with the current state of research on the text (and Updike's own exegetical perspicacity, not so incidentally, is also revealed here, just as he demonstrates his theological acumen later in *Roger's Version*), then goes on to emphasize and approve Jesus' unequivocal words against adultery and divorce; but then he becomes tangled in his rhetoric, and in an effort to propose a paradoxical truth and to demonstrate how the biblical word is a scandal, he comes round to praising adultery as a desirable modern condition. He argues that, in the homogenization of contemporary life, the sphere of adultery is a rare remaining place where men and women can meet in freedom and authenticity. In his exaggeration he turns absurdly lyrical: 'Verily, the sacrament of marriage, as instituted in its adamant impossibility by our Saviour, exists but as a precondition for the sacrament of adultery. . . . Why else, I ask you, did Jesus institute marriage as an eternal hell but to spawn, for each sublimely defiant couple, a galaxy of little paradises? . . . We *are* an adulterous generation; let us rejoice' (47). The sentiments here remind one of Updike's other investigations into the peculiar exhilarations of adultery (for example, in *Of the Farm*, *Couples* and *Marry Me*), but in none of those do his characters ever engage in such an astonishing celebration and theological endorsement of it. Marshfield at this point seems still unhinged by his own marital and extramarital problems and is trying to justify himself through elaborate sophistry.

In his second sermon, written during the next Sunday with the portentous date of the 13th, Marshfield appears even less in control. He rambles through a part-brilliant, part-perverse commentary on Jesus' miracles and concludes with a sudden curse upon his imagined audience. Although he takes as his text a phrase from the account of Jesus' miracle at the Cana wedding where he turns water into wine, Marshfield thereafter virtually ignores that scene and speaks on the miracles as a whole, declaring that the faith they were to inspire has disappeared and pronouncing a curse on the phantom congregation for its unbelief:

'may you depart from this place forever sterile; may your generation wither at the roots, and a better be fed by its rot' (107).
Another sequence late in this sermon indicates that Marshfield is
still in the depths of his personal dilemma and explains his rage.
Abruptly he says: 'Imagine a man married to goodness, and hating
goodness as darkness hates the light; yet he cannot budge that
marriage and his hate by a thumb's-width, and his spirit curses
God' (106). This, beyond the hyperbole, is Marshfield's situation
(his own wife is indeed a good woman), and his vengeful words
at the end are in some measure an expression of his frustration.
His prophetic stance here is presumptuous, of course ('I curse
you, then, as our Lord cursed the fig tree', he says – 107), and his
judgement on others is really a half-recognized condemnation of
himself.

But in the third sermon, 'delivered' on the twentieth day of the
month, sanity asserts itself. Marshfield finally allows the
symbolism of the desert to work on him. Taking an Old Testament
text on Jacob in the wilderness as his inspiration, he meditates on
the barrenness and waste that the desert connotes and on the
insidious spreading of the modern technological wasteland. But
he also effusively describes the rich plant and animal life of the
desert, often unseen and unappreciated, that witnesses to the
ability of organisms to flourish there and, as one would expect,
transforms these observations into a metaphor of encouragement
and renewal: the errant preachers, literally and spiritually stranded
in a dry place, can yet find a blessing in it and endure towards a
better time. After the initial self-justification that Marshfield
attempts, and then after the rage, in other words, comes the
adjustment to reality, and although it is not an expression of a
classical 'dark night of the soul' experience that is turned into faith
triumphant, it is at least a recovery of a fairly normal perspective,
a chastened perspective, that sets Marshfield on the way back to
competent functioning in the world.

Yet even the final sermon, composed four days before Marshfield returns home and evaluated by Ms Prynne as respectable
enough for an actual airing, would confuse and shock most real
congregations. Addressing again his fellow pastors at the retreat,
he preaches on a Pauline resurrection text, but not in a manner
that would comfort those wishing to believe in bodily resurrection
and immortality. He stresses the impossibility of such a physical
renewal from death, the difficulty of faith in the light of such

knowledge, and the resultant abiding mystery of existence as expressed by Pascal: *'Qui m'y a mis?* Who has set me here?' (211). Marshfield's response, which concludes the sermon, is this: 'To ask the question is to imply an answer: there is a *qui*, a *Who*, who has set; we have not accidentally fallen, we have been placed. As of course we already know in our marrow' (212). This is a fudging and unoriginal reply to an inquiry focusing at the start on the possibilities of resurrection and eternal life, but if it is the best that Marshfield can do, it is also, at least, an answer that does not promise too much, that avoids the excesses of his earlier efforts and shows that he is ready to return to the ambiguities of the world outside.

But following this display of competency Marshfield proceeds to cajole and bully Ms Prynne in his final days of therapeutic writing until she does, at last, bed down with him before he leaves. He is unfaithful on the day of his trip home to a wife and church. Has it all been a farce, and has he learned nothing? This is a possibility. Marshfield may be incorrigible and an example of bad faith in both the Christian and existential sense. More likely, though, is that Updike wants him to stand as an image of the great difficulties involved in living clearheadedly and clearsightedly in our era. Even without referring to the major sections of the novel I have ignored, the chapters that are not sermons, one recognizes this as post-modern narration: the four sermons display an attitude, beyond a pose of existential alienation, that is mainly confusion; technology is no longer viewed as potentially redemptive but as out of control; language itself is tricky, unmanageable, even demonic; intense self-consciousness frustrates attempts to know and love others. In the context of this mood Marshfield's struggles to accommodate the demands of *eros* and *theos*, if possible together, assume a desperate quality, so that his seduction of his keeper is a sorry but predictable last step of his therapy; in making love to the silent mentor of his religious convalescence he finds, momentarily, the missing erotic dimension of his faith. Why couldn't he find this dimension in his marriage? Because, it seems, his mate doesn't sufficiently represent the *other* in its mystery and excitement. One could argue that Updike's protagonist simply doesn't try hard enough to break through to the other who is behind the familiarity of the marriage partner, but this failing too illustrates a post-modernist trait: one lacks the time, patience and incentive to establish the deepest and most valuable relationships

– as Updike's fiction discloses, even if largely by negative and ironic example.

The non-homiletic passages of *A Month of Sundays*, especially those eventually addressed as 'love letters' to Ms Prynne, are such examples. They display strikingly those traits of the love letter I described in Chapter 2, yet largely without the balancing redemptive characteristics. Instead of tempering the sado-masochistic tendencies of love relationships, Marshfield's letters intensify them and reveal a hostility towards the would-be lover ('Then don't come, you bitch', he writes close to the end of his month). They are cunning and dissembling, further, in ways that disclose Marshfield's acute insecurity and his need to dominate women in order to bolster his precarious sense of self-worth. And instead of aiding him in learning to live valuably with absence, they are his vehicle for the frustrated drive towards gratification and closure – so that when these are granted by Ms Prynne's last-minute coupling with him, nothing is really satisfied or resolved. He has not discovered, in his convalescence, how to celebrate the body but remains prisoner of his appetites.

Updike's sermons are thus paradigmatic of his fiction as a whole, and these later ones especially convey the thrust of his recent narration generally. Their preachers, hearers and substance reflect the uncertainty, confusion and cynicism of a culture that has had to abandon the once-fashionable existentialist pose, with its belief in the freedom to make meaningful decisions, and simply confess that life has become too complicated to be managed. Updike's sermons certainly do not substitute for a dramatization of this condition in his fiction, which condition his protagonist Marshfield describes as an 'Inbetweentimes', a liminal era of lost belief between the old religiosity and a hoped-for future rebirth of faith, but the sermons do summarize, in concentrated form, the traits and effects of this faithless interlude. Especially the stress on sex and religion in the homilies, in terms of the desire to get body and spirit together, reflects the wish simultaneously to eroticize and spiritualize the arid technology that surrounds and pervades contemporary life.

THE WITCHES OF EASTWICK: DESIGNING EVIL

Robert W. Funk in *Jesus as Precursor* recalls the painter Peter Caldwell in Updike's *The Centaur* describing his lineage from his grandfather to himself as 'Priest, teacher, artist – the classic degeneration', and suggests that this declension might be supplemented by a fourth vocation: the sorcerer.[5] The stress on sex and religion and their relations with technology takes on a curious and perverse twist in *The Witches of Eastwick* (1984) that makes Funk's comment seem prophetic. Two sermons appear in the latter pages of this novel which, in a highly eroticized context, comment on the nature of evil in the age of technology. Because these are also, especially the second one, in an important way texts of pain as I treated them in Chapter 2, I will explicate them in detail.

The Witches of Eastwick depicts the lives of three women in a Rhode Island town of the late 1960s who practise witchcraft and who yield to the influence of the newcomer to Eastwick (the name reminds one of Updike's own town of Ipswich), the demonic Darryl Van Horne. In presenting the first of the sermons Updike (as at other places in the narrative) indulges his version of Latin-American magical realism, whereby highly improbable or literally impossible occurrences are described as plausible events. The sermon is given on a July Sunday morning by Brenda Parsley, who has assumed the pastor's duties of the Unitarian Church after her husband, the Reverend Ed Parsley, runs off to New Jersey with a local teenage girl (and eventually blows himself up while handling terrorists' explosives). Brenda's sermon begins as a reflection on the nature of evil but slides quickly into 'radical chic' Sixties rhetoric that in turn shifts to an attack on the three witches Sukie, Jane and Alexandra (none of whom are in the audience) and their malevolent spell on the community. Evil 'is not a word we like to use', she says at the start, seeking to rehabilitate the term: 'We prefer to say "unfortunate" or "lacking" or "misguided" or "disadvantaged".' Then a few sentences later comes the fashionable political criticism that changes into a condemnation of local behaviour:

As we have turned outward to the evil in the world at large, . . . turned our indignation outward toward evil wrought in Southeast Asia by fascist politicians and an oppressive capitalism seeking to secure and enlarge its markets for anti-ecological luxuries, while we have been so turned we have been guilty – yes guilty, for guilt attaches to *o*missions as well as *co*missions – guilty of overlooking evil brewing in these very homes of Eastwick, our tranquil, solid-appearing homes. Private discontent and personal frustration have brewed mischief out of superstitions which our ancestors pronounced heinous and which indeed . . . *are* heinous. (302–3)

But she is not able to finish her denunciation of the witches themselves; strange things intervene to prevent her. 'With their foul acts and unspeakable charms they have driven some men to deranged acts', Brenda announces at the height of her fervour, herself now an apt embodiment of righteous indignation. 'They have driven some men – I firmly believe this – have driven some men to their deaths.' Here she is sabotaged by what looks like sorcery. Insects – a bumblebee, moths, a butterfly – slip from her mouth, impede her speech, make her panic and break off her talk. ' "Pray!" Brenda shouted, seeing she had lost control of the occasion. Something was pouring over her lower lip, making her chin shine. "Pray!" she shouted in a hollow man's voice, as if she were a ventriloquist's dummy' (306).

This scene, although it startles the congregation and ends the service, is never given rational explanation, nor is it in fact referred to again in the remaining forty-odd pages of the novel. Yet its surreal nature leads one to recall the atmosphere of seventeenth- and early eighteenth-century New England, where witchcraft was widely believed in, as reported in, for example, Cotton Mather's *The Wonders of the Invisible World* (1693). It is ironic that Brenda – a modern, female, unordained Unitarian pastor – would be precisely the wrong person, according to the colonial Puritans, to preach a sermon on witchcraft, yet does so with a passion and force that seem to provoke a punishing reaction from the witches of Eastwick themselves. The sermon is thus doubly out of place: as one of a number of unsettling surreal intrusions into a realistic novel, and as the vehicle for an assault on an outmoded superstition by a singularly inappropriate speaker.

What is the effect of this inordinate stress on witchcraft in and through this sermon? It accomplishes three things and fails significantly at another. First, it reminds one of the obdurate mystery of evil. Witchcraft itself can be regarded as a failed attempt to explain and manipulate evil, in so far as it interprets evil as operative in supernatural creatures (the devil and his demons) who interact with humans loyal to them. That this is an inadequate understanding of evil was manifest to many even in those centuries when the witchcraft mania was strong. That sorcery is likewise patently implausible in the context of Updike's novel, yet both active and unexplained rationally there, 'decentres' it and returns one to dwell on a more primordial incomprehensibility of evil.

One is not converted to a belief in witchcraft through Updike's novel, that is to say. But one is led to realize that the twentieth century, in substituting other myths for the myth of witchcraft to deal with evil, has had little success in resolving its mystery.

Second, that Brenda is apparently defeated by the mischief of sorcery in her effort to expose witchcraft as evil recalls for us a prominent guise in which evil appears in our age: in the form of banality, as Hannah Arendt and others have taught us.[6] Brenda's utterance is turned comic; the insects in her mouth cause her to lisp and misspeak, and she is made ridiculous to her congregation. Most of the three witches' magical power in the novel is deployed in such mean and petty ways, in nasty tricks they play on each other, so that witchcraft in its representation of evil is trivialized – rendered banal. Yet behind these gestures of witchery are also lethal intentions – and perhaps successes. The witches join strength to get rid of Jenny, the young woman who outwits them all in the contest for Darryl Van Horne's affections and, to their dismay, marries him. Whether any cause and effect actually obtains between the witches' tangible curse on Jenny – a voodoo doll that they fashion and employ as focus of their incantations – and Jenny's slow death from cancer is left open. The fact is, though, that they *intend* evil, shaping a surrogate figure meant to harm and destroy out of the stuff of the everyday, just as they themselves, superficially ordinary women of the Rhode Island town, half-disguise an obsession with a secret power that makes them *extra*ordinary even as it feeds off their worst instincts.

Third, that the three witches are absent from Brenda's disastrous sermon performance and not directly responsible for it suggests that the power of mischief has spread beyond them to other women in the town, who exercise it at the service. Reminiscent of Hawthorne's familiar story 'Young Goodman Brown', in which the naive protagonist believes he has discovered most of his

Puritan fellow citizens infected by satanism, the sorcery in *The Witches of Eastwick* is also taken up by more and more practitioners. Yet it is not only that the power is thus dispersed 'laterally' but that it deepens into genuine evil – another way in which the banality of evil appears.

What is this 'genuine evil'? It emerges at last not as a universal force channelled through individuals but as the desire to harm others, and the ability to do so, that individuals themselves generate in order to indulge an exaggerated sense of self. It is as if one of the selves that constitute a personality comes to dominate the others, destructively and autodestructively, so that evil takes shape as an aberration of personality in a fundamental way. Such a view of evil differs from Reinhold Niebuhr's influential definition of it as generated by institutions, but I think it has a claim to be as valid. One recalls that one of the great Western myths of the origin of evil, featuring the fall of the angel Lucifer from heaven, stresses the obsession with the glorification of a *self* and the conjunctive will to power to achieve that self-aggrandizement, and in the deployment of this power – the organization of others to achieve the goals of a single will – can be seen a continuity from the genesis of evil in a self to its maturation in a collective.

Such insights disclose themselves, of course, not through an exegesis of the Unitarian sermon but through a reading of it in its communal context. One is able partially to demythologize the witchcraft that the sermon condemns and interpret it as a disguise for the greater and more basic mystery of evil (which mystery reveals itself, partially, in the evidence of the novel's *plot*): that evil is attached to the ordinary, needs the ordinary as its seedbed, and thrives on self-inflation that strives to transcend the ordinary. Perhaps a major aspect of evil's essence is that it renders a person incapable of transcending the ordinary in positive, healthful ways.

It is disappointing that *The Witches of Eastwick* depicts witchcraft simplistically instead of as a vehicle of such salutary transcendence, and it is surprising that Updike, so *au courant* on a multitude of contemporary issues, should perpetrate the old view of witches as purveyors of mischief, if not of outright malevolence. Although reports of modern witchcraft as a positive religious force had been in the news nearly a decade before the publication of *The Witches of Eastwick*, and although Updike displays at least minimal knowledge of good witchcraft in a book review of 1979, he has apparently not taken it seriously. Thus the potential for delineating the vitality and communal power in the goddess religions and in feminist witchcraft is lost on this novel. Indeed, at the end of a review of a 'woman's novel' (the sceptical quotation marks are Updike's own) he refers to 'the quality of femininity, static and wary, its final recourse the bleak dignity of solitude', yet it is just such ultimate loneliness that the vibrant solidarity of modern witchcraft denies.[7] After the small Eastwick coven breaks up, two of the witches are 'saved' by marriage and one (Sukie) disappears. In the plots of contemporary witchcraft, the three would more likely find fulfilment among a sisterhood whose magic consists of shaping a worship of the 'great goddess' centred in the self and grounded on nature.

In order to remain fair to Updike, however, I must return to what he does accomplish in *The Witches of Eastwick* rather than continuing commentary on what he might have done. If witchcraft is treated there as an allegory, of sorts, of evil via the depiction of the effects of spell-casting on Brenda as she preaches, in the lay sermon preached later by Van Horne evil is addressed discursively and straight-on. This is also a text of pain, love and even of worship that, as we shall see, deepens our discussion of such writing as presented in Chapter 2. Here Updike has the rambunctious inventor, a latter-day Roger Chillingworth now no longer as satanic as earlier in the novel, deliver from the Unitarian pulpit a grim lecture on evil in the natural universe that reminds one, on the one hand, of Robert Frost's bleak vision of nature (expressed in poems such as 'Design') and, on the other, of the science teacher George Caldwell's brilliant discourse on time in Updike's 1963 novel *The Centaur*. Van Horne's performance suggests the obverse of Bonhoeffer's 'religionless Christianity': a theologized secularism. Instead of using a Bible, Van Horne pages through a volume of *Webster's Collegiate Dictionary*, selects a few terms – centipede, tapeworm, tarantula – and takes these, along with scattered notes, as his inspiration for a rambling and profane meditation on the malevolence of nature as demonstrated by the dumb voraciousness of poisonous insects and parasites. Contrary to the classical theologians, he declares that the evidence of nature's design (an argument that has fascinated Updike throughout his career) indicates not a kind and loving creator but rather a cruel and malicious force at work. His talk is advertised on the church marquee, in fact, as 'THIS IS A TERRIBLE CREATION' (322).

The undertone of this grim secular sermon is that Van Horne's

new wife, the young Jenny (née Gabriel) is in the hospital dying
of cancer, and his stress on parasites eating away inside human
bodies is an only slightly displaced allusion to the cancer cells
destroying his mate, causing her to bleed to death. It is a sermon
provoked by his wife's literal suffering and even provided with
dignity, in spite of its coarseness, through his own anguish. It is
also, both in spite of and because of its defiance, a religious reading
of the book of nature, and one that interprets pain in a defiantly
different way than the Judeo-Christian tradition has done. Pain
according to Van Horne is neither divine punishment for sin nor
a crucible through which the sufferer can be refined towards holiness. It is the state and condition of the universe.

It is a view that is also markedly different from Heidegger's, for
whom pain is a condition of *Dasein*, yet one through which *Dasein*
comes to know itself and the world. Pain interprets death
according to Heidegger; it is a *Vorahnung*, a premonition of death
and reminds us as participants in *Dasein* that we live toward death
and can choose to make our lives valuable against the awareness
of impending death. That this is the way things are, that existence
is permeated and circumscribed by pain and death is neither good
nor bad for Heidegger: it is, simply, the way things are – a view he
learns via 'poetic thinking', by discovering the poetry of Romantic
writers such as Hölderlin and Trakl (surely a late Romantic even
as a twentieth-century writer), whose very language, with its colli-
sion of images and doomed struggle towards complete expression,
incorporates the ubiquity of pain and death.[8]

This attitude, as well as the Judeo-Christian one, Van Horne
cannot abide. He is portrayed as a Luciferian figure, and his
defiance and vision of a hellish universe are appropriate to a
rebellious Satan who sees the 'evil' of his disobedience for which
he has been condemned as actually the possibility for a better
world than the one that humans inhabit – and as an inventor he
tries to better the human lot. As Van Horne says at the end of
his talk, having just sarcastically depicted parasites, in disgusting
graphic detail, as examples of 'noble' deific design: 'Couldn't you
have done better, given the resources? I sure as hell could have.
So vote for me next time. OK? Amen' (328). His question is fundamentally the perplexing one of theodicy: of why an omnipotent
creator did not make a world free of suffering, and his response
is that the creator who chose not to must himself be evil. Such an

answer identifies pain and suffering as inherently evil: evil is that which is painful and causes suffering.

Van Horne's assumption here, although he is in the midst of an assault on Christian thought, is actually reinforced by Christian mythology, in which hell is imagined as a place of eternal pain and suffering as punishment for those who have lived evil lives, and thus a close connection between pain and evil is established. The difference – to state it again – is that Van Horne wishes to identify pain as evil itself, as evidence of an evil creator, whereas in the Christian tradition pain is an instrument with which God chastises and Satan sometimes (with God's tolerance) advertises and indulges his evil power. Van Horne's view is a foreshortening of the Christian one and attempts to read pain 'religiously' in a secular world. The extension of his argument would run, 'if there were a creator, he would have to be evil, for he has permitted pain. Hence it is better to believe in no creator at all than in a malevolent one, and to accept the fact of a cruel, unthinking universe.'

This argument has at least two fallacies. First, the existence of pain and suffering does not posit the impossibility of a good creator. If the theological/philosophical argument from design to demonstrate a benevolent creator is not tenable (and it is not taken seriously by many nowadays), neither is its negative counterpart. Second, although the universe may be designated as unthinking, it is not cruel. It is only what humans by extension, attributing affect and motivation to nature, consider to be cruel. Van Horne, although a modern non-believer, still wants to divert the blame for human suffering from humankind and shift it to an ill-defined and probably non-existent supreme being, or to a universe that has assumed the cruel properties of such a being. Yet the community of Eastwick is at fault for much of its suffering; the lusts, insecurities and selfish acts of its citizens have intensified the pain already simply present in the world. Van Horne himself, although cast as a Satan figure, is not a purveyor and channel of evil from some supernatural force. He is rather a catalyst for excessive behaviour, a Lord of Misrule, a patron of carnival who provides the context for indulgence in which others, especially the three witches, choose to exercise their worst instincts. Thus evil here is ultimately not addressed as a theological/philosophical issue (in spite of Van Horne's secular sermon) but is portrayed as arising from a refusal of individuals to form an authentic community which would be characterized by compassion and commitment and by the desire to relieve pain rather than inflict it. What Eastwick has not learned is that the challenge of pain for the secular world is not to identify its origins speculatively but to learn to channel it toward humaneness and hope rather than toward mere self-preservation and nihilism. Evil, whatever else it may be, is failure to take on this responsibility.

Van Horne's coarsely eloquent address is curiously like Ernest Becker's grim vision at the start of his profound, posthumously published *Escape from Evil*:

> At its most elemental level the human organism, like crawling life, has a mouth, digestive tract, and anus, a skin to keep it intact, and appendages with which to acquire food. Existence, for all organismic life, is a constant struggle to feed – a struggle to incorporate whatever other organisms they can fit into their mouths and press down their gullets without choking. Seen in these stark terms, life on this planet is a gory spectacle, a science-fiction nightmare in which digestive tracts fitted with teeth at one end are tearing away at whatever flesh they can reach, and at the other end are piling up the fuming waste excrement as they move along in search of more flesh.[9]

Becker understands human evil as a *panicked* response to this necessary death-ridden condition of existence and hopes that in learning to recognize the worst about itself, that we incessantly destroy in order to transcend our fear of death, humanity can yet temper its irrationality, at least enough to avoid total destruction.

Its seems to me that the response of Heidegger (whose own life and career were marked and marred by his struggle to come to terms with the monstrous evil of the Nazi era) is at least more bearable and potentially more effective than Becker's. If we can expand his practice of reading the poets in their own terms, adapting philosophy to their language and image (anticipating the post-structuralist dethroning of philosophy as privileged discourse) rather than translating the poetry into analytical discourse, we arrive once more at the possibility of creating recuperative fictions. The writing and reading of these, and the conversations on them, can provide alternatives to the belief in the inevitability of the dominance of evil and to an acceptance of the practice of evil, by imagining the worst and the best: by facing the horror of existence and playing through it, learning how to envision the richness of being while tempering its nihilating power.

The gospel narratives culminating in the crucifixion of Jesus provide a foundational recuperative fiction in Western culture. The stark horror of the crucifixion remains an image that grasps the imagination and impels us to recall the condition of life as suffering towards death, yet the radically compassionate behaviour of Jesus practised against the sense of his ending is a model for the community's choice of healing and wholeness.

Updike's narratives, and those of other writers discussed in these chapters, are also, at least when well-constructed, such fictions of recuperation. They probe the painful points of their characters' lives not as a prelude to presenting resolutions but for the opposite reason: to portray humanity always held in the tension of suffering and health, yet to encourage the imagination's play of *Gelassenheit* with this elemental condition as a strategy for making meaning and wholeness on the way to death.

FICTIONS OF KERYGMA

What is one to make, finally, of Updike's sermons? That they appear so often and so strategically placed in his narratives suggests that he regards them as somehow privileged texts that carry a special significance. On the other hand, that most of them are preached by persons ill-established to serve as moral or spiritual leaders suggests that these discourses are anything but Updike's attempt to offer his own homilies transparently disguised as fiction. What hermeneutical role, then, do they fill? We can observe first that they are preached, for the most part, by remarkably 'unreliable narrators'.[10] The fumbling Reverend Eccles, the lustful theology student of 'Lifeguard', the shallow Reverend Pedrick of *Couples*, the duplicitous and wayward Tom Marshfield, the earnest but barely competent Brenda Parsley and the demonic Darryl Van Horne are hardly types to whom one would wish to entrust one's moral and religious education. Yet they occupy (very tenuously, in the case of the lifeguard and of Van Horne) the vocation in which persons function as super-reliable narrators, traditionally speaking not only the truth but the truth of God. 'Ordinary' unreliable narrators in texts of fiction cause the reader to doubt the veracity of the teller's account and lead her to search for meanings of the story other than those that the literal (but flawed) narration prompts. The presence of the unreliable narrator in modern and post-modern fiction has greatly complicated the hermeneutical task but also made it vastly more challenging and offered the reader a much greater interpretive responsibility.

The presence of unreliable narrators, such as Updike's clergy, who ought to be especially reliable gives another turn of the screw. The use of such narrators confirms that literary artists do not hesitate to involve religious discourse, with its at least residual persuasive powers, in the service of fiction to deepen its quality of undecidability and lead the reader still further into the realm of what Hillis Miller calls the Nietzschean concept of repetition, whereby the novel does not represent reality mainly via similarity, by offering 'Platonic' reflections of it, but more by simulacra of that reality that stress difference and cause the reader to construct his own fiction of that reality rather than merely absorb an imitation of it.[11] Updike's preachers as unreliable narrators do, of course, evince a similarity to real clergy: none of us needs to be told how religious huckstering by the so-called evangelists, especially those who use the electronic media, has brought on widespread mistrust of the ministerial profession. But the effect of the unreliable preacher-narrators is more to make religious discourse, in the context of fiction, a modality of unbelief, or at least scepticism, a testimony to the *Abgrund* of interpretation: the gap that opens up between text and referent, text and reader, through the realization that language, the text, the image, always necessarily falsify what they cause us to recognize and constrain us to 'correct' that recognition through our own inventions. Updike's sermons thus have a privileged place in his writing as especially vivid signals of suspicion, warning the reader that these representations of belief are in fact misrepresentations and that they stand for the unreliability of all discourse, which unreliability sets the conditions for interpretation.

The term *suspicion* leads us to another way of understanding the role of Updike's sermons: via Paul Ricoeur's hermeneutics of suspicion and affirmation. Ricoeur treats the phenomenon of unreliability in terms of 'false consciousness' (employing the Marxian term as important to the thought of Nietzsche and Freud as well – the other two in his triumvirate of 'masters of suspicion'), arguing that our post-Cartesian capacity for doubting consciousness itself has led us to suspect our ability to interpret whatever we take to be the objects of our scrutiny.[12] As Freud, for example, has shown us, we may think we are interpreting logically a particular text, problem, situation, when we are actually responding to an unrecognized reactivation of an infantile trauma. Or as Hillis Miller puts it, borrowing from Gerard Manley Hopkins, the underthought gets in the way of the overthought.[13]

Hermeneutics for Ricoeur is a kind of interpretation particularly well suited to deal with the significantly hidden:

> What distinguishes false-consciousness from error or falsehood and what motivates a particular type of critique, of denunciation, is the possibility of signifying another than what one believes was signified, that is, the possibility of the masked consciousness. . . . Consciousness, far from being transparent to itself, is at the same time what reveals and what conceals; it is this relation of conceal/reveal which calls for a specific reading, a *hermeneutics*. The task of hermeneutics . . . has always been to read a text and to distinguish the true sense from the apparent sense, to search for the sense under the sense, to search for the intelligible text under the unintelligible text.[14]

Such demystifying of the Cartesian consciousness, Ricoeur says, is matched by the demythologizing of religion (he means Western Christianity) by theologians such as Bultmann, who have identified the false consciousness of Christianity as mistaking the old mythological world view (in which Christianity arose) as the obstacle to modern belief, whereas the real problem remains 'the folly and the scandal of the Cross and the Resurrection': the incredibility, to the 'natural' mind, of the Christian kerygma.[15] To confront this incredibility at the authentic point is to discover what the kerygma can mean to contemporary humanity apart from the 'stumbling block' of the scientific world view: 'we know now that in deciphering the cultural vehicle of the text, we have to discover what is more than text, what is the preaching of the Person and of the event of Christ.'[16] And further:

> to preach is not to capitulate before the believable and the unbelievable of modern man, but to struggle with the presuppositions of his culture, in order *to restore this interval of interrogation* in which the question can have meaning. If we consider the

problem of secularization no longer only as the end of myth-ology and the religious era, . . . but as an estrangement from the kerygmatic situation itself, then the whole problem of myth will from this point of view become immediately changed.[17]

Hermeneutics, then, having effected this critique of culture via its strategy of suspicion, works to re-establish the possibility of belief through engaging the language of imagination that transforms suspicion into affirmation. 'It is at this ultimate level that I confront the three princes of necessity: man, they say, must come to love necessity – to love fate – to love things as they are and accept the fact that his life disappears, that reality continues, anonymous and silent. Such is the atheistic *affirmation* of my culture.'[18] Ricoeur is not, of course, content to leave it at this but discovers

the moment in the other hermeneutics when I encounter the problem of what I will call the grace of imagination, the surging up of the possible: how is man a possible, not a necessary reality?
. . . As I understand it, man is always sustained by his mythicopoetic core: he is always created and recreated by a generative word.
I believe that the fundamental theme of Revelation is this awakening and this call, into the heart of existence, of the imagination of the possible. The possibilities are opened before man which fundamentally constitute what is revealed. The revealed as such is an opening to existence, a possibility of existence. Consequently, the circle of the atheistic hermeneutics recloses on the necessary, but the circle of the kerygmatic hermeneutics opens on the generation of possibility in the heart of imagination of our language.[19]

The genre that Ricoeur draws on here to illustrate the power of the hermeneutics of affirmation is the New Testament parable, which is both preaching and narrative fiction (although he – mistakenly, to my mind – refers to them as 'short dramas'), and he writes at the end of this particular essay, 'If we look at the Parables as a word addressed first to our imagination rather than to our will, we shall not be tempted to reduce them to mere didactic devices, to moralizing allegories. We will let their poetic power display itself within us.'[20]

The composers of the New Testament gospels presenting Jesus as the preacher of kerygma have little in common with Updike creating *his* preachers, but provocative points of comparison nevertheless obtain. One could ask, for example, if Jesus is not, however inadvertently and in fact against all intention, described in the gospels as a version of the unreliable narrator, and whether this unreliability does not substantially complicate the interpretation of the kerygma. That question, however, addresses a text different from those under discussion here – Updike's sermons – so we should ask instead if and how a hermeneutics of suspicion and affirmation can reveal something in Updike's fictional homilies beyond what I have called the unreliability of all discourse. If the sermons are (like the New Testament parables) a fictional religious discourse that is also 'a word addressed first to our imagination rather than to our will', they do not yet overcome the obstacles to belief. But they *can* suggest what it might be *like* to believe. Such a leap of the imagination is not the prelude to a leap of faith, but it can constitute the conditions for Ricoeur's familiar concept of the 'second naivete': that result of imaginative hermeneutics through which one can experience something of the lost innocence of faith. But Updike's sermons, precisely by engaging the reader in unreliability, also point beyond fiduciary nostalgia and toward a redefinition of faith that pays attention to our 'estrangement from the kerygmatic situation itself'. It is, significantly, in the postmodern temper with its ironic recapitulation of modern – that is, realistic – forms that we experience both the second naivete and the estrangement from the kerygmatic situation. That estrangement consists in part, at least, in a reflex that has caused realism to flourish: a refusal to remain open to mystery, to infinite possibility. Such openness is 'unproductive', illusory, and leads to chaos, we object as we accelerate into a world out of control.

Yet the deconstruction of realism that also marks our era provides an occasion to revalorize mystery. Ricoeur suggests that this can happen via the poetic word. I believe that it can happen particularly through narrative fictions, those of the sort that, like some of Updike's sermons, dramatize a prophetic mode that can cause a community to rethink its identity – to consider whether it is, in fact, a community. Lyotard's claim in *The Postmodern Condition* that narratives have lost their power is true only in reference to the narratives of realism (and is only partially true there) and is belied otherwise by the fact that his discourse in that very book can be effectively and easily recast in narrative form.[21] I believe that in the necessary continuities of narrative itself – its metonymic, contiguous dimension – can be found a model (in this case a simulacrum) of wholeness and integrity in the very midst of fragmentation and dislocation. To put it most simply: it is very hard, if not impossible, for us not to tell stories, and even if these stories plot our lives of disorientation, their very telling is at least an impulse toward reaching an *other* and occasionally even a gesture of community. Fiction such as Updike's, in which the sermon, as model of *in*authenticity in its various guises, still manages to tease us *through* a nostalgia for a naïve faith and into imagining what a post-faith faith might be like, can bring us within hearing range of kerygma. Or we could say that the fictional sermon, by so strikingly portraying the absence of kerygma through the medium that once conveyed it, provokes us into imagining its presence. If, as Herbert Schneidau says, 'kerygma is literature's secret life, its closet fantasy', then the fictional sermon may offer a way of coming out.[22]

The immensity of what has been lost through the decline of communities where telling God's story was the dominant sacramental and civic act, but also the inevitability of that loss, are conveyed by Harry S. Stout's remarkable book *The New England Soul*.[23] Stout describes how the seventeenth- and early eighteenth-century preacher and his sermons were the absolute centre of Puritan colonial society, which, in the absence of competing media such as newspapers or magazines, received its civic as well as its spiritual and cultural instruction from the homily preached twice on Sundays, sometimes during the week, and at all public events such as holidays and elections. The preachers were accepted as the channel of God's revealed word to these outposts of the elect, and took altogether seriously their duty as translators of the theocratic message. Indeed the preacher, often the town's only intellectual and well trained as Bible interpreter, nevertheless sought to efface himself in the pulpit, refrained from injecting his personality into the sermon and strove instead to be a pure conduit – while the congregations assumed the critic's role and scrutinized the sermons to be sure that they did not stray from orthodoxy.

Inhabitants of the late twentieth century would find such a society intolerably repressive, of course, and in our judgement of its restrictions we overlook its positive traits: that it promoted unity, identity, a sense of order and direction. We tend to overlook also how the sermon in this society was a form of transition from the storytelling, oral-aural orientation to the discursive, chirographic cultures in which narrative fiction absorbs the storytelling impulse. The Puritan sermon, both narrating and interpreting a compelling and dominating version of the Judeo-Christian story, would soon give way in form and substance to the more imaginative and individualizing preaching of the evangelists speaking *outside* of the church (Stout marks the Great Awakening of 1740–3 as the first major challenge to the Puritan pulpit culture). These itinerant sermonizers, often speaking extemporaneously and encouraging personal interpretation of scripture, were just as much the harbingers of bourgeois realism as were their countrymen (some of them clergy) and -women back in Britain writing the first examples of the modern English-language novel. But whereas these novels subverted authority by offering social criticism in the 'harmless' form of fiction, the evangelists did so by inviting their hearers to accept only the authority of the Bible, which meant a reliance on individual interpretations – a situation that would result in conflicting 'authorities' and the rise of denominational pluralism that characterizes American Protestant life.

Thus it is not surprising that the subversions practised by the novel and by the post-Puritan homily should find a convergence of sorts in the fictionalized sermons that have been, if not popular, at least surprisingly hardy in the unfavourable climate of twentieth-century literature. Nor is it surprising, then, seen in the context of this convergence, that the fictional sermon is used by a subtle writer like Updike to undermine the novel of realism itself, to cast doubt upon the conventions of realism and thereby upon its authority, in order to leave us more open to the possibilities of mystery that individual readers as well as reading communities can explore.[24]

Notes

1. The first quotation is from Paul Tillich, *Dynamics of Faith* (New York: Harper & Row, 1957) p. 106. The second quotation is from Martin Buber, *I and Thou*, 2nd edn, tr. Ronald Gregor Smith (New York: Charles Scribner's Sons, 1958) p. 119.
2. Representative reviews and essays can be found in Updike's *Assorted Prose* (New York: Alfred A. Knopf, 1965), *Picked-Up Pieces*

(New York: Alfred A. Knopf, 1975), and *Hugging the Shore* (New York: Alfred A. Knopf, 1983).

3. *The Poorhouse Fair* (1958); *Rabbit, Run* (1960); 'Lifeguard' in *Pigeon Feathers* (1962); *Of the Farm* (1965); *Couples* (1968); *A Month of Sundays* (1975); *Rabbit Is Rich* (1981); *The Witches of Eastwick* (1984); *Roger's Version* (1986). All of these texts were first published by Alfred A. Knopf, Inc. in New York. Although the protagonist of *Roger's Version* is a divinity school professor who was once a parish minister, and although the novel is full of theological discourse, no actual sermons appear in it, and hence I have not included a discussion of it. Page numbers of the texts from which quotations are taken are given in parentheses following the citation.

4. This review, entitled 'More Love in the Western World', appears in *Assorted Prose* pp. 283–300.

5. Robert W. Funk, *Jesus as Precursor* (Philadelphia and Missoula, Montana: Fortress Press and Scholars Press, 1975) pp. 34, 44.

6. Hannah Arendt, *Eichmann in Jerusalem: A Report on the Banality of Evil* (New York: Viking Press, 1963).

7. The book review in which Updike shows some knowledge of modern witchcraft as a positive force is of a reissue of *Lolly Willowes*, the first novel of Sylvia Townsend Warner, originally published in 1926. The review is collected in Updike's *Hugging the Shore*, pp. 303–7. Updike's review of the 'woman's novel' is actually of two novels: *Eva's Man* by Gayl Jones and *Miss Herbert* by Christina Stead. The review is in *Hugging the Shore*, pp. 532–8. Sympathetic accounts of feminist witchcraft and goddess religions are found in Naomi R. Goldenberg, *Changing the Gods: Feminism and the End of Traditional Religions* (Boston: Beacon Press, 1979); Starhawk (Miriam Simos), *The Spiral Dance: A Rebirth of the Ancient Religion of the Great Goddess* (San Francisco: Harper & Row, 1979); and Carol P. Christ and Judith Plaskow (eds), *Womanspirit Rising: A Feminist Reader in Religion* (San Francisco: Harper & Row, 1979).

8. Cf. Martin Heidegger, 'Language in the Poem: A Discussion on Georg Trakl's Work', in his *On the Way to Language*, tr. Peter D. Hertz (New York: Harper & Row, 1971).

9. Ernest Becker, *Escape from Evil* (New York: The Free Press, 1975) p. 1.

10. Shlomith Rimmon-Kenan gives a concise definition of the unreliable narrator in *Narrative Fiction: Contemporary Poetics* (London: Methuen, 1983) pp. 100–3.

11. J. Hillis Miller, *Fiction and Repetition: Seven English Novels* (Cambridge, Mass.: Harvard University Press, 1982) pp. 15–16.

12. Paul Ricoeur, 'The Critique of Religion', tr. R. Bradley DeFord, in Charles E. Reagan and David Stewart (eds), *The Philosophy of Paul Ricoeur* (Boston: Beacon Press, 1978).

13. Miller, *Fiction and Repetition*, p. 16.

14. Ricoeur, 'The Critique of Religion', p. 215.

15. Ibid., p. 221.

16. Ibid.

17. Ricoeur, 'The Language of Faith', tr. R. Bradley DeFord, in Reagan and Stewart (eds), *The Philosophy of Paul Ricoeur*, p. 227.
18. Ibid., p. 237.
19. Ibid.
20. Ricoeur, 'Listening to the Parables of Jesus', in Reagan and Stewart (eds), *The Philosophy of Paul Ricoeur*, p. 244.
21. Jean-François Lyotard, *The Postmodern Condition: A Report on Knowledge*, trs Geoff Bennington and Brian Massumi (Minneapolis: University of Minnesota Press, 1984), especially pp. 37ff. Cf. also my article, 'Squabbles of Science and Narrative: Lyotard's *The Postmodern Condition*', *Art Papers*, vol. 10/1 (January–February, 1986) pp. 18–20.
22. Herbert N. Schneidau, *Sacred Discontent: The Bible and Western Tradition* (Baton Rouge: Louisiana State University Press, 1976) p. 303.
23. Harry S. Stout, *The New England Soul* (New York and Oxford: Oxford University Press, 1986).
24. This undermining of realism could also be understood in terms of Bakhtin's concept of dialogism. Dialogic novels according to Bakhtin play off differing kinds of discourse against each other and, unlike realistic narratives, not only resist their reconciliation but celebrate the impossibility of resolution. The sermons in *A Month of Sundays* and *The Witches of Eastwick* are kinds of discourse that make these dialogic novels. Cf. Mikhail Bakhtin, *Problems of Dostoevsky's Poetics*, tr. Caryl Emerson (Minneapolis: University of Minnesota Press, 1984), and Katarina Clark and Michael Holquist, *Mikhail Bakhtin* (Cambridge, Mass.: Harvard University Press, 1984).

5

Sacred Texts/Sacred Space

Jesus bent down and wrote with his finger on the ground.

. . . [I]f we are able imaginatively to grasp the symbolic trajectory that leads from tattoos and ritual mutilations to the constitution of erogenous zones in modern men and women, we would have gone a long way toward sensing the historicity of the sexual phenomenon.[1]

NATURE'S BOOK ON BODIES

In a short story entitled 'The God's Script', the Argentine writer Jorge Luis Borges has Tzinacán, an Aztec priest, tell the tale of his incarceration.[2] The priest, who has conducted ceremonies of human sacrifice, has been captured by Spanish conquistadores, tortured and condemned to life-long imprisonment in a hemispheric dungeon. The dungeon is divided in half down the middle, and the other half, across from the priest, is inhabited by a jaguar. Once a day a keeper opens a trap door at the top of the dungeon to let down food and water, and during those few seconds of light the priest can see the jaguar through a barred opening between the two cells. Tzinacán, after languishing many years underground, remembers that somewhere in the world is written a secret magical message of God, and then later recalls that the jaguar is 'one of the attributes of God' (170). He spends many more years studying the patterns of the animal's spots and at last, in an ecstatic, revelatory moment, discovers the divine message there. It is a fourteen-word formula that, were he to utter it, would make him all-powerful. But Tzinacán does nothing. The experience has transformed him so that he no longer has interest in mundane things, and the story concludes with him lying in his dark cell, looking forward to nothing but death.

It was this remarkable tale that first provoked my reflection on the relationship between sacred texts and sacred space, on how in the process of making and finding meaning we discover texts in unexpected places, valorize and even sacralize certain texts and their locales because of a creative interaction they establish. This reflection reminded me of other stories in which texts appear on unusual surfaces, and these suggested that concepts such as 'the scene of writing' and 'metatext' have significance at once more literal and more figural (there is a pun here that will soon become clear) than has been assigned to them by the structuralist and post-structuralist critics. Since most of the novels and stories containing or comprising these texts call attention, at some crucial point, to their own artifice – in essence deconstruct themselves – I will follow the strategies by which they do this and, in the process, provoke an awareness of the sacred. I will be concerned to show how a sense of the sacred emerges from the interplay of two 'impasses': from the frustration of these texts' efforts to be subsumed in the full embodiment they strive toward, and from the inability of the corporeal addressed by these texts to come fully to word, to express itself adequately in language. The narratives, in other words, describe charged texts that are too much for their context, and a charged corporeality too forceful to be fully articulated in language. In this dual, joined surplus is a mystery that elicits the sacred.

I will be guided in this chapter by four kinds of fictions of strange inscribing. The first kind describes texts in nature, those unwritten by humans that are yet 'read' by us as keys to the secrets of the universe. These are above all texts of mystery. The second kind, to which I will give most attention, depicts texts inscribed on the body, those that attempt a radical incorporation, incarnation, absorption of word and image – or that seek to block or bypass the internalization process by employing the body itself as text. These are predominantly texts of pain. The third kind projects texts written or sketched at locations that become holy because the inscriptions are already sacred, or where the inscriptions gain numinosity because the space they inhabit has been sacralized. This interdependency of inscription and space casts light on certain problems of the 'linguistic universe', for example on the relation of signifier to signified. Such texts involve pain, love and mystery. The fourth kind concerns inscriptions that seek to sacralize and also transform space by textualizing it. The opposite of the first kind that depicts the book in nature and nature as book, this kind portrays human inscription that wishes literally to substitute itself for the world and thus efface it. These are texts of technology that are, nonetheless, texts of recuperation.

'The God's Script' seems, for all its characteristic Borgesian novelty of plot, at first merely a version of the familiar metaphor of reading nature. No text has been composed here as such; there is not even any writing or even, at first, any scene of writing. The priest first discovers the presence of a hidden message, then takes on the role of its decoder. He is intent on discovering a pattern in nature and then interpreting it in a way that will give him insight into the divine mind: 'I considered that we were now, as always, at the end of time and that my destiny as the last priest of the god would give me access to the privilege of intuiting the script' (170). There is no question in Tzinacán's mind that there *is* a message – he is confident of that – and although he does not know what form it will take, he assumes it will be a written text: 'perhaps I had seen the script of Qaholom [the god] a thousand times and needed only to fathom it' (170). For Borges these two assumptions betray a constellation of biases underlying Western hermeneutics: that ultimate meaning exists, that it is accessible to individuals if they only know where and how to look, that it will probably come in the shape of a text, and that it can be employed to fill out one's days and defend against the anxiety caused by the knowledge of impending death. All of these can be subsumed under the image of nature's book. God is its enigmatic, immensely difficult author who writes on nature; humankind must become the infinitely patient, ingenious reader absolutely committed to the calling of intepretation in order to meet the conditions for a life- and world-transforming revelation that might eventually occur.

Why should the image be of a book? Why should nature in Western culture be so ruthlessly texted? The Aztec priest provides an answer. Reflecting on 'the generic enigma of a sentence written by a god' (171), he says:

What type of sentence (I asked myself) will an absolute mind construct? I considered that even in the human languages there is no proposition that does not imply the entire universe. . . . I considered that in the language of a god every word would enunciate that infinite concatenation of facts, and not in an implicit but in an explicit manner, and not progressively but instantaneously. In time, the notion of a divine sentence seemed puerile or blasphemous. A god, I reflected, ought to utter only a single word and in that word absolute fullness. (171)

Comprehending nature, the world, as text is part of a tactic of radical reduction that seeks to subjugate the world and, finally, to approximate divinity. The image of the world as text, nature as book, belongs to our vocabulary of ontological imperialism.

Tzinacán is, of course, an unreliable narrator, and he is so because he is mad. His years of dark incarceration have driven him relentlessly inward, and his imagination inspires him to invent the memory of the mysterious god's script, the magical sentence that is the distillation of all knowledge into a fourteen-word formula. Yet the attitude and method that guide him in his madness correspond to those of the sciences. He becomes a thoroughgoing observer and categorizer.

I devoted long years to learning the order and the configuration of the spots. Each period of darkness conceded an instant of light, and I was able thus to fix in my mind the black forms running through the yellow fur. Some of them included points, others formed cross lines on the inner side of the legs; others, ring-shaped, were repeated. Perhaps they were a single sound or a single word. Many of them had red edges. (171)

This effort of painstaking scrutiny of the object under investigation is matched by the desire for the flash of insight that will cause disparate units of information to join into a meaningful whole, and the priest's attempt to read the jaguar's spots emerges as an image of the scientist's task, for he too, via a combination of patient, systematic observation and creative conjecture, tries to learn a hidden order and explicate it. Geneticists, for example, even employ the language of ciphering, referring to the DNA and RNA 'codes' (Watson and Crick 'cracked' the genetic code in 1953) and the 'messages' carried by the DNA-RNA molecules.[3] Thus in the genetic model the world as book becomes the body as book, and the geneticist reads a text embedded in the body as one way of one aspect of solving the 'mystery of life' or even the 'riddle of the universe'.

In a certain way at least, then, the space on which the hidden messages are found is rendered as sacred for the scientist as for the religious seeker, since for both that space is the context of the secret knowledge that, once disclosed, will provide ultimate power – over suffering and death, over all lacks that mark existence. The space is seldom appreciated for itself in Western culture, whether by mystic or scientist, and even the artist, for whom space is highly significant, tends to use it and transform it toward the creation of a 'something more'. He also wants the secret revealed in the formula of a sacred text that provides power.

In the end Tzinacán does approximate divinity and gains ultimate power, but he does not exploit it. His omnipotence, paradoxically, generates impotence. The divine revelation he receives is so overwhelming that it obliterates his individuality, so that he remains 'lying here in the darkness' and waiting for death. Would a perfect reading in fact destroy one's individuality? It would at least radically alter that individuality, for a full understanding of another perspective could not help but profoundly influence one's own. Something of this happens in conversion experiences, where – to be sure, without 'perfect readings' – one's individuality is overcome by the force of another perspective, to the extent that one adopts a good part of that system. If the perfect reading – to follow Borges' fictional logic further – were of the divine mind, one would no doubt succumb to that totality and have one's individuality lost in the omniscience. The paradox of reading to achieve ultimate knowledge and power is that full success would mean the sacrifice of the self. In this sense, reading can be a nihilating activity.

Why *else* would one read? An answer is in Borges' own project of writing. One grasps that in this story he has played with the metaphor of reading the book of nature in order to dissolve it. It is dissolved both through a Borgesian deployment of something like Derrida's 'trace' and through Borges' implied author's attitude. The elusive concept of the trace in Derrida's thinking has to do with the argument that meaning can never be fully present to us, that we can experience it only as an already-happened, and a something-else, as we reflect on events and assign them value, or as a not-yet, that we can experience only as anticipation and difference.[4] Meaning is thus 'present' only as a trace of, a hint of, a clue to the fullness of an already-happened, or as a tracing, tracking or scouting of the future to project its meaning. Yet 'trace' as noun or verb is a spatial concept and suggests the need to think of the search for meaning in spatial as well as temporal terms. Thinking of it in terms of presence and absence, of plenitude and lack, are possibilities. In 'The God's Script' the trace is of the omnipotent divine formula, the existence of which is a vague memory (that he probably invented) in the priest's mind and an anticipation, but it is also an absence and a lack (the script is missing or unrecognizable) that needs to be tracked down and made explicit. Borges has Tzinacán actually do this, accomplish the impossible, yet then refuse to act on this trace become fullness. His reading, which has cost him his individuality, has risen to the status of an end in itself – but the loss of individuality is also only the loss of the imperial and colonizing self that wants to understand and control everything. It is the self to which mystery is a threat and a challenge. The self that is transformed and remains is in unchanged circumstances yet in repose with the universe, in a state of pure *Gelassenheit zu den Dingen*. One can read, then, in order to find in the activity itself a trace of such repose.

Borges not only in this story but in scores of others addresses the question of why read – if it is an imperialist, control-seeking and ultimately nihilating act – also with the gesture of play. Most of his fiction has its implied author – that presence behind the text who both is and is not Borges – involved in dramatizations of and reflections on philosophical and theological problems that have obsessed the West for millenia, yet he never pretends to resolve them. Or better, he does *pretend* to resolve them, and in that gesture of the imagination his play with meaning as an alternative to the drive to find absolute meaning is conveyed. One reads, according to this attitude, to engage in deep play, to enjoy the sensuality of the mind's possibilities, and especially to do so in the interactions of writing, reading and tracing that involve one with the others. The sacred text, then, appears as no text that claims the status of sacred and as every text that contributes to the endless and always unfulfilled play of meaning. The space sacralized by such texts is the space that the reader occupies and embodies as she tracks toward the ludic, communal conversation that indulges the pleasure of others rather than avoiding them or seeking to control them.

A passage that can be read as a fascinating counterpiece to 'The God's Script' is the opening paragraphs of Annie Dillard's *Pilgrim at Tinker Creek*.

I used to have a cat, an old fighting tom, who would jump
through the open window by my bed in the middle of the night
and land on my chest. I'd half-awaken. He'd stick his skull
under my nose and purr, stinking of urine and blood. Some
nights he kneaded my bare chest with his front paws, powerfully, arching his back, as if sharpening his claws, or pummelling
a mother for milk. And some mornings I'd wake up in daylight
to find my body covered with paw prints in blood; I looked as
though I'd been painted with roses.

      . . . What blood was this and what roses? It could have been
the rose of union, the blood of murder, or the rose of beauty
bare and the blood of some unspeakable sacrifice of birth. The
sign on my body could have been an emblem or a stain, the
keys to the kingdom or the mark of Cain. I never knew as I
washed, and the blood streamed, faded, and finally disappeared, whether I'd purified myself or ruined the blood sign of
the passover. (1–2)

This somewhat – to my mind – overwrought and overwritten
passage is evocative not least because of the sexual imagery that
pervades the depiction of interaction between cat and woman, but
also because of a scatter-shot of allusions that sends the reader to
an old network of writing on the uncanny. 'What blood?' and
'what roses?', for instance, remind one of the stylized interrogation
of William Blake's 'Tyger': the rhetoric that controls the poem
consists of questions such as 'What immortal hand?' 'What the
hammer? What the chain?' The 'fearful symmetry' of Blake's beast,
moreover, becomes clear through Dillard's vignette and especially
Borges' jaguar story as the pattern on its pelt that is written by a
divine designer.

But still more instructive is how Dillard appropriates the imagery
of strange inscribing in this text of eloquent non-fiction. The author
at the beginning of her naturalist's autobiographical account (more
or less in the tradition of Henry David Thoreau) that comprises
Pilgrim at Tinker Creek borrows a shaman-like authority. She
describes her own body as the space chosen by nature to be a
place for the mysterious 'sign' of bloody paw prints that may be
the literal trace of some primal act (sexual union, birth, killing) or
reminiscent of a ritual moment (condemnation, expiation).
Dillard's drastic overdetermination of this sign suggests that here
the metaphor of reading the book of nature is supplemented by

that of the body both incorporating nature and being incorporated by it, so that nature is read on and in the human body, and the shaman-like authority is made to derive from a virtually involuntary, even visceral meditation on this force indwelling and surrounding the body.

Dillard's strategy does not at first appear persuasive – not until, in reading the whole of *Pilgrim*, one recognizes what she is about. It does not seem convincing, initially, because she situates her metaphors in an age not conducive to them. Fredric Jameson helps one to see this disparity. Explicating the modern 'master narrative' of psychoanalysis and tracking a 'metaphysic of desire', he draws on William Blake and Northrop Frye to show how the human body has been employed as 'a symbol of the organic community', as an 'image of the cosmic body'.[5] This has occurred, Jameson says, via anagogic interpretation (as employed by the medieval theologians and Blake) or archetypal criticism (as employed by Frye) to express the most community-orientated kind of reading. Dillard, positing the tracks on her skin as signs of universal import that she hopes to read for us (the community) in and as the body of her text, ventures a metaphoric equation that our era does not support. However much she tries to mythicize her own body in this opening vignette, expanding it to fill the space of the cosmic body that (in the language of myth and poetry) envelopes nature, her modern, alienating, historic individuality renders that project suspect.

One sees no grounds at first for granting Dillard licence to portray her body as sacred space in an age that in good part denies the master narratives of sacrality. Her tactic is not unlike that of a Jonathan Edwards, who over two centuries ago in texts such as *Images or Shadows of Divine Things* employed nature and the historical, personal self as figures to read divinity in and around him. Yet Edwards's language was plausible and generally persuasive to a culture that confessed a Christian metaphysics. Dillard, who does not have the luxury of that context, faces at the outset of her account a sceptical audience rather than a believers' community.

It gradually becomes clear, however, as Dillard proceeds that the tomcat vignette does not introduce a believers' book of nature, wherein God's benevolence is proven in the grandeur of divine design, but rather a struggle with the problems of theodicy at least as profound as that experienced by Updike's inhabitants of

Eastwick. Rather than dramatizing, through a variety of fictional
devices (characters' voices and behaviour, plot structures, etc.),
the agonies of coming to terms with a brutal world, Dillard
portrays *herself* as experiencing the conflicts of theodicy sensuously
(and sometimes sensually): she sees, hears, feels, tastes, smells
them, in other words encounters them bodily in particularly
intense ways and transfers, or transcribes, their inscription on her
into her autobiographical text. In doing so she plays on our familiar
themes, from earlier chapters, of falling, *Gelassenheit* and mystery
and expands their significance.

Recalling the athletic exuberance of a mockingbird's daring dive
('Just a breath before he would have been dashed to the ground,
he unfolded his wings with exact, deliberate care' – 8), Dillard
senses the gratuitous plenitude of cosmic 'beauty and grace' that
this falling represents; while her description of the 'kayak sickness'
that afflicts Greenland Eskimo seal hunters – the glare and reflection of the fjords gives them the sensation of sinking into a void
– projects cosmic vertigo. Later she perceives herself falling: 'like
Adam . . . I plunge, waft, arc, pour, and dive' (221), and this
metaphoric-corporeal experience, exhilarating and dizzying, is her
deepest response to the puzzle of why pointless and random
suffering permeates existence.

This is, of course, a non-answer, intellectually speaking, to the
questions of theodicy, but it is one that Dillard insists on and one
that she expresses also via a version of *Gelassenheit*. She identifies
a 'kind of seeing that involves a letting go. When I see this way I
sway transfixed and emptied. . . . When I see this second [non-
analytical] way I am above all an unscrupulous observer' (31).
Such nonchalance does not place her in *mind*, aloof from nature
as a disinterested observer. To the contrary, she locates herself
thoroughly in the fullness of the natural: 'I retreat not inside
myself, but outside myself, so that I am a tissue of senses' (201).
It is a position she does not adopt to ignore or soften the gruesome-
ness of life; her depictions of parasites eating away inside bodies
are as graphically grim as Darryl Van Horne's sermon in *The
Witches of Eastwick*. Yet she can 'find a balance and repose' (201)
because she has learned to write with her body. 'Our life is a faint
tracing on the surface of mystery', she says (143). It is a mystery
that is impenetrable ('we know now for sure that there is no
knowing' – 203), but it can be met in its horror and loveliness.
Our recognition that Dillard has been marked by these, by horror

and beauty, authenticates the shaman-like authority she asserts: we can read her as a text that has struggled through to a celebration of the world's own awesome nonchalance.

Yet another – far better known but little read – text that, as an overwhelming mythicizing fiction, can evoke human corporeality as cosmic even in the secular age is suggested by Jameson in an analysis of Northrop Frye. He writes, 'we glimpse the human body itself when in Joycean fashion the landscape slowly turns into a sleeping giant'.[6] The allusion here to the great central figure of *Finnegans Wake*, who is both setting and hero and within whose enveloping absence the world's plot occurs, leads one to see how the body can still be profoundly imagined as sacred and cosmic even in profane and alienated times. Joyce's novel, which to my mind comes as close to sacred status as any written in the modern secular West, achieves mystery, offers the reader mystery as the (non) end result of a deep play with it. It provides, magnificently, as fiction what Dillard offers as meditative autobiography: a view of the body as nexus of sacred text and sacred space.

WRITING AS MUTILATION

Foucault commenting on Nietzsche says that 'The body is the inscribed surface of events (traced by language and dissolved by ideas), the locus of a dissociated Self (adopting the illusion of a substantial unity), and a volume in perpetual disintegration.'[7] A tone, if not of apocalypse (as marks the work of Borges that I just discussed), at least of social disintegration, pervades one of the most remarkable modern fictions of writing on the body: Franz Kafka's 'In the Penal Colony'. Published in 1919, this expressionist story is as instructively bizarre as anything written in the post-modern era. In its fantastic plot a text is supposed to be cut into – incised or deeply tattooed rather than inscribed – a living human body, in a lethal process through which the victim as reader is simultaneously his own scene of writing – his own *mise en scène* of a dramatic performance that is writing – and whose reading is intended to be a horribly painful corporeal absorption of the text. Further, the sense of the body that we have already observed, of the body-as-text serving somehow as a victim (the imprisoned jaguar, Dillard 'pummelled' by her cat) is here paramount: writing on/in the body in Kafka's tale is above all punishment. It is, in fact, a death *sentence*, and although that pun does not work in the original German, one thinks of a familiar German idiom, 'auf den Leib geschrieben' (literally,'written on the body' but meaning 'fitting perfectly') that has its own punning significance.

As the fanatic officer in charge of the deadly writing machine explains to the narrator, an explorer from Europe visiting this remote penal colony somewhere in the tropics, the point of this kind of execution is to produce in the condemned person an understanding of justice. This particular prisoner, the officer reveals, does not know his sentence, nor even that he has been found guilty (he is 'a soldier condemned to death for disobedience and insulting behavior to a superior' – 180), yet the officer anticipates that he, like previous prisoners, will literally learn that sentence on his body: 'Er erfährt es ja auf seinem Leib' ('He will experience it on his body' – 187). The execution will be by a huge writing machine or etching apparatus consisting of a vibrating bed to which the condemned person is bound, a 'designer' suspended two metres above it which contains the machinery, and in between a 'harrow', a sheet of glass in which needles are embedded and which is lowered onto the body so that the needles can write (actually punch or perforate) their script. The machine slowly revolves the victim's body on the bed so that the harrow can write its message deeper and deeper, until the penetration produces death.

The officer, who claims to have conducted many such executions, declares that the victim's moment of recognition is the inspiring part of the process:

> But how quiet he grows at just about the sixth hour! Enlightenment comes to the most dull-witted. It begins around the eyes. From there it radiates. A moment that might tempt one to go under the Harrow oneself. Nothing more happens than that the man begins to understand the inscription, he purses his mouth as if he were listening. You have seen how difficult it is to decipher the script with one's eyes; but our man deciphers it with his wounds. To be sure, that is a hard task; he needs six hours to accomplish it. (190–1)

Somewhat later the officer becomes nostalgic about how, under the regime of the sterner old commandant (now dead), the executions became a virtual religious ritual:

. . . in those days the writing needles let drop an acid fluid, which we're no longer permitted to use. Well, and then came the sixth hour! It was impossible to grant all the requests to be allowed to watch it from near by. . . . How we absorbed the look of transfiguration on the face of the sufferer, how we bathed our cheeks in the radiance of that justice, achieved at last and fading so quickly! (195)

Just how this *anagnorisis* and enlightenment happen the officer does not explain, but pain is obviously the transforming force, the purifying element that prompts transcendent insight. Pain, however, as we observed in Chapter 2, does not actually function this way. Rather, at least at its worst, it paralyses mind and body by demanding a concentration on itself. Kafka in this story significantly confuses pain with suffering. Suffering – and suffering laced with pain but not dominated but it – can indeed generate enlightenment and spiritual transformation. This conflation of pain and suffering allows one to see how the whole story exercises a tactic of elision: writing is mutilation, writing causes pain, death comes by writing, yet in all of these sequences some step is omitted, something sprung over. In ordinary (realistic) situations of capital punishment, the death sentence is both spoken and written on paper, *then* carried out by another medium: hanging, shooting, gas, electric chair or whatever. To have the sentence etched into the body by a lethal writing machine, however, is a conflation and elision that can also be comprehended as a pun: the execution of the sentence is the execution of the victim. Viewed grammatically, the punishment process described by the officer involves the collapsing of metaphor into metonymy, or the convergence of symbolic and literal action.[8]

From Kafka's game of conflation and elision one can derive a four-fold commentary on facets of this deadly somatography: on justice, fetishizing, sacrality and writing fiction itself.

The ostensible reason for this barbarous punishment in the penal colony is to produce a state of enlightenment in which the dying victim *feels* justice. Only the mad logic of a totalitarian system would try to force illumination by inhumane methods, one would think, yet the examples of the Inquisition, of the Austro-Hungarian bureaucracy in which Kafka himself participated and of the ever more refined combinations of torture and mind control in our age remind us that the logic inhabiting this fiction has in fact permeated our culture and our sense of justice.

The sentences are read tactilely by the condemned soldier after hours of pain, the officer in charge claims, but the satisfaction is mainly for those looking on and reading 'normally' through the glass harrow. Yet the calligraphy, with all of its embellishments, and because of the blood from the perforated flesh, is very hard for the observers to read (the explorer cannot even decipher the 'guiding plans' on paper that the officer shows him), and the body as text thus gradually appears as a fetishized object with voyeuristic and exhibitionistic apeal. What the text *says* is shown not to matter; the watchers are fascinated by what the fatal writing *does*. They study the suffering and dying victim, excited by their incursion into his intimacy and helplessness, and (as is generally the case with fetishes) assign a magical, erotic and sacral quality to the abused, simultaneously overvalued and undervalued body. That the body is believed capable of reading an intricate message cut into it attests to the magical quality; that the penetration of it leads to an ecstatic, transforming climax of death indicates the erotic aspect; that it calls forth a ritual of awed observation and vicarious participation shows the sacred dimension.

The power of the body thus fetishized as text is revealed in the officer's shift from voyeur to exhibitionist. His identification with the fetishized body becomes so strong and obtrusive that he substitutes himself for the condemned soldier as victim and – in yet another of Kafka's conflations and elisions – turns a vicarious experience into a first-hand one that, perversely, destroys the whole system.

In Kafka's story, then, as in the metafiction of Borges and the personal mythicizing of Dillard, the texted body as sacred space risks losing its numinosity precisely then when that numinosity is manipulated. In 'The God's Script' Tzinacán refuses to exploit the power of the divine formula discovered on the jaguar's pelt, and the text becomes meaningless, fades back into nature. In *Pilgrim at Tinker Creek* the author's own attempt to invest the paw prints' bloody design on her body with religious-ritualistic import at first rings false. In 'In the Penal Colony' the officer's attempt to revive the failing authority of the old commandant – what he sees as a sacred tradition – by his own exemplary and sacrificial death under the harrow of the writing machine ends in the disintegration of both the machine and the tradition. According to the plots of these three narratives, bodies can be maintained as sacred space only when the texts that render them sacred, and the rituals that convey the sacrality, are not turned into instruments of power.

The whole text of 'In the Penal Colony' is, of course, in one sense a disclosure of such abuse of power, and the key to seeing it this way is the officer's unreliability as secondary narrator. There is no reason to doubt the veracity of the primary narrative voice, which presents events as focalized by the alien perspective of the explorer, but the officer's behaviour raises questions of his credibility. Although his explanation of the execution/writing machine's history, function and purpose *seems* plausible, within the surreal premises of the fiction, his irrational and compulsive actions as the plot unfolds cause one, in retrospect, to suspect his whole story. One has, after all, only his word that the machine has functioned as he claims. In the only instance when the explorer sees it in use, on the officer's own body, it botches the job horribly and kills its volunteer victim brutally, without writing at all.

This possibility of the officer's unreliability as a narrator casts all previous interpretation of the story in doubt and permits one to find yet another reason for Kafka's conflations and elisions. The collapsing of metaphor into metonymy, the melding of symbolic and literal action (which is at last still symbolic action, as an articulation of language) as strategies that distinguish this tale, culminate in the disintegration of the reading process itself. The officer's failure to make the machine write on/for him, the explorer's failure (and lack of opportunity) to read any text on paper or on bodies, the reader's failure to read this story *conclusively* all conflate into a *mise en abyme* (a self-reflexive gesture) that warns of abusive reading: a sort that desires the subjection of all narration to a single, absolute, unquestioned authority. The officer's subjugation of his body to the writing machine, to persuade the explorer (the reader) of the rightness and justice of the old authoritarian system, is a monstrous act of self-abuse lost on the explorer, an assumption of a massively self-contained system that can recognize nothing outside itself, no alternatives. Hence the explorer as foreigner, alien to this totalitarianism, rejects it as the reader resists an encompassing allegorical interpretation. The officer is himself, finally, *aufgehoben*, impaled on the wrecked harrow, suspended over the pit, and 'cancelled', just as the story's 'proper' ending is suspended and a determinate reading cancelled.

In this tale of traumatic writing and reading, the only text that the explorer can read is, at the end, an inscription on the old commandant's gravestone. It is a religious text in the stone, calling for faith in the resurrection of the commandant lying dead beneath it. The bystanders watching the explorer's reaction do not have this faith – indeed, no one in the penal colony seems to, now that the officer is dead – yet the little shrine has remained known. For although the old commandant's kind of justice seems transcended, it remains potent as a reflex and tempting as a possible absolute foundation of order and meaning. As Michel de Certeau puts it,

> . . . the law constantly writes itself on bodies. It engraves itself on parchments made from the skin of its subjects. It articulates them in a juridical corpus. It makes its books out of them. These writings carry out two complementary operations: through them, living beings are 'packed into a text' (in the sense that products are canned or packed), transformed into signifiers of rules (a sort of 'intextuation') and, on the other hand, the reason or *Logos* of a society 'becomes flesh' (an incarnation).[9]

Kafka's story suggests how such intextuation and incarnation can go wrong, how their operations can become demonic, ends in themselves. The punishing discipline here does not sustain the law nor recover justice. Rather, the autodestruction of the old order, and the suspension of a conventional ending, prepare for a new reading beyond this text: one in which the law of retribution is succeeded by the play of grace.

Simone de Beauvoir wrote nearly four decades ago that 'Woman feels inferior because, in fact, the requirements of femininity *do* belittle her. She spontaneously chooses to be a complete person, a subject and a free being with the world and the future open to her; if this choice is confused with virility, it is so to the extent that femininity today means mutilation.'[10] The text I will address next could be read as a fictional dramatization of de Beauvoir's statement. This is the notorious *Story of O* by Pauline Réage (a pseudonym), a novel that describes the subjugation of the female body and the power of total fetishizing through painful inscription. Published in France in 1954 but not available in a complete English translation until 1965, *Story of O* recounts the sexual debasement of the beautiful young Parisian fashion photographer O, who is not further named, and the absence of whose proper name helps the text define, at the end, a surviving sanctity of female space. O, to please her lover René, consents to join a 'gyneceum' at Roissy where she is initiated into the rites of sado-masochistic pain, humiliation and sex and eventually comes under the control of Sir Stephen, her 'master', who inflicts on her increasingly intense forms of sexual abuse and gradually transforms her into a slave virtually devoid of subjecthood.

In the sequence of scenes I want to comment on, writing connected to the body and writing directly on the body are performed as mutilations – mutilations that confirm the woman's degraded role in a perverse relationship, that reinforce the simultaneous over- and undervaluation of the body, and that encourage voyeurism and exhibitionism as aspects of the ritualized fetishism. This writing, moreover, comments on pornography in an instructive way. The Greek term *pornographos*, originally 'writing about prostitutes', characterizes what this novel, in part, is: O and the other women at Roissy, perhaps not technically prostitutes since they are not paid for their services, are nonetheless elaborately *kept* women for a number of men and in that sense are prostitutes. But *Story of O* is also about writing *on* prostitutes, and this curious combination – writing about and the painful writing on – suggests what we are coming to recognize as truly pornographic: the depiction, for sexual arousal, of the *damaging* appropriation of another's body sheerly for the satisfaction of one's desires. As is evident from my italics, I consider the depiction of the damaging or destructive use of another's body as that which makes portrayals of erotically exciting acts pornographic.

Yet *Story of O* does not strike me as sexually arousing in any sense precisely because O's own reflection on her debasement (described by a narrator who is external to the story but privy to O's thoughts and feelings) conveys her precarious subjecthood fairly distinctly to the reader and mitigates somewhat the sense she herself and others have of her as an object for sexual use. That is to say, although she learns to function as a vessel of sexual exploitation, the reader responds to many more facets of her personality – to many of the other selves in her repertoire – and thus cannot view her from the disengaged, objective perspective that pornography encourages.

Thus, although *Story of O* employs the conventional themes of pornography, it actually provokes a reflection on the nature and style of pornography rather than sexual stimulation. Its twin modalities are pain and mutilation, and these together provide a particularly strong articulation of debasement in a series of scenes in Part III, late in the text. These passages connect pain and mutilation to inscriptions as sexual possession.

The novel up to this point is full of various sexual penetrations of O – mouth, anus, vagina – by fingers and penises, nearly all of them to demonstrate to her that she can be taken at will as an object for satisfying lust. That her masters (Sir Stephen and others to whom he grants the use of O) indulge a more or less refined sadism goes without saying. In these scenes inscriptions serve as a supplemental, more incisive kind of penetration done formally and ritualistically to confirm O's identity as a possession. O has been taken to the house of Anne-Marie (an older woman who co-operates with Sir Stephen) outside Paris, where O's labia are pierced by Anne-Marie and, later, a stainless steel ring inserted. Prior to this a ceremony takes place in which the naked O kneels before Sir Stephen and listens to Anne-Marie's query: 'Do you consent, O, to wear the rings and monogram with which Sir Stephen desires you to be marked, without knowing how they will be placed upon you?' (151). To which O replies, 'I do'.

After some days, during which O is whipped and otherwise sexually used and abused, Anne-Marie, with Sir Stephen and another woman present, replaces the stainless steel ring with a gold-plated lead ring to which another similar ring is attached, and to each of these a gold and lead disk: 'On the blank side will be your name, your title, and Sir Stephen's family and given names . . . with, below it, a design composed of a crossed whip and riding crop' (158). After these are in place, O is taken to another room where she is bound upright to a column and has her buttocks branded: 'The marks made by the branding iron, about three inches in height and half that in width, had been burned into the flesh as though by a gouging tool, and were almost half an inch deep: the lightest stroke of the finger revealed them' (167).

This mutilating causes O great pain, of course, yet 'From these irons and these marks, O derived a feeling of inordinate pride' (167). A main reason why O endures great pain, here and elsewhere, is that in an era that stresses alienation (*Story of O* was written during the flourishing of French existentialism) and in which the affections seem benumbed, anesthetized, experiencing pain could be mistaken for the recovery of true feeling – and O commits this error. Suffering intense pain, and doing so for the sake of the men who abuse her, permits her to believe that the agony of her body is actually a *feeling* – and a reciprocated feeling – of deep love. A main reason for her pride in her mutilation is that she sees in the rings and in the brand the signs of something very much like a marriage; yet it is, in fact, a relationship based on the dynamics of possession.[11] This possessing is developed and reinforced not only by mutilation but also by the voyeurism/exhibitionism and by the over- and undervaluation of the body that accompany the ritualized fetishism. That O allows herself to be pierced and branded demonstrates her willingness to exist as the property of a 'husband'. Her role is an intensification of the traditional female role in marriage. The ring through her labia, unlike a wedding ring, cannot be removed except by filing through the metal: she is in perpetual bondage. The brand on her buttocks, unlike the marriage certificate, is likewise a permanently inscribed sign that she is owned by another. The rings and disk are, further, encumbrances to independence and choice. They hang a third of the way down her thighs, obstruct her movements, and determine her clothing styles, thus limiting her still more to the status of male property.

The effectiveness of these signs on O's body depends on their visibility, and they are in fact applied and used in a context of insistent voyeurism and exhibitionism. It is important to O's masters that she be visually as well as sexually accessible virtually at all times. Her genitals are often exposed, and her labia parted, with others looking on, as if the effort literally to see inside her were also an effort to push past her last intimacy, know her totally and make the others the possessors of her subjectivity.[12] This absorption with O's body renders it fetishized and, like the body in Kafka's tale, causes it to be at the same time over- and under-valued – overvalued as the target of such excessive, obsessive attention and undervalued as the object of humiliation and abuse. O is always the object of the others' gaze, even when she is being taken sexually, and the voyeurism is never actually relieved by sexual participation. The voyeurism remains constant as the medium of the fetishizing and as a means of maintaining control over the woman's body-as-possession, and as a kind of distancing, of non-participation even as one takes part.

O (by profession a photographer and thus one who herself enhances the objectifying gaze through technology) responds to the voyeurism and the fetishizing it involves with her own exhibitionism. For example, after she has been pierced and branded she wishes that her friend Jacqueline were present, so that she could show her the rings and disks and the large letters burned into her skin. Because she has come to accept herself as the fetishized object, simultaneously ascribing too much and too little worth to her body, she can show herself off, proud of her mutilations, as one who has special status in the eyes of others. She learns to derive her identity not from her individuality in relation to others but sheerly as the focus of others. Or: her individuality has been absorbed into the gaze of the others. The many roles that constitute her selfhood are concentrated into this one, the sexual object.

The voyeurism and exhibitionism interact by interpreting the mutilations as deeper penetrations. O is regularly entered in mouth, anus and vagina: to have the labia pierced and the buttocks branded is a permanent penetration of the body, keeping her 'occupied' even when the penis is absent and confirming the penetration, the constant violation via the others' gaze, and the woman's subservient reception of it by which she identifies herself.

Story of O, finally, relates painful writing on the body to sexuality in ways the other examples we have studied do not. The inscribed rings and disks are much like standard wedding rings and identification tags. What makes them different is that they are worn on the vagina. Significant about the branding is that it is done on the buttocks, traditionally a part of the body associated with erotic shame and punishment. This writing, which consists of O's name, her master's name and monogram, and the sado-masochistic symbol of crossed whip and riding crop, is intended as a mark of sexual ownership much like a contract: the names of the possessor and the possessed pressed against the woman's genitals and the possessor's validating initials burned into the private flesh, 'proclaiming in bold letters that she was Sir Stephen's personal property' (167).

Does the site of writing here, then, become sacred space? It does in so far as the dynamics of sexual possession, representing the ownership of another person, substitutes for traditional religion. The writing on and against O's body, placed there in ritualized fashion, registers a consecration of that body as the place where her master worships himself. For O has consecrated herself to Sir Stephen so that, in taking on her subjecthood – knowing her in the most intimate ways in public surroundings – he becomes self-sufficient, a little god.

This celebration of male dominance in at least a quasi-religious atmosphere, using writing on the scandalized female body to establish it as sacred *masculine* space, seems to illustrate Susan Gubar's point in ' "The Blank Page" and the Issues of Female Creativity'. There, after a discussion of male literary creation (featuring Henry James, Conrad, Roland Barthes, Ishmael Reed and others), in which the artists perceive the act of writing as sexual penetration, she summarizes: 'This model of the pen-penis writing on the virgin page participates in a long tradition identifying the author as a male who is primary and the female as his passive creation – a secondary object lacking autonomy, endowed with often contradictory meaning but denied intentionality. Clearly this tradition excludes woman from the creation of culture, even as it reifies her as an artifact within culture. It is therefore particularly problematic for women who want to appropriate the pen by becoming writers.'[13]

Although O is emphatically not a virgin, the branding of the 'intact . . . smooth, rounded area' (164) of her buttocks is an action that fits Gubar's model, yet *Story of O* qualifies and complicates her theory. For one, although O never knows who actually does the branding, it is undertaken in any case not by a man alone but in complicity between Sir Stephen and the three women participating; it is not only a male penetration. More important, since it is now fairly well established that 'Pauline Réage' is a pseudonym for a woman and not for a male pornographer (as some have speculated) as author of the novel, one finds here the curious situation of a female artist perpetrating 'the pen-penis writing on the virgin page'. I believe that this is an instance of a woman taking over a male-oriented metaphor in order to neutralize it on the way to creating an 'improper' ending to the text – not unlike the way in which the story's right conclusion and the reader's determinate reading are *aufgehoben* in 'In the Penal Colony'. A critical part of the author's neutralizing strategy involves the enigma of naming. The mystery of Pauline Réage's true name parallels the mystery of O's full name inscribed on the ring/disk that presses against her vagina: we do not know either of them, and thus the author, in this most revealing of texts, maintains a secrecy that returns us to the mystery of writing and sexuality and their interaction. Both writing and sexuality can be exploited and abused by those wishing to gain power, but the price they pay is to engage in writing and sexuality as acts of compulsion rather than to experience them as acts, shared willingly, of revelation and love.

The intentional failure of proper naming prepares the absence of a proper conclusion. *Story of O* breaks off abruptly, summarizes a missing last chapter in a laconic, enigmatic sentence (*'In a final chapter, which has been suppressed, O returned to Roissy, where she was abandoned by Sir Stephen'*), then in a concluding, equally enigmatic paragraph announces *'a second ending to the story of O, according to which O, seeing that Sir Stephen was about to leave her, said she would prefer to die. Sir Stephen gave her his consent'* (204). Whatever else these three sentences may be, they strike me as contemptuous, as the throwaway conclusion by a writer who declares her freedom to quit the pen/penis-marks-virgin-page model, now that she has demonstrated how it can be neutralized. In a way the female body here, as a textualized sacred space, maintains its inviolability after all.

In the same essay on female creativity mentioned above Susan Gubar writes, 'Like Kafka's victim in "The Penal Colony", [sic] women have had to experience cultural scripts in their lives by suffering them in their bodies. This is why Maxine Hong Kingston writes so movingly about her resemblance to the mythic woman warrior who went into battle scarred by the thin blades which her parents literally used to write fine lines of script on her body.'[14] I want to gloss the scene that Gubar refers to in Kingston's *The Woman Warrior: Memoirs of a Girlhood Among Ghosts*. This text, published in 1976, is an autobiographical account of Kingston's own adolescence as a Chinese-American in Stockton, California, an account that is interwoven with Chinese myths and fairy tales. The focus of the memoir is the double difficulty of growing up as a Chinese-American girl, suffering both the prejudice of the old society in which girls are considered inferior creatures and the second-rate status of Oriental immigrants in a culture barely tolerant of them (the 'ghosts' of the subtitle refer, among other things, to the Caucasians, whom the Chinese consider 'unreal' in retaliation for their racism). In her second chapter Kingston tells (and perhaps embellishes) the tale of Fa Mu Lan, the Chinese peasant girl who goes off at age seven into a fifteen-year apprenticeship, with two immortals disguised as an aged couple, to become a woman warrior and liberate her people from their oppressors. When she returns home as a magnificent young woman at the end of her training, her parents in an elaborate ceremony carve a long list of grievances against the oppressors into their daughter's back. The beautifully evocative passage is worth quoting in full.

My mother put a pillow before the ancestors. 'Kneel here' she said. 'Now take off your shirt.' I kneeled with my back to my parents so none of us felt embarrassed. My mother washed my back as if I had left for only a day and were her baby yet. 'We are going to carve revenge on your back,' my father said. 'We'll write out oaths and names.'

'Wherever you go, whatever happens to you, people will know our sacrifice,' my mother said. 'And you will never forget either.' She meant that if I got killed, the people could use my dead body for a weapon, but we do not like to talk out loud about dying.

My father first brushed the words in ink and they fluttered down my back row after row. Then he began cutting; to make fine lines and points he used thin blades, for the stems, large blades.

My mother caught the blood and wiped the cuts with a cold towel soaked in wine. It hurt terribly – the cuts sharp; the air burning; the alcohol cold, then hot – pain so various, I gripped my knees. I released them. Neither tension nor relaxation helped, I wanted to cry. If not for the fifteen years of training, I would have writhed on the floor. . . . The list of grievances went on and on. If an enemy should flay me, the light would shine through my skin like lace.

At the end of the last word, I fell forward. Together my parents sang what they had written, then let me rest. My mother fanned my back. 'We'll have you with us until your back heals,' she said.

When I could sit up again, my mother brought two mirrors, and I saw my back covered entirely with words in red and black files, like an army, like my army. My parents nursed me just as

if I had fallen in battle after many victories. Soon I was strong
again. (41–2)

The young heroine of this mythic episode takes the injustices
committed against her people, their pain and humiliation, onto
her back, voluntarily endures a ritual mutilation in order to serve
both as the vicarious sufferer – the one who absorbs their hurt –
and their deliverer. Important, of course, is that it is a woman –
and a disguised woman at that (her army thinks she is a man) –
who is the saviour, for in this role she hopes also eventually to
redeem her sex. And indeed, in the rest of the tale the woman
warrior frees the country and returns to liberate her own village
last and accept the adulation of her husband, son and other
relatives.

This fantastic 'talk-story' told to the author by her mother, an
accomplished raconteur, serves as a crucial metaphor for her. As
an author she too has gone off (she lives in Honolulu with husband
and son) and from a distance employs her woman's writerly
weapons to fight the twofold injustices against sex and race. As
she puts it, 'The swordswoman and I are not so dissimilar. May
my people understand the resemblance soon so that I can return
to them. What we have in common are the words at our backs.
The ideographs for *revenge* are "report a crime" and "report to five
families." The reporting is the vengeance – not the beheading, not
the gutting, but the words. And I have so many words – "chink"
words and "gook" words too – that they do not fit on my skin'
(62–3). The difference between her and the woman warrior, of
course, is that her writing brings no happy end. The prejudices
are too much for her powers. Nevertheless, there is a depth of
commitment to community here, coupled with a remarkable power
of language, that constitutes this text very nearly as a redemptive
narrative. It may at last be little more hopeful than the fictions of
Kafka and Réage, yet here the swordswoman's/author's inscribed
body is the place where mutilation produces strength and resolve.
Here the woman challenges her status as 'a secondary object
lacking autonomy' and creates, in the forceful reminiscence *cum*
art work, a space where reconciliation can be imagined to begin.

Sharon Willis concludes her fine study of bodily inscription in
the fiction of Marguerite Duras with the assertion that Duras' texts
'invite us to work within the contradiction of body and discourse,
since body is socially inscribed but always exceeding discourse

and representation, and since discourse, while propped on the body, inevitably outruns it, into the field of social agency.'[15] It seems to me that Kingston, far less prolific and influential than Duras has been, is nonetheless more adept at modulating the contradictions of body and discourse. Duras, a Frenchwoman at home in the Orient until the age of eighteen, returns again and again to the East in her writing, as if to a primal scene, perhaps to exorcise the shocks of youthful vision, in any case always trying but never managing to resolve the mystery of her double heritage. Kingston, an Oriental growing up in America and now at home in Hawaii, has also taken a mediating position between East and West in her writing. It permits her to present the burden of her prose, the words at her back, in an international context and in ways that, however guardedly, call for an international community. Kingston's writing also portrays what Willis calls, in Duras' fiction, 'hysterical discourse', but whereas writing on the body in Duras projects fragmentation, in Kingston it expresses wholeness, however flawed. 'If an enemy should flay me,' Fa Mu Lan says, 'the light would shine through my skin like lace' (41). The fragile, obstinate beauty of such images generates the sacred space of Kingston's work.

SIGNIFYING THE DESERT

The first kind of inscription I addressed in this chapter had to do with texts written by nature on itself: nature's self-inscriptions. The second kind presents texts written by humans on human bodies: various sorts of somatographics. I will turn briefly to a third kind, to texts written by humans on nature. What I have in mind becomes clearer from a quotation in the only narrative I will interpret here, the Australian author Patrick White's 1957 novel *Voss*. Early in this text, in a significant passage of free indirect discourse, Voss ponders his goal and his name, which seems to him 'a crystal in his mouth'.

If he were to leave that name on the land, irrevocably, his material body swallowed by what it had named, it would be rather on some desert place, a perfect abstraction, that would rouse no feeling of tenderness in posterity. He had no more

need for sentimental admiration than he had for love. He was
complete. (41)

Four hundred pages later and twenty years after Voss had indeed
been put to death, swallowed by the Australian wilderness, the
sole survivor of the fated expedition he led reports to the woman
with whom Voss became as obsessed as with the desert: 'Voss left
his mark on the country. . . . He was cutting his initials in the
trees. . . . The blacks talk about him to this day. He is still
there . . . he is there in the country, and always will be' (443).

    This magnificent novel (one of the most accomplished and one
of the most underrated of all the narratives I deal with in this
study) is a fictional version of the attempt of the German explorer
Ludwig Leichhardt to be the first, with a small band of men, to
cross the Australian continent. The fictive counterpart of Leichhardt (who undertook the journey in 1845) is Johann Ulrich Voss,
who launches his journey in 1848, suffers terrible hardship with
his men and dies en route. White portrays Voss as a tormented
personality, a man of uncompromising will and possessed by his
doomed desire to conquer the Australian desert – which epic
journey is also a quest for the self and, against his protestations,
for God.

    Besides Voss, the novel has two other foci. One is Laura
Trevelyan, the orphaned young woman who lives with relatives
in the Colony outside Sydney. The other is the desert itself, which
is so powerful and pervasive that (like Thomas Hardy's Egdon
Heath in *The Return of the Native*) it functions virtually as a protagonist, or as an antagonist to Voss and Laura as protagonists. These
three are involved in the inscriptions that establish or confirm
sacred space in the novel. Voss intent on making his mark constitutes one such inscription; Voss and Laura writing love letters
produce a second kind; and the wilderness generates a third.

    The account to Laura at the end by the lone survivor Judd (who
is yet another version of an unreliable narrator) of Voss cutting
his initials into trees is an ironic trivialization, for Voss' desire to
leave his imprint on the Australian landscape is an egomaniacal
drive only weakly reflected in the adolescent practice of carving
on wood, although this too betrays the intensity of his obsession.
Voss is an embodiment of the Victorian imperialist spirit, although
he is both an intellectual and a mystic. His lust to penetrate the
interior, where no white man has gone before, is a classic case of

sublimated sexuality, just as it is a textbook example of an effort simultaneously to deny and accommodate the death wish. Thus Voss wants to inscribe himself on nature in the most audacious sense and in the process transform both himself and the landscape into sacred space. It is already an audacious action in its foolhardiness (Voss prepares his team poorly for survival in the outback); but more than that, Voss not only wants to conquer nature but to learn its secrets as well, force it to yield up its intimacy without giving anything of himself. Hence the journal he keeps as he pushes deeper into the barren wilderness, recording his observations of the land he thinks to mark by his transit. Expecting to gain an immortality – his name remembered – by his feat of endurance, he projects himself as a sacred text embodied as sacred space – an overweening self-image, to be sure, but a powerful one. Further, he struggles to emulate his inimitable God and to assume God-like attributes such as absolute purity, discipline and compassion, and thus strives through his presence to confer sanctity on the landscape. It is an act of innocent arrogance not unlike the assumption of Victorian missionaries that they could, by force of their superior Christian word, enlighten areas of heathen darkness.

Amazingly (but typical of the artistic challenges that White sets for himself), this ascetic and fanatic creature Voss is also portrayed persuasively as a man who falls deeply in love. He has only one significant encounter with Laura, consisting of an intense and private dialogue following a dinner party on the eve of his departure for the desert, yet this is enough to impel them toward a spiritual union that evolves during their separation. They never see each other again, but Voss proposes marriage to Laura via his first letter to her, and she writes back to accept, at first with certain reservations and qualifications. These are the only letters that the two ever exchange. Others are written that do not reach their destinations, true love letters whose content remains known only to the authors (and the novel's readers), for the letters go astray or are never completed. These letters that never arrive comprise human inscriptions that, if not written directly on nature, surely gloss such writing.

That their correspondence becomes this gloss is anticipated in their single, foreboding conversation after the dinner party. There Laura, caught up in her ambivalence toward Voss, exclaims, 'You are so vast and ugly. . . . I can imagine some desert, with rocks,

rocks of prejudice, and, yes, even hatred. You are so isolated. . . .
Everything is for yourself' (87–8). When she tells him this, and
more, Voss asks, 'Do you hate me, perhaps?' and Laura replies,
'I am fascinated by you. . . . *You* are *my* desert' (88). Voss for his
part, as the ordeal of the cross-country trek worsens and debilitates
him, increasingly hallucinates Laura's presence, and she merges
with his wasteland surroundings more and more as he approaches
death.

It is of course an irony that these passionate letters do not reach
the suffering lovers, now that, as Voss puts it, 'distance has united
us thus closely' (217), yet because each has become the other's
landscape the writing is actually superfluous. They can imagine
each other so intensely that their representations to each other
in writing are unnecessary. The writing is transcended by the
inscription of each on the other as felt presence. They experience
the impossible ideal that lovers wish their letters to accomplish,
to be so packed with desire that they overcome space and time
and fill the other with their presence. It is as if the lovers' absence
as I described it in Chapter 2, that inspires love letters in the first
place, is here encountered not as the opposite of presence but as
its fulfilment. This is a projection of the body through nature that
needs no script. Thus the destruction of Voss' second letter to
Laura, from the outback, is portentous. Voss entrusts it to Dugald,
an old aborigine returning to an outpost, to pass on to the network
of whites, but Dugald once back among his people simply tears it
up: 'the pieces of paper fluttered round him and settled on the
grass, like a mob of cockatoos' (220) – a literal, gratuitous inscription of man on nature.

The distanced spiritual lovers commune without letters only
because they are sick, Voss through the deprivations of body that
make him hallucinate and Laura through her sympathetic 'brain
fever' that parallels Voss' distress and nearly kills her. As Voss
slides further into illusion, Laura's presence to him becomes more
constant and intimate. Shortly before Voss and those left of his
band are captured by the aborigines, he imagines Laura riding
horseback beside him, in a vision of suffering and *eros:* he 'saw
that they had cut off her hair, and below the surprising stubble
that remained, they had pared the flesh from her face. She was
now quite naked. And beautiful. Her eyes were drenching him'
(367). And then, in a new paragraph: 'So they rode on above the
dust, in which they were writing their own legend.' Inscription

joins Voss' fantasy when actual writing is no longer needed. Laura meanwhile has, under doctor's orders, indeed had her hair cut off to make the suffering of her fever more bearable.

Not long before Voss is killed he has a vision of near-total union with Laura:

> As she lay beside him, his boyhood slipped from him in a rustling of water and a rough towel. . . . Leaves were in her lips, that he bit off, and from her breasts the full, silky, milky buds. They were holding each other's heads and looking into them, as remorselessly as children looking at secrets, and seeing all too clearly. . . .
>
> So they were growing together, and loving. No sore was so scrofulous on his body that she would not touch it with her kindness. He would kiss her wounds, even the deepest ones, that he had inflicted himself and left to suppurate. (383)

And Laura in her delirium throughout the final days of Voss' ordeal shares his intimate agony. As Voss is pricked by his black captors to see if he bleeds, Laura is bled with leeches by her doctor. Anticipating his decapitation (although she has no knowledge of his situation) by the aborigine youth, Laura's own throat hurts, and after Voss is finally slaughtered, Laura is released and her fever breaks: ' "Oh God," cried the girl at last, tearing it out. "It is over. It is over" ' (395).

Such 'soulmating' via hallucination and delirium produces, then, what was difficult for Laura and virtually impossible for Voss: a sharing of the self. It is, in fact, almost a merging of the two selves. The description of it could easily be maudlin from a lesser artist than White, and its mode is unbelievable by any standards of realism. This impasse for the reader, constituted by the difficulty of one's taking the novel seriously, finally, as literary realism, reminds one that *Voss* is, after all, part of the linguistic universe, and to see how the characters' implausible relationship as representational realism modulates into a particularly revealing anatomy of a foundational linguistic structure. Quite simply, Voss' and Laura's convergence can be read as coming to form a linguistic sign. They draw closer to each other, for the reader, in a rhythm of signified and signifier that eventually crystallizes into a unit of meaning. If Voss is Laura's desert, for example, a vast territory waiting to be known and named, she provides the gaze through

which he explores and is explored. Laura is Voss' desert vision in
a double sense: she is with him as his illusion and as his insight.
Voss breaks down in its later pages as realistic fiction but can
therefore be recuperated as an allegory of linguistic sign formation.
To see the novel like this is to follow through on the recognition
that these two lovers, each of whose letters do not reach the other,
replace inscription as a felt presence articulated by the other. And
in joining together their own interpretive action, the reader is able
to express them as a sign.

A sign of what? They are a sign of how the linguistic and
physical universes are always intentional, never merely abstractions, empty spaces, wastelands. Voss aspiring to leave his name
on the landscape as 'perfect abstraction' instead leaves it as numinous imprint there that gives the desert significant density. For
Laura and a few others, at least, it becomes sacred space. This
imprint is possible because Voss' 'abstraction' is transformed into
vitality by Laura's pervasive signifying present to him. Yet the
awesome lesson that Voss and his band learn on their deathward
trek is that the great Australian desert constantly inscribes itself
as sacred space apart from their incursion and in spite of it. In
one sense they die because they trespass on and desecrate
primeval sacred territory. Voss is killed outright, his head cut off
by the boy Jackie, a former aborigine member of the expedition,
in a ceremony of exorcism ('He must break the terrible magic that
bound him remorselessly, endlessly, to the white men' – 394) in
which 'the spirits of the place were kind to Jackie'. Others of the
band are left by the watchful aborigines to die of exhaustion or by
their own hands.

Just how this seemingly trackless wasteland is in fact a sacred
place that *can* be desecrated by arrogant and ignorant outsiders is
explained by Max Charlesworth in his comments on 'aboriginal
dreaming'. 'For the Aboriginal his land is a kind of religious icon,
since it represents the power of the Dreamtime beings and also
effects and transmits that power.'[16] Such dreaming is the aborigines' way of comprehending and functioning in their harsh land:
by blending ancient myth and contemporary geography with ritual
wandering. Because certain sites are permeated since primordial
time with the sense of the ancestral sacred, the aborigine learns
to identify them and to chart his course, in what appears to others
as mere desert, in relation to them. And indeed, the Australian
desert in *Voss* emerges in a profound way as such a locus of the

holy. It is alive with the mythic and animistic presences that the aborigines see, feel and worship, and Voss' band is made to sense the beauty and the horror of this savage sacredness. The outback is the scene of great natural and supernatural forces coupling and clashing, so violently that the Western concept of reading the book of nature or of viewing God's handiwork in nature is made to seem merely quaint. Here the landscape itself is ecstatic and demonic, shot through with elemental energy – and always with the aborigines as nature spirits incarnating this mysterious atmosphere of the wasteland and serving as its guardians.

Although the aborigines are illiterate by Western standards, they can read the sacred inscriptions – cave drawings – of their ancestors on this numinous space. Voss and his men find such drawings in a cave where they take refuge from the grim winter weather. Some of the drawings are sexually explicit and embarrass these prim Victorians, yet, aided by the blacks, they grasp something of the 'dreamtime' power emitting from the ancient art. This art is a direct writing on the landscape that the insiders can read. As David Lewis, a modern explorer of the Australian desert, states it, 'When an Aboriginal depicts a stretch of country he generally incorporates its mythical with its physical features, so stressing the inseparable interrelation between the two. Such paintings cannot be interpreted without inside knowledge, yet their emphasis on the spiritual attributes of places makes them doubly memorable to the initiated.'[17] This painting-drawing-writing is not merely representational, as we Westerners employ that designation. In fact, it is barely representational and is much more a merging-with, an articulation and elaboration of its context. In its innocent refusal to separate art and environment it simultaneously creates and reinforces sacred text and sacred space together. It forms a holy sign that seems never to have been asunder and thus offers, to the mythology of our imagination, an image of wholeness that, even though alien to *our* ancestry, is something we need to tell.

Laura herself takes defiant comfort in her version of such a merging-with at the end of the novel. Responding to a drunken Englishman who, these two decades later, inquires about 'this familiar spirit . . . the German fellow who died,' she says, 'Voss did not die. . . . He is still there, it is said, in the country, and always will be. His legend will be written down, eventually, by those who have been troubled by it' (448). In a significant way that legend has already been written.

RECOVERING WORDS

Two contemporary short stories, finally, focus on the commonest kind of non-textual writing – on graffiti, or writing (usually) on walls – yet in highly original ways. They are stories that do not deal in pain such as marks the narratives of Kafka, Réage, Kingston, White and others. Rather, they show such writing as symptomatic of mental and relational breakdowns and as attempted recuperations. The earliest of these is 'The Anatomy of Bliss', published by the American author John L'Heureux in 1977. The other is 'Crazy, Crazy, Now Showing Everywhere' by Ellen Gilchrist, also American, as part of her 1984 collection *Victory Over Japan*.

'The Anatomy of Bliss' focuses on a young couple: Calder, 'a promising assistant professor of comparative literature', and Honey-Mae, an interior decorator who furtively writes on the interior walls of their house. Although their marriage is passionate, it is threatened by Honey-Mae's writing, the authorship of which she at first denies when Calder confronts her with it, and then admits. The handwriting, moreover, which begins with three words in tiny script inside the bedroom closet and eventually expands to whole walls throughout the house, is in an unknown language – something especially galling to Calder, who has 'learned five languages'. His obsession with Honey-Mae's undecipherable graffiti only exacerbates her compulsion, so that she writes all the more, and in desperate reaction he writes 'I HATE YOU' repeatedly in huge letters on the bedroom wall.

At last the import of their psychiatrist's simple explanation for her compulsive behaviour – she writes because she is unhappy – breaks into Calder's awareness. He rushes home to find her covering the wall of his study, the only room she had spared hitherto, but here the writing assumes form and comprehensibility:

But not columns of words this time, not random scratchings. No, the words grow from the baseboard and rise up the long length of white wall into airy patterns of trees and flowers and animals. The words are all in different colors, written close together, so that you do not see *happy unhappy happy*, you see only the flowering tree the words have formed, and on the tip of the longest thinnest branch, the delicate shining blossom that says *bliss*, over and over. (74)

Calder, who 'has never actually seen her writing before', gently offers her his acceptance of her actions and 'watches, astounded, as slowly the madness drains from her eyes' (74). The story ends with the couple, the writing ignored, in a quiet embrace on the floor.

My summary does not convey the comic or ironic dimensions of 'The Anatomy of Bliss'. Surely one of its key generative ironies is that Honey-Mae, an interior decorator, here defaces a house – her own – and thus acts against the purpose of her profession. Her mysterious graffiti mar their dwelling, just as public space is violated by scrawled or spray-painted messages, and a similar kind of defiance, a demand of the powerless to be recognized, is her motivation. Yet she is almost certainly not aware of this motivation. Rather, the unknown language appears to surge out of her like some surplus welling-over from a Freudian unconscious. In fact, that she can express this language apparently without understanding it (and what she writes may not be a real language) makes it seem something like chirographic glossolalia, an uncontrolled and ecstatic 'writing in tongues'. Inarticulate desire, that is to say, flows from her and literally marks her surroundings.

That this situation is intensely erotic, in spite of the grief it causes both of them, is evident. During the months of Honey-Mae's compulsive writing they continue to make love, as a way of communicating that postpones the need to address this flaw in their life together, and as a kind of comfort against its terrors. The writing, in this context, can be regarded as a desperate love letter from wife to husband, its language unintelligible but its unconscious intention clear. Her husband needs to accept her as she is, without attempting to shape her to his desires and to his assumptions of what she should be.

Viewing this handwriting on the wall as a sort of love letter returns us to my discussion of love letters in Chapter 2, and one can see how 'The Anatomy of Bliss' both reinforces and extends the traits of love letters described there. I mentioned there how the love letter can suspend 'the text inscribed on the body in/as pain, acting as a civilizing agent against the human tendency to conduct erotic encounters aggressively' (50). Calder, who has 'got this vicious streak', evinces sadistic impulses (his 'I HATE YOU' on the wall is the result of one of them), and Honey-Mae, who shows masochistic reflexes, deflects her husband's aggression and simultaneously forces a confrontation (that she consciously avoids) by indirectly addressing him through her enigmatic graffiti. Her transgression of the white walls, defacing them by writing, deeply offends him and eventually causes him to see how he has transgressed her selfhood by trying to mould her in his image.

Like most love letters, Honey-Mae's wall writing is dissembling. Always written when Calder is away (until the final scene), it fills up the void of his absence and asks for reassurance of his love. Precisely by its unintelligibility and bizarre locus it asks for his trust. 'Love me in spite of my madness', is its message, and in that sense it demands just what it seems to negate.

The climax arrives when Honey-Mae invades Calder's most private space, his office, and he returns home to catch her in the act. But by now his passion has deepened into compassion; he is able to see enough beyond himself to recognize her need and accepts her as she is. She, in turn, found at his most intimate place, has become artistically articulate. The graceful tree of words that she creates, reading *happy unhappy happy* and *bliss*, is just as much a gift to him as it is an instance of her right to be at the centre of his life.

Whether or not one wishes to see the logical traces of grace in this story (in that unconditional acceptance generates reconciliation and wholeness), one can in any case observe how technologized space is textualized, as the walls of a modern home are covered with writing in an attempt to recover, or originate, a deep love relationship. If we wish nowadays to play with and profit from the metaphor of the linguistic universe, and think of it as something more encompassing than 'the book of nature', then it follows that certain textualized spaces will become, however provisionally, sacred, and will become so because we project onto them our most insistent longings. The 'love letters' of 'The Anatomy of Bliss' act as such a momentary convergence of sacred text and sacred space, and the story can be seen as recuperative.

The writing on the wall by the madwoman of Gilchrist's 'Crazy, Crazy, Now Showing Everywhere' emphatically cannot be construed as any sort of love letter. Rather, she writes out of defiance, to protest about the conditions of her life with her wealthy family and to construct a refuge of words. The woman is the fifty-year-old Fanny Yellin, who has been in and out of a mental institution and now, back home with her millionaire husband in Alexandria, Virginia, remains functional through tranquillizers but seldom leaves her bed. Fanny's sister-in-law Lilly, the narrator of the story, describes her 'madness museum', her message-covered bedroom as it looked before she was admitted to the hospital:

> From the door the mural spread inward, onto the four walls of the high-ceilinged rectangular room. Water colours, crayons, oils, acrylics, long sections marked 'Conspiracies' and 'Swindles,' names and dates and anecdotes from her fifty years' war with the wealthy Jewish world into which she was born.
>
> There were crossword puzzles made of jargon cut from newspapers. WHOSELIFEISITANYWAY was glued to a chair. There were quotations from thick books on psychiatry. The east wall was devoted to R. D. Laing. The floor was littered with paintbrushes and jars of paint and hundreds of Marks-A-Lot pens. (136)

Over the door Fanny has written 'Crazy, Crazy, Now Showing Everywhere', a pun that reads like a title on a theatre marquee but that also indicates the ubiquity of Fanny's madness as she herself feels it. And it is because she feels so vulnerable and exposed, terrified that her family will commit her to 'the Looney Bin', as she herself calls it, that she retreats to her room and turns to words for her defence and attack. 'Bring me words,' she pleads to Lilly. 'I need more words. I need all the words I can get' (139). Fanny wishes literally to scripturalize space, to surround herself totally with texts, hide within them and employ them as weapons against her conspiring family. 'When I find the right words I will expose them. . . . I will have it all out in the open where everyone can see. Then they will not be able to deny it. Then everyone will know' (137). What it is that she wants to expose is never clear, but it concerns her conviction that she has been held captive all her life in a prison of social and familial constraints that have driven her mad.

Fanny's condition hardly improves during her period of treatment in the institution, during which time her text-covered room is painted and the offending words hidden. She returns home, back to her now pristine bedroom, and, bolstered by her drugs, carries on her fight indirectly but with the old wit and obsessiveness. As she tells Lilly, 'I'm going to play their game. I'm going to put them on paper and have them framed and nail nails into the wall and hang them up' (141). She shows Lilly her sketch of 'seven garbage cans, all in a row with the tops down nice and tight' (141), and representing, of course, the 'trash' of her pre-institution life. But she still demands words from Lilly: 'I want you to bring me words every day this week.' Her room, once a shrine of sacred texts, is now a palimpsest within which she survives: desperately, cynically, humorously. The old words are painted over, to be covered by the proper drawings and texts (which will function as a *mise en abyme* and as a trace), but they are still there like a textual unconscious, hidden but active and influential.

Fanny fails to maintain her technologized, textualized space. Her pharmaceuticals, in fact, are the technology that enables her to mount her defence of words at all. But words are still recuperative for Lilly, whose solitary reflection concludes the narrative. Sitting on her front steps in autumn dusk and frustrated by her failure to gain family sympathy for her mad sister-in-law, she says:

> I like to sit here this time of day, watching the jays and nightjars fight above the city roofs, turning and swooping and diving, calling, caw, caw, caw, calling good news, good news, good news, calling hunger, hunger, hunger. (142)

Caw. Good news. Hunger. The first of these is mere scripted sound, nature's noise signalling, among the fighting birds of day and night, the claims of territory and dominance. The second, the good news, hints at gospel, proclamation. The good news proclaimed to and by the embattled Jewish narrator may be the love between her and her mad relative. They wish to save each other, and the words that pass back and forth, however inept, are redemptive, helping them at least to survive in their brittle, neurotic world. The third, the hunger, tells that survival is not enough.

They long for words to set them free. What words these are they do not know (they could be the words of liturgy) but the very longing is a sign of hope.

Notes

1. The first quotation is from the Gospel of John 8:6. The second quotation is from Fredric Jameson, *The Political Unconscious: Narrative as a Socially Symbolic Act* (Ithaca, New York: Cornell University Press, 1981) p. 64.

2. Publishing information on all creative texts discussed in this chapter is listed below. Page numbers of the texts from which quotations are taken are given in parentheses following the citation.
   Jorge Luis Borges, 'The God's Script', tr. L. A. Murillo, in *Labyrinths* (New York: New Directions, 1964) pp. 169–73.
   Annie Dillard, *Pilgrim at Tinker Creek* (New York: Harper & Row, 1974).
   Ellen Gilchrist, 'Crazy, Crazy, Now Showing Everywhere', in *Victory Over Japan* (Boston: Little, Brown and Company, 1984) pp. 129–42.
   Franz Kafka, 'In the Penal Colony', tr. Edwin and Willa Muir, in Stephen Spender (ed.), *Great German Short Stories* (New York: Dell, 1960) pp. 180–209. 'In der Strafkolonie', in Franz Kafka, *Erzählungen und kleine Prosa*, vol. 1 (New York: Schocken Books, 1946) pp. 181–213.
   Maxine Hong Kingston, *The Woman Warrior: Memoirs of a Girlhood Among Ghosts* (New York: Vintage Books, 1977).
   John L'Heureux, 'The Anatomy of Bliss', *The Atlantic Monthly*, vol. 239/4 (April, 1977) pp. 66–74.
   Pauline Réage, *Story of O*, tr. Sabine d'Estree (New York: Ballantine Books, 1965).
   Patrick White, *Voss* (Harmondsworth, Middlesex: Penguin Books, 1960).

3. Cf. James D. Watson, *The Double Helix* (New York: New American Library, 1969).

4. For more on Derrida and the concept of trace, cf. Jacques Derrida in (among other places) *Speech and Phenomena*, tr. D. B. Allison (Evanston, Illinois: Northwestern University Press, 1973). Cf. also Mark C. Taylor's excellent discussion of Derrida's 'trace' in his *Erring: A Postmodern A/theology* (University of Chicago Press, 1984).

5. Jameson, *The Political Unconscious*, pp. 72–3.

6. Ibid., p. 72.

7. Michel Foucault, 'Nietzsche, Genealogy, History', in Donald F. Bouchard (ed.), *Language, Counter-Memory, Practice: Selected Essays and Interviews by Michel Foucault*, trs Donald F. Bouchard and Sherry Simon (Ithaca, New York: Cornell University Press, 1977) p. 148.

8. I mean metaphor and metonymy here as Peter Brooks, summarizing Todorov, treats them in *Reading for the Plot* (91). Writing the sentence on the body sublates the metaphoric action (based on resemblance)

in favour of the contiguity that marks metonymic action. Even the etymology of contiguity (Latin *contiguus* = 'touching') suggests how the syntagmatic, or relentlessly 'literal', tries to establish itself as the tangible and 'real'.

9.   Michel de Certeau, *The Practice of Everyday Life*, tr. Steven F. Rendall (Berkeley: University of California Press, 1984) p. 140.

10.   Simone de Beauvoir, *The Second Sex*, tr. H. M. Parshley (New York: Alfred A. Knopf, 1952) p. 429. That *Story of O* may be an *intentional* fictional commentary on de Beauvoir's work – a possibility suggested to me by Sharon E. Greene – is reinforced by Jean Paulhan's declaration in his preface to *Story of O*. He says, 'And yet, in her own way O expresses a virile ideal. Virile, or at least masculine. At last a woman who admits it!' (xxv).

   Other texts on writing, mutilation and the body that were helpful to me are Francis Barker, *The Tremulous Private Body: Essays on Subjection* (London: Methuen, 1984); Alphonso Lingis, *Excesses: Eros and Culture* (Albany: State University of New York Press, 1983); Gabriele Schwab, 'Genesis of the Subject, Imaginary Functions, and Poetic Language', *New Literary History*, vol. 15/3 (Spring, 1984) pp. 453–74; and Allan Stoekl, *Politics, Writing, Mutilation: The Cases of Bataille, Blanchot, Roussel, Leiris, and Ponge* (Minneapolis: University of Minnesota Press, 1985).

11.   I am indebted to Sharon E. Greene for pointing out the pervasive marriage imagery in *Story of O*. For a Marxist analysis of the fetishized female body in the evolution of the novel cf. Jon Stratton, *The Virgin Text: Fiction, Sexuality, and Ideology* (Norman: University of Oklahoma Press, 1987).

12.   Luce Irigaray writes of the male 'desire to force open, to penetrate, to appropriate for himself the mystery of the stomach in which he was conceived, the secret of his conception, of his "origin".' Luce Irigaray, 'This Sex Which Is Not One', in Elaine Marks and Isabelle de Courtivron (eds), *New French Feminisms* (New York: Schocken Books, 1981) p. 100.

13.   Susan Gubar, ' "The Blank Page" and the Issues of Female Creativity,' in Elizabeth Abel (ed.), *Writing and Sexual Difference* (University of Chicago Press, 1982) p. 77.

14.   Ibid., p. 81.

15.   Sharon Willis, *Marguerite Duras: Writing on the Body* (Urbana: University of Illinois Press, 1987) p. 169.

16.   Max Charlesworth, *Religion in Aboriginal Australia: An Anthology* (St Lucia, Queensland: University of Queensland Press, 1984) p. 10. Quoted by Geoffrey R. Lilburne, 'Religious and Scientific Views of Space: Aboriginal Dreaming and Our Own' (unpublished).

17.   David Lewis, 'The Way of the Nomad', *Hemisphere: An Aboriginal Anthology* (1978), pp. 79, 81. Quoted by Geoffrey R. Lilburne in 'Religious and Scientific Views of Space'. I am grateful to Professor Lilburne for making me aware of scholarship on Australian aboriginal culture. The concluding pages of Naomi R. Goldenberg's *Changing of the Gods* (137–40) consist of a fascinating account of 'Australian dream space' in a context which suggests that the author knows nothing of aboriginal dreamtime.

6
Scheherazade's Fellowship
Telling against the End

... a mutilated, incomplete self, composed of nostalgia and a sense of guilt.

Now weare coming to the curse roads of it ... now weare getting down to terpitation.[1]

LIVING OUT THE APOCALYPSE

Some of the narratives I discussed in the previous chapter present 'bad' communities, others describe 'good' communities in disarray, and still others portray the absence of communities altogether. The gyneceum at Roissy in *Story of O*, where women live in sexual subjugation to men, is an intact but negative community. Kafka's penal colony, not a positive model in the first place, seems like the execution machine itself to be disintegrating. The Chinese-Americans in California in *The Woman Warrior* cannot maintain the solidarity – which itself was often sustained by brutality – of their villages back in old China. The desert expedition 'community' of *Voss* stumbles toward fragmentation and death, while the Colony outside Sydney (in a country partly settled as a penal colony!) is troubled by all sorts of tensions and conflicts. The couple in 'The Anatomy of Bliss' seem to have no community at all to turn to, only the psychiatrist, and the extended family of 'Crazy, Crazy, Now Showing Everywhere' fails to give the necessary support to its most troubled member.

In this chapter I will expand and deepen my discussion of community. I will address two novels that depict two future societies as dystopias and in the process describe a range of religious – or at least 'believers' ' – communities that have both positive and negative traits. These communities function in 'post-

159

chirographic' societies and depend crucially on religious ritual that is at least in part reinforced by spurious theology. Against this authoritarian theology the novels' narrators tell corrective stories that constitute much of the narratives' substance. I hope to show how this personal and ritualized oral narrative both 'remembers' and envisions better communities than their tellers endure and thus tries to provide a more vital context for an education in a liberating and sustaining mystery. I will also be guided here by the argument of Clifford Geertz that I discussed in Chapter 2: how the religion of a culture takes over when the rational mind feels deeply threatened by the fear that chaos is the ultimate reality, and how that religion then elaborates itself as myth and ritual to provide a bearable view and experience of existence.

The novels I will treat are *Riddley Walker* (1980) by Russell Hoban, an American living in England, and *The Handmaid's Tale* (1986) by the well-known Canadian Margaret Atwood.[2] Hoban's novel especially is a fiction-writer's textbook example of Geertz' version of the 'Scheherazade syndrome': as the sultan's clever wife tells nightly stories to him to prolong her life, whole cultures create their believers' fictions against the threat of the end.[3] In *Riddley Walker* the end has, in a sense, already happened, and the remnant still alive invents a religion out of the elements of chaos and destruction. That kind of situation is complicated in *The Handmaid's Tale*; there the religion imposed by the authorities against the threat of death, which is also the religion that is maintained by the threat *of* death, is opposed by a type of Scheherazade who can tell her death-defying tale only after her escape.

Because I will be examining the 'anatomies' of two religions created by Hoban and Atwood, I will offer considerably more descriptive renarration, quotation and glossing of passages in this chapter than in the previous ones. It is not inappropriate to do this, I think, in the final chapter of a study that argues for a greater religious appreciation of storytelling.

Riddley Walker is also the name of that novel's narrator and chief actor. He is a twelve-year-old boy who belongs to a band of salvagers and foragers in devastated Kent, the descendants of a culture virtually destroyed some two millenia earlier in a nuclear disaster. The catastrophic 'Bad Time' is recalled, confusingly, in the tribal memory as the explosion of the proton accelerator at Canterbury but also as nuclear war. No descendants of the survivors seem to exist anywhere else in 'Inland' (England), although people do live across the channel in 'Outland'. The degeneracy of the scattered groups subsisting in the wasted Kentish countryside is manifested by technological regression since their holocaust, by the near-disappearance of writing and by the butchered English that they speak. Riddley, who succeeds his father (killed in a salvaging accident) as a 'connexion man' – a sort of shaman who interprets the travelling puppet shows mounted periodically in the settlements by the government elders – is one of the few who can read and write. His first sentence, that introduces the novel, illustrates graphically the colourful semi-literacy of this decayed culture: 'On my naming day when I come 12 I gone front spear and kilt a wyld boar he parbly ben the las wyld pig on the Bundel Downs any how there hadnt ben none for a long time befor him nor I aint looking to see none agen' (1). Since the whole narration is composed in this idiom, full of strange vocabulary, syntax and spelling, it makes for slow reading and helps to account for the fact that the novel, although highly praised upon its publication, has not enjoyed a wide readership. Yet this decelerated reading has its advantages. It enables one to enter into the fiction of a regressed future society, whereby the very ponderousness of puzzling out the dialect provides a parallel to the confused conceptualizing of the characters themselves.

Their language and culture are animated above all by a glorification of their remote technological, nuclear-era past into a religion. Nuclear power and electronic/computer technology are the main elements of this now mythicized past, representing an energy and exploitation of nature's 'seakerts' that these people hope, doggedly, to regain through various kinds of divination and ritual. Their 'theology' focuses on the 'Eusa Story', an amazing corruption of the legend of St Eustace, the second-century Christian general who was martyred with his family by the Roman Emperor Hadrian. Sometime after the nuclear holocaust that is the background of *Riddley Walker* its survivors discover a fifteenth-century wall painting in Canterbury Cathedral (perhaps in its ruins) depicting an episode in the life of St Eustace: 'At the bottom of the painting St Eustace is seen on his knees before his quarry, a stag, between whose antlers appears, on a cross of radiant light, the figure of the crucified Saviour' (123). The luminous crucifix is misconstrued as 'the Littl Shyning Man the Addom' (127) who is torn in two by 'Eusa', and out of whose rending (atomic fission) great power is released that eventually leads to 'Bad Time', to nuclear destruction.

This is the story that is the core of the 'Eusa shows' of the peripatetic government leaders Goodparley and Orfing, the Pry Mincer and Wes Mincer (corruptions of 'prime minister' and 'Westminster') who perform variations of the story with hand puppets in a freewheeling fashion in the scattered settlements, followed by the 'terpitations' of the local connexion men. Goodparley and Orfing are a combination of itinerant preachers, showmen and political bosses who keep the Eusa Story alive as an oral tradition that is also religion and entertainment.

Some forty-five 'Eusa folk' also exist incarcerated in various of the 'dead towns'. These are mutants, made that way by radiation and centuries of inbreeding, a sort of priestly class and the descendants of the 'Puter Leat' and 'Power Leat'' (computer élite and power élite) who were once the scientists, technologists and political and spiritual leaders of pre-holocaust society; 'Eusa' might also be a play on 'USA'. Their stock is maintained, in spite of the grotesque creatures it produces, because the others hope that one day some of them will join forces ('pul datter' and 'do some poasyum') and piece together enough of the old knowledge to return this sorry remnant, miraculously, to the greatness of the late twentieth century.

The action involving Riddley in this effort is so intricate that concise summary is impossible. In brief sketch: Riddley, who is both blessed and plagued with a strong sixth sense, incurs the hostility of some of his 'tribe', runs away, finds and frees a blind, mutant Eusa boy who turns out to be the 'Ardship of Cambry' (Archbishop of Canterbury). They travel about, protected by a pack of lethal wild dogs, and become involved in plots to assume political power of the region and to recreate the old mysterious energy. They, with others, manage to mix sulphur, potassium nitrate and charcoal and thus reinvent gunpowder – which experiments result in two very messy explosions that kill off a number of people, mostly Eusa folk and including the young 'Ardship'. Riddley, who is somewhat more of a witness than participant, survives all this and devotes himself to replacing the Eusa Story with Punch and Judy material, the puppet figures of which he has discovered and puts to work – or into play. At the end, in the company of the now deposed Orfing, he begins to travel the blighted countryside, bringing his 'secular' substitution for the Eusa show to the settlements.

My summary does not begin to capture the wit, charm and wild inventiveness of *Riddley Walker*. In spite of its utterly grim wasteland setting, the novel conveys a humour, an ingenuous drive to *believe* and interpret in the absence of real comprehension, a persuasive dramatization of the uncanny and a tenacious coping in the context of near-hopeless adversity. Hoban, known mainly as a successful author of children's books, here transfers the fresh vitality of that genre at its best to what is formally a novel of enervation.

Atwood's *The Handmaid's Tale*, in contrast, although it describes a less forbidding environment, is unremittingly bleak. Her Republic of Gilead, formerly the United States of America, is a totalitarian society of the 1990s born in violence: '. . . when they shot the president and machine-gunned the Congress and the army declared a state of emergency. . . . That was when they suspended the Constitution' (174). In this 'monolithic theocracy' a reactionary Christianity and high technology have combined in the hands of a ruthless powerful few to control the lives of everyone else.[4] Whereas religion in *Riddley Walker* consists in the confused interpretation of events and documents of a distant past, in *The Handmaid's Tale* it is a calculated literalist enactment – one could say deployment – of strategic Old Testament passages. Crucial is the story of the patriarch Jacob and his wife Rachel recounted in Genesis, in which Rachel, unable to bear children, proposes to her husband: 'Behold my maid Bilhah, go in unto her; and she shall bear upon my knees, that I may also have children by her (Genesis 30:3). This narrative provides inspiration for the power class in Gilead, especially the ageing childless couples among them. They have access to women of childbearing age who have been conscripted as 'handmaids' and who copulate in regularly scheduled household ceremonies with their masters in the hope of producing offspring who will be taken over by the élite married pairs.

The narrator of the novel is one such prospective surrogate mother, identified only as Offred (of-Fred, the first name of her master). Her account, found preserved on some thirty tapes, is the subject of scholarly speculation at a symposium on Gileadean Studies, presented as the concluding section of the novel. This symposium takes place in 2195, two centuries after the events of *The Handmaid's Tale*, and one learns here that the Republic of Gilead no longer exists, although what has taken its place is not made clear. Since Offred, like most subjects of Gilead, is not permitted to read and write (most texts have been destroyed), she records her story after her escape from her servitude and possibly from Gilead itself. Her narrative describes how, after the revolution that brought the religious fascists into power, she was separated from her mate and daughter, forced into novitiate-like training as a handmaid, and assigned ('offered') as a potential childbearer to her 'family', the Commander and Commander's Wife, in an unidentified city.

The thirty-three-year-old Offred, with her fellow breeders, leads a nun-like existence (apart from her sexual duties) that includes the wearing of an enveloping red habit; she is kept under stringent surveillance and suffers the contempt and resentment of her mistress. She endures a repressive and hyperpuritan society in which pornography (which had become increasingly rampant in the late twentieth century) has been abolished and all other non-sanctioned sexual activity, from rape to extra-marital affairs, is punishable by death. Because of this threat Offred is terrified when her elderly Commander requests a forbidden secret evening assignation with her. Yet it turns out when she appears that he wants merely – of all things – to play Scrabble with her and hold casual conversation. Subsequent clandestine meetings with her Commander, a highly-placed government official, bring Offred some minor privileges and lead her into reluctant private intimacy with him. But soon she begins a series of highly dangerous sexual encounters with Nick, the Commander's chauffeur. When Offred's indiscretion with her master is discovered by the Commander's Wife and her life thus placed in jeopardy, she is rescued by an underground group of which Nick is a member and disappears.

DYSTOPIC PLOTTING

This is, obviously, not a very substantial plot of action, and Atwood seems in fact even less concerned to construct a traditional narrative with balanced beginning, middle and ending than in her previous novels, choosing instead to stress a scenic-descriptive and recollective-evocative mode of storytelling both for her narrator and for herself as controlling author. The focus of the scenic effort is not scenic at all in the usual sense of that term; rather it is on the ecological and social disaster that comprises this dystopia. The focus of the recollective effort is on nostalgia (cf. Greek *nostos* = homecoming and *algos* = pain), a painful dwelling on the loss of the intimate and domestic past.

A main reason why the United States has been replaced by the totalitarian Gilead, and why Offred is forced into her 'biblical' vocation, involves the corruption of environment and society. The scholar summarizing the history of Gilead at the late twenty-second-century symposium describes the catastrophic conditions both dramatically and succinctly:

> Need I remind you that this was the age of the R-strain syphilis and also of the infamous AIDS epidemic, which, once they spread to the population at large, eliminated many young sexually active people from the reproductive pool? Stillbirths, miscarriages, and genetic deformities were widespread and on the increase, and this trend has been linked to the various nuclear-plant accidents, shut-downs, and incidents of sabotage that characterized the period, as well as to leakages from chemical- and biological-warfare stockpiles and toxic-waste disposal sites . . . and to the uncontrolled use of chemical insecticides, herbicides, and other sprays. (304)

And Offred in her own accounts connects the blighted environment to the genetic mess.

> What will Ofwarren [a pregnant handmaid] give birth to? A baby, as we all hope? Or something else, an Unbaby, with a pinhead or a snout like a dog's, or two bodies, or a hole in its heart or no arms, or webbed hands and feet? . . . They could tell once, with machines, but that is now outlawed. What would be the point of knowing, anyway? You can't have them taken out; whatever it is must be carried to term.
>
> The chances are one in four, we learned that at the Center. The air got too full, once, of chemicals, rays, radiation, the water swarmed with toxic molecules, all of that takes years to clean

up, and meanwhile they creep into your body, camp out in your
fatty cells. (112)

The destruction of the physical world is equated with the debasing
of sexuality. The handmaids during their training period are
shown hard-core pornographic violence films from the late twentieth century ('Women, kneeling, sucking penises or guns . . .
hanging from trees, or upside-down, naked . . . being raped,
beaten up, killed.' – 118); and after the revolution 'The Pornomarts
were shut . . . and there were no longer any Feels on Wheels vans
and Bun-Dle Buggies circling the Square' (174). Yet although the
Gilead regime has been able to police and regulate sexual behaviour, it seems helpless to revive the diseased environment, and
thus most of the children born to the handmaids are abnormal. It
is not surprising, therefore, that Offred's mind is often drawn to
her free, pre-Gilead past, to her healthy family and to her chaotic
but reasonably happy life then with husband, child, mother and
friends. Although it was a corrupt culture in many ways, it was
one in which difference, the right to disagree and protest, freedom
to make even the obvious bad choice, tolerance and privacy constituted the nature of the community. Indoctrinated to a degree by
the Gilead theocracy, Offred is ambivalent about the values of the
old United States versus those of Gilead, but there is no doubt
that she would far rather be living her old life. Thus she embodies
the dilemma of late twentieth-century consumerist culture. She
feels concerned and vaguely guilty about having contributed to a
society in her own past that depended on the production of waste,
yet she also identifies that waste as concomitant with a largesse
of spirit and goods that furthers tolerance and comfortable living,
and she finds an efficient (such as it is) totalitarianism worse than
a profligate democracy.

Offred's lack of fervour for the reactionary reforms of Gilead –
for the puritan community – and her desire for individual fulfilment thus involve her in plots against authority that, however
dangerously, provide her life with passion, hope and meaning.
This plotting, in fact, becomes virtually identical with the plot of
the novel. This is not surprising in terms of narrational strategy;
Walter Ong reminds us that oral narration tends to be episodic
rather than finely plotted, and Offred telling her story after her
escape – the culmination of a plot – to a tape recorder would
naturally describe the plots of her Gilead sojourn in the form of

the casually interconnected episodes that shape the novel.[5] But the point is that what is secret and subversive gives structure and meaning to those forced to exist in unsatisfactory, usually repressive and highly organized societies. As the tattoo on her ankle (like O's branding) reminds her, Offred is identified as a number, one of the mass, so that to be subversive is to assert one's individuality and personhood. To plot is to keep a sense of self alive and to search for other, sympathetic selves to join one in a community of difference.

The power that the rulers of Gilead display and exert baldly to control a restless populace assumes a more complicated form in *Riddley Walker*. In the Gilead theocracy state power is asserted to carry out the will of God, although the authorities must constantly persuade a sceptical citizenry that they indeed know the divine will and how to effect it. In the blasted world of *Riddley Walker* power is construed as simultaneously political, spiritual and physical and is literally worshipped. Because the awesome nuclear force that destroyed this culture millenia earlier has been mythicized into something still greater in the collective memory, and because almost all technology vanished during the cataclysm, power itself is apotheosized and made the subject of mystery, nostalgia and hope. This backward folk worships what its forbears had mastered; yet whereas the high technology culture of the late twentieth century was (is, from our perspective) also enslaved by its accomplishments, Riddley's people, who have no technology to seduce and bind them, yearn for just such subjection. Their religion is in large part inspired by a nostalgia for the old power, to possess it and be possessed by it. Riddley standing amazed amid the ruins of the giant generators at Folkestone weeps and says, 'O what we ben! And what we come to! . . . How cud any 1 not want to get that shyning Power back from time back way back?' (100).

But the nostalgic worship of this dissipated power is also marked by the appalling conditions for survival. '*Riddley*,' Goodparley says, '*we aint as good as them befor us. Weve come way way down from what they ben time back way back. May be it wer the barms what done it poysening the lan or when they made a hoal in what they callit the O Zoan. Which that O Zoan you cant see it but its there* its holding in the air we breave. You make a hoal in it and Whoosh! No mor air' (125). The lives of these primitives would not be bearable if they did not have the veneration of their great past to mitigate their bleak present. For what else is left to the survivors of the apocalypse, or the survivors of the survivors, who have to look back on the eschaton and see themselves passed by, occupying its far side, the side beyond hope?

Since it is not possible to abandon hope even in this infernal (or post-infernal) landscape, these people must have more than nostalgia. Friedrich Heer writes in *The Medieval World* that 'Dante's constructive purpose was to set Christendom on the right road to the apocalypse', and it is not too grand to associate Hoban's post-apocalyptic vision with a dark and brilliant imagery reminiscent of *The Divine Comedy*, even if on an ironically reduced scale.[6] Thus instead of Beatrice as symbol of light one finds 'the Littl Shyning Man the Addom', for example, and instead of the conflagrations of hell one has the campfires against marauders and the elements in this place of suffering. But above all, like Dante's obsessive and tormented creatures, and like the subversives of Atwood's Gilead, the people of blighted Kent refocus their nostalgia by plotting, and by plotting even in circumstances of despair. Their strategies are technological, political and religious, all interconnected. The Eusa folk, mutant descendants of the old 'Puter Leat' and 'Power Leat', conspire to take over power from their masters, the shadowy government figures who hold them captive as the keepers (however flawed) of the secrets of nuclear energy. The government representatives conspire to keep the isolated settlements under control by intimidation and by performances and prophecies of the Eusa faith. Many, including Riddley and his Eusa friend the Ardship, conspire to unite the mysterious three elements that they believe will create a 'littl' version of nuclear force but that is actually gunpower. When they succeed, the explosions at the two sites take lives but do not improve anyone's lot or political position. Riddley himself as new connexion man succeeding his father contrives to create a new puppet show using Punch and Judy instead of Eusa figures and thus challenges the 'state religion'.

Does anything come from these conspiracies, subversions and power struggles? Essentially not, in terms of changing the grim conditions for survival. If anything, matters have been made worse, for now the formula for gunpowder is known as well as the sources of its ingredients, so that the ominous possibility of a new cycle of ever more efficient destruction arises. Yet the plotting is necessary, even inevitable. It is, as we saw in the case of *The Handmaid's Tale*, a fumbling and stumbling toward meaning, a simultaneous performing and shaping of one's life story, the acting out of one's narration that gives the narration its substance and structure. That the plotting of *Riddley Walker* takes on so much of the nature of conspiracy and power struggle is the result of the precarious state of the enervated post-holocaust communities there. How a community can move through plotting to conceive itself in story and provide its own meaning under the worst of circumstances is what I wish to discuss next, on the basis of these two dystopias as negative examples.

RITUALS TOWARD DEATH AND LIFE

The settlements of the decaying Kentish countryside of *Riddley Walker* survive by a story. Even though it is one in which they are emplotted through the conspiracy of their leaders at the Mincery (who themselves appear to believe in the story also), and even though we readers, placed at a fundamentally ironic distance from the story, know it to be false, it determines their past as history, their present as ritual and their future as faith.

The 'history' of Riddley's people is, as we have seen, a mythologizing of twentieth-century 'fizzics', 'chemistery' and computer science mainly through the vehicle of a greatly corrupted second-century martyr's tale, the legend of St Eustace. Absolutely none of the science is comprehended in even the most elementary fashion, and the Christian legend is thoroughly (and delightfully) misconstrued, yet what emerges is a remarkably apt way of re-counting the rise and fall of the nuclear age and how this blighted society's misfortune struck it. Especially effective is the hermeneutic of the saint's legend whereby Eustace replaces Christ – Jesus becomes Eusa – and the focus of Christianity as we know it shifts to this minor figure whose deeds form the basis for a theology of nuclear fission and fusion. Goodparley, at this point still 'Pry Mincer', offers a masterpiece of misinterpretation of the legend. After showing Riddley the modern English ('old spel') account of the St Eustace material (the only normal English in the whole novel), he proceeds to 'as plain' it to the boy. For example, reacting to the passage I quoted earlier, in which Eustace is

depicted on his knees before a stag who has a radiant crucifix
between his antlers, Goodparley offers this tortured exegesis in
which he uses the biblically-derived phrase, 'a little salt and no
savour' (he has no idea of its Sermon on the Mount background),
as his key:

> Any how I wer reading over this here Legend like I use to do
> some times and I come to 'the figure of the crucified Saviour.'
> Number of the crucified Saviour and wunnering how that be
> come the Littl Shyning Man the Addom. Suddn it jumpt in to
> my mynd 'A little salting and no saver.' I dint have no idear
> what *crucified* myt be nor up to then I hadnt give *Saviour* much
> thot I thot it myt mean some 1 as saves only that didnt connect
> with nothing. Id never put it to gether with saver like in *savery*.
> Not sweet. Salty. A salt crucified. I gone to the chemistery
> working I asket 1 Stoan Phist [a senior member of the group] . . .
> what *crucified* myt be nor he wernt cern but he thot itwd be
> some thing you done in a cruciboal. 1st time Id heard the word.
> Thats a hard firet boal they use it doing a chemistery try out
> which you cud call that crucifrying or crucifying. Which that
> crucified Saviour or crucifryed salt thats our Littl Shyning Man
> him as got pult in 2 by Eusa. So 'the figure of the crucified Saviour'
> is the number of the salt de vydit in 2 parts in the cruciboal and
> radiating lite coming acrost on it. The salt and the saver. 1ce
> you got the salt youre on your way to the hoal chemistery and
> fizzics of it. (128–9)

All this may be a more than faint parody of the manner in which
reckless exegetes exploit religious texts toward any conclusion,
however ludicrous, that they want, but it is also an instance of
the human need simply to make and have meaning. It is 'terpitation' with a vengeance, in which any explanation, no matter how
far-fetched, is better than none at all, since undecidability and lack
of closure seem well-nigh intolerable to us. Riddley, as we shall
soon see, becomes much more expert than his seniors at practising
negative capability and living without final answers.

The proper English version of the St Eustace legend that Goodparley shows to Riddley is not the only basis of the Eusa story
that informs the travelling government puppet shows. The oral
tradition of Eusa and the Bad Time is mingled with other folk tales,
songs and riddles that together complete this living mythology for

the post-holocaust remnant. One of Hoban's greatest accomplishments in the novel, in fact, is his providing body and density to
this futurist fiction, giving the illusion of credibility by creating the
resemblance of a real mythology – essentially a paramythology –
from elements of religion, folklore, history and science, most of
which are also invented.

One could think of this rich oral culture fashioned by Hoban as
consisting of a core enveloped by a larger sphere which is in
turn surrounded by a still larger one. The peripheral sphere is
comprised of the folk chants, songs and tales that these people
utter in their everyday lives. The middle sphere is the ritual
performances of the puppet shows, and at the centre is the
'connexion', the interpretation and prophecy that the 'connexion
men' provide after the shows.

An example of such a chant is one that the men of Riddley's
settlement speak in unison while working a huge treadmill over
a salvage pit:

> Gone ter morrer here to day
> Pick it up and walk a way
> Dont you know greaf and woe
> Pick it up its time to go
>> Greaf and woe dont you know
>> Pick it up its time to go (9)

Even that simple rhyme expresses the pessimism of these
dispirited people; a song that the children sing to accompany a
game (breaking out of a circle) is more ominous:

> Horny Boy rung Widders Bel
> Stole his Fathers Ham as wel
> Bernt his Arse and Forkt a Stoan
> Done It Over broak a boan
> Out of Good Shoar vackt his wayt
> Scratcht Sams Itch for No. 8
> Gone to senter nex to see
> Cambry coming 3 times 3
>> Sharna pax and get the poal
>> When the Ardship of Cambry comes out of the hoal (5)

The song, which Goodparley interprets for Riddley later (121–2),

actually tells of the suffering and death of the first Ardship of
Inland, the leader (also conflated with Eusa) who survives the
nuclear catastrophe, is made a scapegoat, tortured and mutilated
in the towns named (Horny Boy = Herne Bay, Widders Bel =
Whitstable) that encircle Canterbury, then decapitated and his
head mounted on a pole.[7] Hence the final two lines of the song
in our English: 'Sharpen the axe and get the pole/When the Archbishop of Canterbury comes out of the hole.' This Eusa head,
which talks and prophesies, becomes the focus of a miracle story
much like those actually created during the Middle Ages. It selects
Ramsgate, the only town of the circle round Canterbury that did
not participate in the scapegoating, as the new political and spiritual centre (the Mincery), separates it from the rest of Kent via
a tidal wave, swims across to the island and there orders the
establishment of the Eusa puppet shows as a 'memberment and
for the ansers to your askings' (122).[8]

Still more elaborate are the folk tales that intersperse the
narration: 'The Hart of the Wood', on the devil bringing fire to a
primal post-holocaust couple in exchange for the cannibalism of
their child; 'Why the Dog Wont Show Its Eyes', on how a primal
couple learned '1st knowing' – intuition – from a dog, which led
to scientific experimentation and nuclear destruction; 'The Lissener
and the Other Voyce Owl of the Worl', on the owl that tries to
destroy the world by swallowing its sounds; and 'The Bloak as
Got on Top of Aunty', on the man who tries to outwit death,
which is protrayed as a fierce woman (Aunty = anti) who kills
with her *vagina dentata*. These four, each of which is told by a
different narrator, are themselves miniature plots of destruction
that reinforce the atmosphere of cataclysm permeating the novel.

Rituals are as important to these people as the songs and tales.
When Riddley kills the wild pig in the scene that opens the novel,
he and the other hunters with him perform a ceremony: 'I said,
"Your tern now my tern later." The other spears gone in then and
he wer dead and the steam coming up off him in the rain and
we all yelt, "Offert!" ' [Offered] (1). When Riddley becomes a
connexion man, three horizontal strokes standing for E = Eusa
are cut into his belly, accompanied by ritual phrasing. One of
the most moving passages concerns the funeral immolation of
Riddley's father, during which ceremony the mourners sing what
amounts to a nuclear/space age hymn:

> Pas the sarvering gallack seas and flaming nebyul eye
> [Past the sovereign galaxies and flaming nebulae]
> Power us beyont the farthes reaches of the sky
> Thine the han what shapit the black
> Guyd us there and guyd us back (22)

After this the fires are explained poignantly by a 'tel woman' of the gathering: 'Big fires they use to bern on hy groun to lite them others back to fetch us. Boats in the air o yes. Them air boats as never come back. Becaws them as got a way to the space stations they jus done ther dying out there in stead of down here. Now here we stan and singing that song to bern our dead. No 1 coming back to get us out of this' (23). It is a sad and chilling song of post-apocalyptic hopelessness.

A liturgical ritual begins the Eusa shows themselves. When Goodparley and Orfing perform early on in Riddley's settlement, Riddley as connexion man guides an initial ritual exchange with the watchers that goes in part like this:

> I said, 'Weare going aint we.'
> The crowd said, 'Yes weare going.'
> I said, 'Down the road with Eusa.'
>   . . .
> I said, 'Hes doing it for us.'
> They said, 'Weare doing it for him.' (44)

And when Riddley and Orfing later do their first Punch and Judy show at Weaping, another settlement, and try to secularize the liturgy (since they do not see the Punch material as the equivalent of the Eusa Story's religious nature), the audience refuses and insists on repeating the traditional phrasing that invokes Eusa.

The Eusa show puppetry takes the place of a sermon. As Goodparley and Orfing perform it, it is largely a dialogue accompanying the manipulation of the hand-puppet figures, with Goodparley behind and beneath the portable stage handling the puppets and speaking for them, and Orfing in plain sight as 'straight man' who provides the 'patter'. That a puppet show should dramatize religious texts and doctrine is not as strange as it seems at first. It does show Hoban's awareness of the history of Christian education: until it was forbidden by the Council of Trent (1545–63) puppetry was encouraged by the church to teach Christian scripture. What the men from the Mincery dramatize is not the Bible (which is unknown), of course, and not even the legend of St Eustace that survives there in modern English, but rather a garbled thirty-three-verse version of it that also gives a mythicized account of nuclear fission research, nuclear explosions that caused the Bad Time, and the horrible aftermath. The Eusa shows animate aspects of this account and simultaneously comment on it.

At yet another ceremony on the evening following the show ('Nex Nite') the local connexion man is expected to give his 'reveal'. This too is an event that begins with ritual language, and if the connexion man feels 'on', the group awaits the message. The connexion man is thus seen, like any shaman, as the channel of a transcendent force, a medium through whom a greater power speaks, but he is also seen as one who through temperament or heredity has a particular talent for this prophetic task. Riddley as the son of such a shaman and as demonstrating a strong intuitive sense is aptly named, for he is indeed a 'riddler': one who seeks to solve the puzzles of his dark world but who finds himself able to give such answers as he has mainly in the ambiguous language of mysticism. Indeed, Riddley's first 'reveal' is not a communicative success at all. Barely into his prophecy, he falls into a trance and learns afterwards that he has uttered nothing of the mysterious insights that came to him in that state. What he reports from this trance to the readers, however, the thought that 'EUSAS HEAD IS DREAMING US' (61), gropes toward a fairly sophisticated theology, one that sees the world as a reflection of God's unconscious. Riddley ponders this concept still earlier in his account and there explains how his meditation on it has inspired the narrative that constitutes this novel. At the end of the first chapter he writes, 'Seams like I ben all ways thinking on that thing in us what thinks us but it dont think like us. Our hoal life is a idear we dint think of nor we dont know what it is. What a way to live. / Thats why I finely come to writing all this down. Thinking on what the idear of us myt be. Thinking on that thing whats in us lorn and loan and oansome' (7). What Riddley 'remembers' in his moments of deep play is not a mystery generated merely by 'fizzics'. But it is not the result of metaphysics either. As we shall see, Riddley's dawning awareness of a secularizing faith grows as he digs deeper into his story-performer's bag.

Because the Republic of Gilead in Atwood's novel is a Christian theocracy, its theology and the stories that support it do not depart nearly as far from the Christian tradition as do those of Riddley Walker's world. One could say that whereas a nuclear explosion has caused an irretrievable scattering of the Christian heritage in *Riddley Walker*, in *The Handmaid's Tale* there is an implosion instead: an implosion that comprises the revolution whereby Christianity is turned so radically in on itself, via a literalizing of its texts and praxis, that it subverts itself and becomes demonic.

Although reading and writing are forbidden to many – above all to women – in Gilead, it is not, as a result, like 'Inland' an oral culture. Rather, it is a society marked by three traits: a high technology interacting with repressive strategies, an exploitation of women which is strongly supported by women, and a stress on spectacle.

The religious life of Gilead, which is to say most of existence, is guided by all of these three. An example of how a repressive high tech permeates daily behaviour and determines specific responses is the constant presence of the 'Eyes'. These are the surveillance force of Gilead, the secret police who keep watch on the populace with cameras, microphones and spies and work to ferret out subversives. Thus when the standard ritual words of departure, 'Under His Eye', are uttered, the traditional allusion to the benevolent watchfulness of God doubles as a reminder of the state's intrusive power.

This control of the citizenry depends strongly on the subjugation of women and the collaboration of women in the repressive tactics. At the time of the revolution women were neutralized by the simple manoeuvre of revoking their banking and credit privileges. With no funds available (their finances were turned over to men) they became weak. But many women also joined forces with the revolutionary government to establish the new propagation-oriented order. These are the 'Aunts', powerful females who take charge of the women's re-education centres and train the women conscripted into them to serve as handmaids. This is the context in which religious language and ritual develop most vigorously. Everything is directed toward the success of the handmaids' procreative function. When two meet, the accepted greeting is 'Blessed be the fruit', and the response is 'May the Lord open.' As Offred puts it in succinct religious imagery, 'We are two-legged wombs, that's all: sacred vessels, ambulatory chalices' (136). Since the handmaids of a given area are present at the deliveries of any who manage to bear a child, they learn to participate in ritual fashion: ' "Breathe, breathe," we chant, as we have been taught. "Hold, hold. Expel, expel, expel." . . . The soft chanting envelopes us like a membrane . . . "Pant! Pant! Pant!" we chant' (123–4). Since their lives may depend on conception and child-bearing – those who do not produce are sent off to forced labour camps – the prayers they learn at the centres are desperate and (appropriate for this stress on wombs) hysterical.

> What we prayed for was emptiness, so we
> would be worthy to be filled: with grace,
> with love, with self-denial, semen and babies.
>   Oh God, King of the universe, thank you for
> not creating me a man.
>   Oh god, obliterate me. Make me fruitful.
> Mortify my flesh, that I may be multiplied. (194)

Although there seem to be no traditional community churches where worship services are held (certainly no synagogues: Jews have been deported or forced to convert) religious services are held in the homes and in connection with various special mass events. Offred's Commander, for example, reads aloud from the Bible to the gathered household at the start of the intercourse ceremony, then asks for a silent prayer of blessing. Hymns are sung at large meetings such as the 'Prayvaganzas', and Bible reading takes place there as well. At the one Offred describes, the occasion for a wedding of twenty couples from the élite families, it is a selection of passages on the need for the subjugation of women and how they can be 'saved by childbearing' (221).

The household ceremonies and the birthing occasions are, in a way, public events that condition especially the women of Gilead to act in a manner that is a curious combination of voyeurism and exhibitionism, both religiously coloured, and to succumb to the religious spectacles. Thus in the first of these the handmaid lies, fully clothed except for underpants, with her head between the thighs of the wife, in a literalist imitation of the Genesis example where Bilhad acts as surrogate for Rachel; while all of the other women of the household – the servants – look on, the patriarch, fully clothed as well, couples stoically with the maid.

Similarly, on the birthing occasions the handmaid about to

deliver sits on the lower of two seats of a birthing stool, with the wife of her family above her, so that the maid can bear the child upon the wife's knees in faithful accordance with the Genesis account – all this being observed by the gathering of local hand-maids who chant to encourage a good delivery. These events are orchestrated by an Aunt in charge, moreover, with no men present (the doctors – males – wait outside) and are conducted with a stern matriarchal as well as religious discipline. Offred musing after a delivery in which she participates addresses her absent mother: 'You wanted a women's culture. Well, now there is one. It isn't what you meant, but it exists' (127). But she is wrong; it is not a women's culture but one in which women collude to support a reactionary patriarchy. That women contribute to this society of spectacle, in which moments of intimacy are made public (and in the intercourse ceremony, sexuality by its public exposure is rendered puritanical), is a sign of their exploitation and self-exploitation.

The mass public spectacles, coercive in many ways, are a major part of the religious life of Gilead. The most curious and harmless of these is an invention of electronic technology, the Soul Scrolls. These are stores containing automatic print-out machines that produce texts of prayers. 'There are five different prayers: for health, wealth, a death, a birth, sin' (167). One can order them by computer. 'Ordering prayers from Soul Scrolls is supposed to be a sign of piety and faithfulness to the regime, so of course the Commanders' Wives do it a lot' (167). These are not spectacles in a conventional sense, although one can watch the prayers being endlessly run off; rather, they are computer events used to reinforce orthodoxy and loyalty at the highest levels. More spec-tacular are three other public events with religious dimensions. One, the Prayvaganza I have already mentioned, is designated either for women or men. The women's Prayvaganzas generally celebrate group weddings, the men's military successes – Gilead is constantly at war. Since these mass meetings, held outdoors, are tightly organized and also televised, they serve as indoctrination rituals.

More fearsome are the Salvagings and a ritual growing out of these called Particicution. The term 'Salvaging' is an ominous euphemism, for the people 'salvaged' are actually savaged. These are the occasions, also segregated by sex and with obligatory attendance, on which convicted criminals are executed. At the one described by Offred and conducted by an Aunt, two maids and a wife are hanged. The bodies are then displayed, hung from hooks, on the huge wall that has stood in the city for more than a century. Atwood, who lived in West Berlin while writing part of *The Handmaid's Tale*, clearly uses the notorious wall that divides that city as her model. Her description of spotlights, barbed wire and armed guards at this barrier evokes the image of the Berlin Wall. Here it is the grisly backdrop for a regime of religious totalitarian ruthlessness – the bodies of priests and nuns (such as still exist), adulterers, abortionists, schemers against the theocracy are displayed there – and a site of voyeuristic attraction. Offred, like many others, is drawn there to stare at the hooded corpses suspended from the hooks, curious about who the latest victims are and what crimes they committed.

This fascination with death, where the watcher could well be the victim, is exploited by the regime in the most sensational spectacle-ceremony of all, called Particicution. It is a ritual in which a condemned male is killed by the handmaids. Following the Salvaging that Offred depicts, a surprise Particicution takes place in which the aroused maids kick, beat and tear to death an alleged rapist. Particicution (participation-in-execution) is a version of an ancient rite in myth known as *sparagmos*, a tearing to pieces.[9] It is how Dionysus, for example, is killed by the frenzied Maenads in Euripides' *The Bacchae*. Offred, who takes no active part in the violence, nevertheless finds herself excited by it. After it is over she discovers that she is ravenous and that she wants to make love. Atwood, commenting on pornography in an interview, observes that 'The thing that is most forbidden is the inside of the body and death.'[10] *Sparagmos* involves both of these; it is a ripping apart, an ultimate exposure of the body, the ultimate voyeurism, and it is not surprising that the handmaids are perversely aroused by it. The speaker at the Gileadean Studies symposium that concludes the novel also has an interpretation of Particicution and an elaboration on the practice.

Scapegoats have been notoriously useful throughout history, and it must have been most gratifying for these Handmaids, so rigidly controlled at other times, to be able to tear a man apart with their bare hands every once in a while. So popular and effective did this practice become that it was regularized in the middle period [of Gilead's existence], when it took place four

times a year, on solstices and equinoxes. There are echoes here
of the fertility rites of early Earth-goddess cults. (308)

In the religious totalitarianism of Gilead, then, the most intense
communal act consists of unrestrained violence and killing
controlled by the authorities who depend on the complicity of their
subjects for the survival of the repressive state. It is bad carnival,
a temporary licence to indulge the most debasing appetites, which
indulgence does not lead back to sane and healthy everyday living
but increases the burden of guilt that is the foundation of puri-
tanism, and that then heightens the overriding sensation of
numbed alienation. Offred, who unlike Riddley Walker cannot dig
deeper into the bag of mysterious figures, needs to find a faith,
to counter her alienation, in a different way.

FICTION MAKES MYSTERY

Although Offred is forced to participate, she is not a true believer
in the Gilead theocracy. The all-exacting state religion itself seems
to be based on only a skeletal theology, so that the dynamic of
faith is transferred largely into a demand for obedience to the
regime. As one learns from the conversations between Offred
and her Commander, the ruling élite are cynical about their own
religious tenets but justify the whole repressive system as a
necessary measure to avert biological and ecological disaster. Had
this revolution not occurred, its proponents argue, the United
States would have destroyed itself. There are few citizens, it
appears, at the time of Offred's narration who do actually believe
the propagandistic principles of the Gilead re-education effort, but
the government knows that history, ironically, is on its side.
Offred attending the Prayvaganza group wedding muses about
the girls being married: 'Even though some of them are no more
than fourteen – *Start them soon* is the policy, *there's not a moment
to be lost* – still they'll remember. And the ones after them will, for
three or four or five years; but after that they won't. They'll always
have been in white, in groups of girls; they'll always have been
silent' (219). This is of course the tactic of repressive regimes
everywhere, and Atwood from her vantage point of Berlin would
have heard enough of its success in the German Democratic
Republic. History shows that if one teaches revisionist history

persistently enough, the repetition will work, and the new generations will indeed become true believers.

If this is the bleak situation that Offred as a first-generation
subject of Gilead must endure, if she cannot believe in her society,
where else can she find her faith and strength? She reaches out
to her past and future through memory and storytelling, and she
bears the present through a very few dangerous liaisons where
she can be her true self, that part of her orchestration of selves
committed to authenticity. Offred employs storytelling to create,
in the absence of an acceptable religious faith, a faith of her own
out of memory, desire and hope.

The nature of this storytelling is as important as its substance.
The circumstances of the narration, for one, are complex. Because
Offred is not permitted to write, she constructs her story at inter-
vals in her head. She calls the process a reconstruction (134), by
which she seems to mean that she wishes to 'get it right', give a
record of how things happened rather than create an embellished
version or even fiction. She wishes, in other words, to produce
an autobiography. But because she cannot record her narrative
until after her escape, when she talks it on tape (which we learn
from a scholar two centuries later, at a time in the future of
Offred's telling), she produces finally a double reconstruction that
is inevitably less history/autobiography and more fiction. That
Offred realizes all this ('. . . if I'm ever able to set this down . . .
it will be a reconstruction then too, at yet another remove' – 134)
means that she needs to believe in the storytelling process, as a
way of presenting truth, in spite of the inability of that process to
remember 'correctly', to be all-inclusive. And she learns this
because she is deprived of the power of writing – that technology
which enables us to maintain the illusion that we can indeed 'make
history', can know and record fully and accurately, and that we
can know and say the whole extent of what we mean. Offred
thus comes to understand truth as an approximation, to be *lived*
approximately, in tolerance and compassion, those virtues that
her society's religion discourages.

'The way love feels is always only approximate' (263), Offred
says, and in that way signals her concern for her audience. The
recipients of her tale are very important to her, above all because
she wants to think that her lost husband and daughter will be
among them.[11] Even though she may not survive her story, she
wishes to believe that those she loves will learn more of her fate.

Why should this matter to her, we might ask, if she is then dead anyway? It is her way, perhaps reflexively, of uniting memory, desire and hope, and thus of making her grim present more bearable. But this concern for her readers as a love of family broadens into a loving address to all who may read her tale:

> But if it's a story, even in my head, I must be telling it to someone. You don't tell a story only to yourself. There's always someone else.
>
> Even when there is no one.
>
> A story is like a letter. *Dear You*, I'll say. Just *you*, without a name. Attaching a name attaches you to the world of fact, which is riskier, more hazardous: who knows what the chances are out there, of survival, yours? I will say *you*, *you*, like an old love song. *You* can mean more than one.
>
> *You* can mean thousands. (39–40)

I discussed in Chapter 2 how authors may think of their texts as love letters addressed to their readers and named *The Handmaid's Tale* as an example. It is of course first of all the narrator who conceives of *her* story as such a love letter, with all of the attendant anxiety and dissembling that belongs to love letters. I mentioned there how the love letter shows a longing that is like the desire of the believer for the fulfilment of his hope and faith through some redemptive event (the return of the lover is envisioned much the same as the appearance of a redeemer), yet how that longing also makes the interval of the lover's absence valuable – which value is celebrated in the letter to the lover. Offred, whose chances of seeing husband and child ever again are slim, cannot celebrate this interval that threatens to become an eternity. Nevertheless, the void that inspires her telling makes the telling itself precious, so that the story as she shapes it becomes the substance of her faith. As it grows and is embellished it begins to substitute for the fragile hope she has of reunion with her family. It mitigates longing with its own density. Offred can become absorbed in it and make it the centre of a private world.

This storytelling against despair that elevates the tale into a semblance of faith is nonetheless painful. Late in the narrative Offred says:

> I'm sorry there is so much pain in this story. . . . I keep on

going with this sad and hungry and sordid, this limping and mutilated story, because after all I want you to hear it, as I will hear yours too if I ever get the chance, if I meet you or if you escape, in the future or in heaven or in prison or underground, some other place. What they have in common is that they're not here. By telling you anything at all I'm at least believing in you, I believe you're there, I believe you into being. Because I'm telling you this story I will your existence. I tell, therefore you are. (267–8)

There is literal, physical pain in this story; Offred tells of punishment and execution. But she means mainly the pain of memory, desire and hope. She suffers from loss and the recollection of what she has lost, from the frustration of present desire, and above all from the fear of hopelessness. She thus suffers through an acutely painful recital – and invention – to create faith and hope. 'By telling you anything at all I'm at least believing in you, I believe you're there, I believe you into being.' This combination of confession and assertion, which could be – perhaps should be – a part of every believer's faith, makes Offred's suffering worthwhile, just as the pain itself sanctifies her narration-as-faith.

Telling stories to keep *others* alive is a variation on the Scheherazade motif, for her concern was for her own neck. Part of Offred's choice in her storytelling that wills the existence of her loved ones, and that relieves her own despair, is a rejection of the religious community that entices her. It offers a vision of an ideal sisterhood that, however unmoved Offred is by it, is still reasonably attractive. An Aunt at the training centre expresses it dramatically: 'The women will live in harmony together, all in one family; you will be like daughters to them. . . . There can be bonds of real affection. . . . Women united for a common end!' (162). The Aunt also flatters and challenges the handmaids to work toward this ideal by identifying them as 'a transitional generation. . . . It is the hardest for you. We know the sacrifices you are being expected to make. It is hard when men revile you. For the ones who come after you, it will be easier' (117). Offred sees through this facile and manipulative evocation of liminality and imagines herself in terms of another image of liminality and marginality: 'I am a blank, here, between parentheses' (228).

Offred finds her identity within another community that is so liminal, marginal and tenuous that it is not even supposed to exist.

This is the underground of resisters, into whose plot Offred finally disappears. The handmaid vanishes at last into her own story, is absorbed by her own narration and through that story becomes, two centuries later, the object of mystery. This abrupt shift of perspective, which wrenches us away from the handmaid's anguish and substitutes the angle of polite scholarly regard, is an effective defamiliarizing tactic. Like the participants in the symposium, we are left to our own conjecture and thus become authors of the handmaid's fate. Shall we have her recaptured? 'Salvaged?' Escape and find her family? But *must* we bring resolution to the story? We can follow Atwood's lead and let the mystery remain. It is in nurturing the mystery, refusing to choose an ending, that we maintain the story. In maintaining the story, learning to merge suspense with *Gelassenheit*, we are instructed in the value of mystery.

The conclusion of *Riddley Walker* is only slightly less open-ended than that of *The Handmaid's Tale*, and its final irresolution is closely connected to storytelling as a way of learning new faith. Riddley goes through three kinds of experience, none of them neatly separated from the others, that impel him toward at least the attitudes in which a new faith can be born. One is ecstatic, one is reflective-redemptive and one is creative.

The ecstatic experience is felt and described in sexual terms and prepared for by the young Ardship's depiction to Riddley, before they part company, of the mysterious gathering that the Eusa folk dream of. It is an astonishing vision of cohesion, of a total absence of differentiation.

> Its where theres all the many nor there aint no end to you there aint no place where you begin nor leave off. Mountains of us valleys of us far far lans and countrys of us. Tits and bellys it wud take you days to walk acrost. Girt roun bums and arms and legs all jynt big and long and long and girt jynt man and woman parts all mullerplying back to gether all what ben de vydit. No more oansome in the gethering. (94)

Later on at Folkestone the Eusa folk try to realize this unification and to recapture, in a mass trance, the secrets of nuclear energy. '. . . the Eusa folk they all took off their cloes and tangelt ther selfs to gether all nekkit and twining like a nes of snakes which they callit that some poasyum [symposium]. Which they done trantsing with it and hy telling' (199). The results are grue-some, however, for in the midst of this 'trantsing' another charge of gunpowder packed in an iron pot is exploded. Orfing, an eyewitness, describes the effects with comic verve: '. . . thats when it gone bang and peaces of iron pot and Eusa folk wizzing all roun. It toar the Ardship all apart and peaces of him raining down . . . plus it kilt three mor Eusa folk and woondit others' (200).

Riddley's own ecstatic experience is more private and more effective. It occurs when he arrives alone in Canterbury and stands on the site of the cathedral ruins which is also 'Zero Groun', the point at which, millenia earlier, the annihilating nuclear blast took place. Hoban, of course, creates his own conflation here. Canter-bury Cathedral, ecclesiastical focus of Christian England, is ident-ified with the locus of nuclear power and is at the epicentre of the accident that destroys the civilization. Riddley (who at age twelve is sexually active) senses the residual spiritual-physical energy in a blatantly sexual way: 'Fealt like it wer the han of power clampt on the back of my neck fealt the Big Old Father spread me and take me' (159). That, and still more graphic intercourse imagery, conveys the intensity of Riddley's enravishment.

This sensation – a familiar phenomenon of religious mysticism – has been prompted by a desire for reconciliation and renewal. As Riddley moves into the 'Power Ring' from the periphery of the dead city, he 'wantit that Spirit of God moving Inland frontwards agen. I wantit the same as Goodparley I wernt agenst him no mor and that wer the hart of the matter' (158). Although Riddley has no notion of what the 'Spirit of God' means (Goodparley has explained it to him, predictably, as 'the chemistery and fizzics' that brought on the discovery of nuclear power), it is obviously something that he wants both to direct and celebrate.

Following his ecstatic and erotic vision he is led by his pack of dogs (also affected by the power of the place) underground to what must be the crypt of the cathedral (the decorated columns he describes as 'stoan trees'), which he thinks of as a great womb, and here imagining and regenerative recollection replace the ecstatic moment. On his knees in the crypt Riddley conceives an image of a face with vines growing out of its apertures, a face he comes to call 'Greanvine', which seems to recollect all faces. This image of organic growth, decay and rebirth (a version of the familiar Wild Man in many mythologies) he combines with a meditation on a graffito he finds nearby under a charcoal cartoon sketch of Goodparley: 'HOAP OF A TREE' (169). The allusion to the crucifixion of Christ, a prominent Christian image of death and rebirth equivalent to the natural one represented by Greanvine, is lost on Riddley. To him it would mean the anonymous expression, probably written by one of the imprisoned Eusa folk, of desire that Goodparley be hanged (Goodparley has already displayed a hanging tree to Riddley in a private performance of Punch and Judy); yet the blended imagery of Greanvine and Hoap of a Tree moves him to restless contemplation and sets the stage for the most significant of his experiences, the one that leads him to a secularizing story performance as a replacement for the old Eusa 'gospel'.

After Goodparley is killed in Riddley's presence (he has already been tortured and blinded by Orfing and his 'hevvys') by the gunpower explosion about the same time that the Ardship and some Eusa folk are blown up by a similar blast at Folkestone, Riddley and Orfing join up to take the Punch and Judy show on the road. With the government at the Mincery now in disarray in the wake of the these deaths, and with the threat of increased violence looming because of the reinvention of explosives, Riddley and Orfing decide to perform shows together as a calming and ordering vehicle throughout the agitated settlements. Why Riddley chooses to perform with Punch and Judy puppets rather than with the Eusa figures is not clear, but it has to do with Riddley's intuition that these chaotic times demand an appropriate story, such as Punch animates, to channel and interpret his life in greater flux than ever.

It does not seem, at first, to be a wise choice, since the violence and salaciousness of the Punch material might well only further enflame the audiences. But Riddley's intuition has its reasons. For one, the Punch and Judy show invites active participation by the audience; the main characters address the viewers and ask for help (in Riddley's performance Judy – here called Pooty – requests that the onlookers warn her when she is offstage if Punch tries to devour her piglet baby). Such involvement is a way, in this disoriented oral culture, of creating stories that become the community's own, as they invest emotion and responsibility in the survival of some of the characters and in the punishment of others. It is a simple strategy, but it helps to relieve the confused settlements of the weight of the now destructive Eusa theology upon them, and it gives them a chance to re-imagine their lives with this elementary – even elemental – material.

Just how elemental the Punch and Judy/Pooty show is becomes manifest in Riddley's production. It deals with violence, sex, deception, eating, the threat of death. Yet ominous as it all is, it is presented in a boisterous, slapstick manner, and the play with meat-eating especially suggests the atmosphere of carnival. In the midst of their near hopeless situation, which threatens to become even worse, Riddley brings his people literal comic relief. Although it may not be the proper preparation for a new expression of faith to follow, in so far as that is conceivable here, this explosive comedy, even with the undertone of foreboding, provides a moment of festivity in which the community can forget its woe and derive strength to go on.

Riddley for his part has already absorbed the lesson of *Gelassenheit*, and this may be what he wants to communicate to his fellows. He entered Canterbury the first time lusting for 'Hy Power' and the nuclear 'Spirit of God', but the reflective experience in the cathedral crypt teaches him something better: 'I cud feel some thing growing in me it wer like a gran sea surging in me it wer saying, LOSE IT. Saying LET GO. Saying THE ONLYES POWER IS NO POWER' (167). Later, after Goodparley is killed and Riddley sets out again for Canterbury, he is able to improve on this revelation.

> Feal the goast of old Power circeling hy over me. Only this time I fealt a Power in me what circelt with it. Membering when that thot came to me: THE ONLYES POWER IS NO POWER. Wel now I sust that wernt qwite it. It aint that its *no* Power. Its the not sturgling for Power thats wher the Power is. Its in jus letting your self be where it is. (197)

This is the condition of mind and spirit that marks Riddley as he undertakes his secular puppetry. It renders him capable of an openness to being at a time of great crisis: 'Ready to cry ready to dy ready for any thing is how I come to it now. In fear and tremmering only not running a way. In emtyness and ready to be fult. Not to lern no body nothing I cant even lern my oan self all I can do is try not to get in front of whats coming' (204).

In this state Riddley glimpses the infinite potential of fiction-making, led to it by an exploration of the figures in the dead Goodparley's bag of puppets. 'Theres figgers in that bag you never seen in a show. You get to wunnering if you gone down deap a nuff in that bag if you mytnt get right the way down to Bad Time and fynd out all what realy happent' (206). He becomes aware of how the storyteller relies on the figures of his imagination to articulate personal and communal experience, and how these figures, then, if allowed to speak and act, tell him and his hearers more than he knows. It is in just this discovery, through the risks of fiction-making in the context of a sympathetic community, making oneself vulnerable to the responsive group, that the possibilities for a new, transcending faith may lie.

THE NARRATIVE IMPERATIVE: FINISHING IN TIME

Has any news of value emerged from this study of two dystopias – two societies, moreover, that are both pathetic and ludicrous in their assumptions and failures? To guide my response to this question I will enlist Paul Ricoeur's brilliant conclusion to the second volume of his *Time and Narrative*. There, borrowing from Bakhtin's distinction between the epic and the novel, Ricoeur writes:

. . . tradition isolates the epic world and its heroic characters from the sphere of the collective and the personal experience of people today. The novel is born out of the destruction of this 'epic distance.' And it is principally under the pressure of laughter, of ridicule, of the 'carnivalesque,' and more generally out of the expressions of serious comedy – culminating in the work of Rabelais, so brilliantly celebrated by Bakhtin himself – that epic distance gave way to the contemporaneousness based on sharing the same ideological and linguistic universe that characterizes the relation between the writer, the characters, and the public in the age of the novel.[12]

I believe that the novels by Atwood and Hoban take the influence of the carnivalesque on narrative a step further by demonstrating how that 'serious comedy' and the language and plots of fictions of degeneration so forcefully enhance each other. Ricoeur says, 'it is the end of epic distance that provides the definitive basis for opposing "low" literature to all the rest of "high" literature.'[13] *Riddley Walker* and *The Handmaid's Tale* are skilfully composed examples of an 'ultra-low' literature that, in its depths, sets conditions of crisis that move us to respond to the real crises of our contemporaneous world. It is a literature that asks urgently for deep play.

Ricoeur writes further,

. . . however deeply we hollow the abyss that separates epic distance and contemporaneousness between the writer and the public, the general features of fiction are not abolished. . . . the modern novel belongs to its time only at the price of another sort of distance, the distance of fiction itself. . . . the representation of a reality in full transformation, the painting of incomplete personalities, and the reference to a present held in suspense, 'without any conclusion' – all this requires a more rigorous formal discipline on the part of the creator of tales than on the part of the storyteller of a heroic world that carries with it its own internal completion.[14]

We have observed how, in *Riddley Walker* and *The Handmaid's Tale*, the creators of tales, functioning in a world of epic disasters yet without the epic mode or tradition to support them, struggle to find such formal discipline, because the stories that they can shape through that discipline are all they have to keep faith. The creators of these creators, the novelists Atwood and Hoban, exercise this rigorous discipline in such remarkable ways as to force the disorder of their dystopias to comment lucidly on our own emplotment in existence. Such awareness of the complications of our emplotment, dramatized radically for us in these novels, provides a condition for letting *Gelassenheit* take over, through which nonchalance we can start to imagine how our stories of faith will proceed.

But the narratives of the handmaid and the youthful connexion man are also prophetic in ways that challenge our carelessness with time and space. As Frank Kermode eloquently informs us in *The Sense of an Ending*, the novel seeks to respond to the anxiety caused by our transitional condition in the world (not too different from what Heidegger calls 'thrownness'), always somewhere between middle and end, by providing us with imaginary conclusions. Yet as our fictions display an increasing awareness of themselves as fictions, they remind us, ironically, through their very conclusions – or lack of them – 'that to live is to live in crisis', in other words without resolution.[15] What about *The Handmaid's Tale* and *Riddley Walker*, two self-aware novels that serve as fictions of life struggling to avert the end (in blighted Gilead) or of life after the end (in post-holocaust Kent)?

They remind us, for one, of what is truly uncanny in our time: that we tolerate the destruction of our environment and our very biological being, and even participate in this destruction. We seem little concerned, perhaps fatalistic or simply negligent, about the acute threats to our global survival through the abuses that these novels dramatize as having already happened: the accumulation of poisonous wastes that cause death and genetic damage, the pollution of atmosphere and ozone that alters our climate, the commitment of incredible sums to the insane development of weaponry and defence systems rather than to the relief of suffering and to ecological and biological protection, and the horror of mass death and mental/physical abnormality not only through nuclear war but just as easily through nuclear accidents. They show with particular clarity the effects of these monstrous acts and events not only on the societies that caused them but also on the generations that follow. Our behaviour that corresponds to *this* sense of an ending – that we permit this wholly irrational drift toward catastrophe – is uncanny in the fullest sense of the term; if novels such as these can make us feel the madness of this behaviour, through the shocking depictions of its probable results, and help us will to change it, they can become actual fictions of survival.[16]

Although *Riddley Walker* and *The Handmaid's Tale* could be construed as narratives of prolonged endings, they are just as crucially fictions of the middle. What Kaja Silverman says about the notion of the text as process applies also to this stress on middles. It suggests 'a reader or viewer who participates in an on-going manufacture of meaning, an activity without a final goal or resting point'.[17] These novels thus portray existence as boundlessly liminal, as a *between* with no beginning or ending, only an inexperienceable start and stop, and hence as both intensely discontinuous and discontiguous. The image of endless falling that Rilke's 'Autumn' poem plays on is appropriate to convey this sensation. They are narratives of and about the impossibility of narrative in a world that refuses to acknowledge its own apocalyptic mode.

How can this impasse be overcome, this fall be braked and broken? A *communitas* of readers, joined at first merely by the fact *that* they read, can learn to confess their need of a shared narrative and encourage the creation and interpretation of a literature that holds in useful tension the doubleness we feel: that we live at once both liminally and in conclusion. It would be a literature that offers us metaphors and plots of alert nonchalance, of crises that are deepened into the play of mystery.

Jameson writes that 'all literature must be read as a symbolic meditation on the destiny of community'.[18] That is profoundly true, but we need to remember that such meditations, then, should lead us back – or on – to narrative again. For the destiny of community is not merely to provide its members with a place to belong. It is also to give them a context where, and a structure of how, they can constantly plot their lives. The story of this plotting is what the reading and interpreting fellowship has to tell.

Notes

1. The first quotation is from Francesco Alberoni, *Falling in love*, tr. Lawrence Venuti (New York: Random House, 1983) p. 94. The second quotation is from *Riddley Walker*, p. 41.
2. Russell Hoban, *Riddley Walker* (London: Jonathan Cape; New York: Washington Square Press, 1980). Margaret Atwood, *The Handmaid's Tale* (Boston: Houghton Mifflin Company, 1986). Page numbers of these texts from which quotations are taken are given in parentheses following the citation.
3. The most recent example of a real-life Scheherazade I have found is the Cambodian Kassie Neou, who was imprisoned as an alleged CIA agent by the Khmer Rouge in 1976 and who told stories to his teenage guards. When 'the jail's 37 inmates were chained together and taken outside to be shot', he was hidden by a guard and a newly-arrived prisoner killed in his place. 'They wanted to save their storyteller.' Cf. *The Houston Post* (6 March, 1987) 19E. Tzvetan Todorov in his *Poétique de la prose* (Paris: Seuil, 1971) treats Scheherazade as a type of 'les hommes récits' or 'story persons' whose lives depend on their narrations; cf. pp. 78–91.
4. 'Monotheocracy' is what Atwood calls the Gilead government in an interview. Cf. Sue Matheson, 'An Interview with Margaret Atwood', *Herizons*, vol. 4/1 (January/February, 1986) p. 20.

5. Walter J. Ong, *Orality and Literacy: The Technologizing of the Word* (London and New York: Methuen & Co., 1982) pp. 147ff.
6. Friedrich Heer, *The Medieval World: Europe 1100–1350*, tr. Janet Sondheimer (New York: New American Library, 1962) p. 366.
7. The other towns mentioned in the song are Bernt Arse = Ashburn, Forkt a Stoan = Folkstone, Do[ne] It Over = Dover, and Sams Itch = Sandwich. I have not been able to find an equivalent to Good Shoar.
8. A town named Minster exists a few miles west of Ramsgate that perhaps helped to inspire Hoban to place the 'Mincery' there.
9. Northrop Frye discusses the concept of *sparagmos* in *Anatomy of Criticism* (Princeton University Press, 1957) p. 192. Cf. also Walter Burkert, *Homo Necans: The Anthropology of Ancient Greek Sacrificial Ritual and Myth*, tr. Peter Bing (Berkeley: University of California Press, 1983). Burkert discusses *sparagmos* in the context of a stimulating Chapter 7 on 'The Sexualization of Ritual Killing: Maiden Sacrifice, Phallus Cult'.
10. Matheson, 'An Interview with Margaret Atwood', p. 22.
11. The concept of the narratee developed in narrative study is helpful here. The narratee is the person or persons to whom the story is addressed within the framework of the fiction, as distinct from the reader of the author's novel. In *The Handmaid's Tale*, the narrator's husband and child are the obvious narratees, but we are also seduced into thinking of ourselves as narratees through Offred's address to the 'You' on p. 40. For more on narratees cf. Rimmon-Kenan, *Narrative Fiction*, pp. 86ff.
12. Paul Ricoeur, *Time and Narrative*, vol. 2, trs Kathleen McLaughlin and David Pellauer (University of Chicago Press, 1985) p. 155.
13. Ibid.
14. Ibid., pp. 155–6.
15. Frank Kermode, *The Sense of an Ending*, p. 26. Kermode is here paraphrasing Karl Jaspers.
16. Sallie McFague's *Models of God* demonstrates skilfully how one can apply a metaphorical theology to respond to the dangers of the nuclear era.
17. Kaja Silverman, *The Subject of Semiotics*, p. 247.
18. Fredric Jameson, *The Political Unconscious*, p. 70. My use of Jameson's sentence does not do justice to the masterful anthropology of religion context in which it is found.

Select Bibliography

Elizabeth Abel (ed.), *Writing and Sexual Difference* (University of Chicago Press, 1982).

Margaret Atwood, *Second Words* (Boston: Beacon Press, 1984).

Mikhail Bakhtin, *Rabelais and His World*, tr. H. Iswolsky (Cambridge, Mass.: MIT Press, 1968).

Ernest Becker, *Escape from Evil* (New York: The Free Press, 1975).

Emile Benveniste, *Problems in General Linguistics*, tr. Mary Elizabeth Meek (Coral Gables, Florida: University of Miami Press, 1971).

Peter Brooks, *Reading for the Plot: Design and Intention in Narrative* (New York: Vintage Books, 1985).

Donald F. Bouchard (ed.), *Language, Counter-Memory, Practice: Selected Essays and Interviews by Michel Foucault* (Ithaca, New York: Cornell University Press, 1977).

Simone de Beauvoir, *The Second Sex*, tr. E. M. Parshley (New York: Harper & Row, 1952).

Kenneth Burke, *Counter-Statement* (University of Chicago Press, 1957).

——, *Language and Symbolic Action: Essays on Life, Literature, and Method* (Berkeley: University of California Press, 1966).

John D. Caputo, *The Mystical Element in Heidegger's Thought* (Athens: Ohio University Press, 1978).

Katarina Clark and Michael Holquist, *Mikhail Bahktin* (Cambridge, Mass.: Harvard University Press, 1984).

Gilles Deleuze, *Différence et répétition* (Paris: PUF, 1969).

——, *Logique du sens* (Paris: Editions de Minuit, 1969).

Jacques Derrida, *Of Grammatology*, tr. Gayatri Chakravorty Spivak (Baltimore: Johns Hopkins University Press, 1976).

——, *Speech and Phenomena*, tr. D. B. Allison (Evanston, Ill.: Northwestern University Press, 1973).

——, *Writing and Difference*, tr. Alan Bass (University of Chicago Press, 1978).

Stanley Fish, *Is There a Text in this Class? The Authority of Interpretive Communities* (Cambridge, Mass.: Harvard University Press, 1980).

Howard Gardner, *Frames of Mind: The Theory of Multiple Intelligences* (New York: Basic Books, 1985).

Peter Gay, *The Bourgeois Experience, Vol. I: Education of the Senses* (New York: Oxford University Press, 1984).

Martin Heidegger, *Being and Time*, trs John Macquarrie and Edward Robinson (New York: Harper & Row, 1962).

——, *Existence and Being* (Chicago: Henry Regnery, 1949).
——, *On the Way to Language*, tr. Peter D. Hertz (New York: Harper & Row, 1972).
James F. Hopewell, *Congregation: Stories and Structures* (Philadelphia: Fortress Press, 1987).
Fredric Jameson, *The Political Unconscious: Narrative as a Socially Symbolic Act* (Ithaca, New York: Cornell University Press, 1981).
Linda Kauffman, *Discourses of Desire: Gender, Genre and Epistolary Fiction* (Ithaca, New York: Cornell University Press, 1986).
Frank Kermode, *The Sense of an Ending* (New York: Oxford University Press, 1967).
William A. Lessa and Evon Z. Vogt (eds), *Reader in Comparative Religion: An Anthropological Approach*, 4th edn (New York: Harper & Row, 1979).
Jean-François Lyotard, *The Postmodern Condition: A Report on Knowledge*, trs Geoff Bennington and Brian Massumi (Minneapolis: University of Minnesota Press, 1984).
Sallie McFague, *Metaphorical Theology: Models of God in Religious Language* (Philadelphia: Fortress Press, 1982).
——, *Models of God: Theology for an Ecological, Nuclear Age* (Philadelphia: Fortress Press, 1987).
Elaine Marks and Isabelle de Courtivron (eds), *New French Feminisms* (New York: Schocken Books, 1981).
J. Hillis Miller, *Fiction and Repetition: Seven English Novels* (Cambridge, Mass.: Harvard University Press, 1982).
Steven Mintz, *A Prison of Expectations: The Family in Victorian Culture* (New York University Press, 1985).
Walter J. Ong, *Orality and Literacy: The Technologizing of the Word* (London and New York: Methuen, 1982).
Walker Percy, *The Message in a Bottle* (New York: Farrar, Straus and Giroux, 1975).
Annis Pratt, *Archetypal Patterns in Women's Fiction* (Bloomington: Indiana University Press, 1981).
Charles E. Reagan and Donald Stewart (eds), *The Philosophy of Paul Ricoeur* (Boston: Beacon Press, 1978).
Paul Ricoeur, *The Conflict of Interpretations* (Evanston, Ill.: Northwestern University Press, 1974).
——, *Fallible Man*, tr. Charles Kelbley (Chicago: Henry Regnery, 1965).
——, *Time and Narrative*, vols 1 and 2, trs Kathleen McLaughlin and David Pellauer (University of Chicago Press, 1985, 1986).
Shlomith Rimmon-Kenan, *Narrative Fiction: Contemporary Poetics* (London and New York: Methuen, 1983).
Elaine Scarry, *The Body in Pain: The Making and Unmaking of the World* (New York: Oxford University Press, 1985).
Kaja Silverman, *The Subject of Semiotics* (New York: Oxford University Press, 1983).
Mihai Spariosu (ed.), *Mimesis and Contemporary Theory: The Literary and Philosophical Debate* (Amsterdam and Philadelphia: John Benjamins, 1984).

Robert J. Stoller, *Observing the Erotic Imagination* (New Haven, Conn.: Yale University Press, 1985).
Harry S. Stout, *The New England Soul* (New York: Oxford University Press, 1986).
Mark C. Taylor, *Erring: A Postmodern A/theology* (University of Chicago Press, 1984).
Gregory Tropea, *Religion, Ideology, and Heidegger's Concept of Falling* (Atlanta: Scholars Press, 1986).
Victor Turner (ed.), *Celebration: Studies in Festivity and Ritual* (Washington, DC: Smithsonian Institution Press, 1982).
John Updike, *Hugging the Shore* (New York: Alfi·d A. Knopf, 1983).
Ian Watt, *The Rise of the Novel* (Berkeley: University of California Press, 1962).

Index